MOOSE

MAX DE RADIGUÈS

CONUNDRUM INTERNATIONAL

To Alec Longstreth

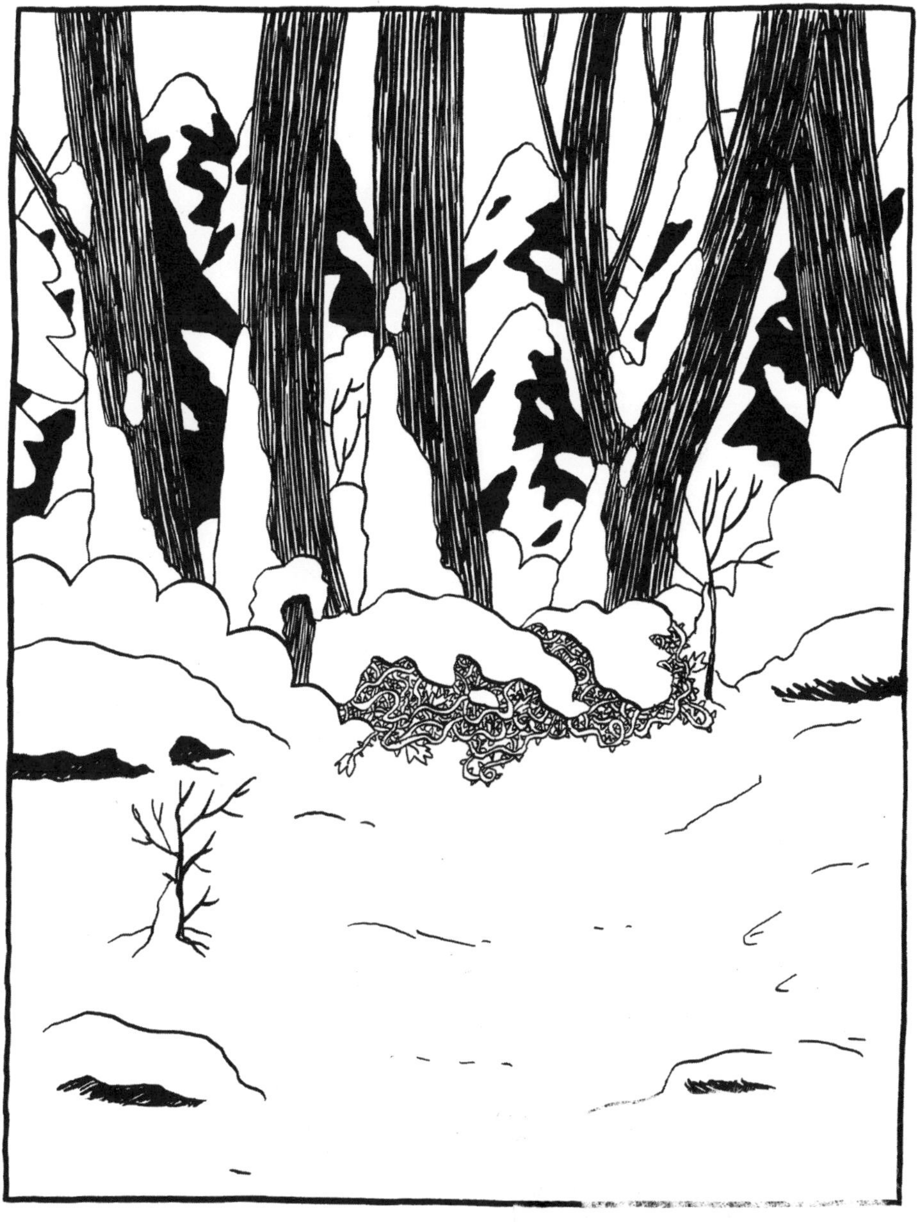

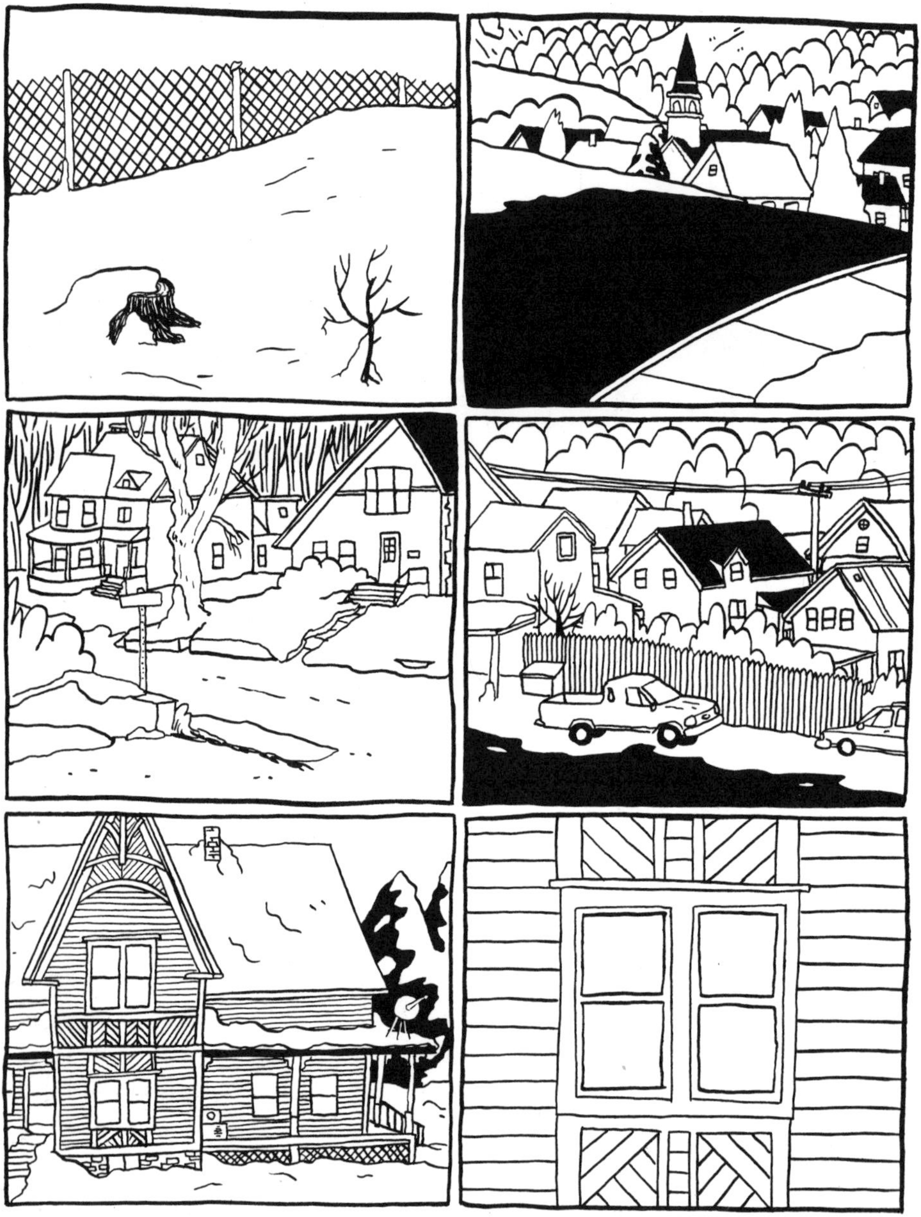

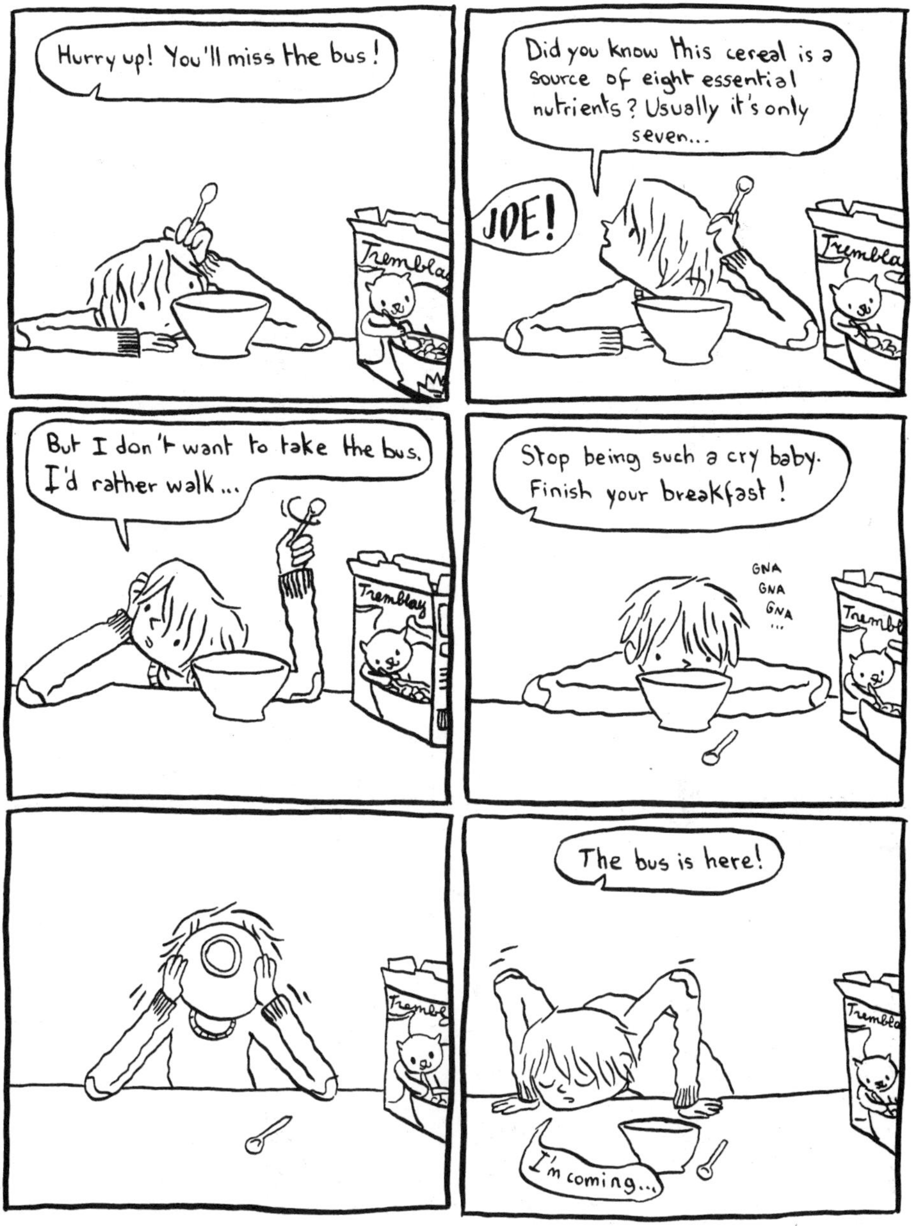
Hurry up! You'll miss the bus!
Did you know this cereal is a source of eight essential nutrients? Usually it's only seven...
JOE!
Tremblay
But I don't want to take the bus. I'd rather walk...
Stop being such a cry baby. Finish your breakfast!
GNA GNA GNA ...
The bus is here!
I'm coming...

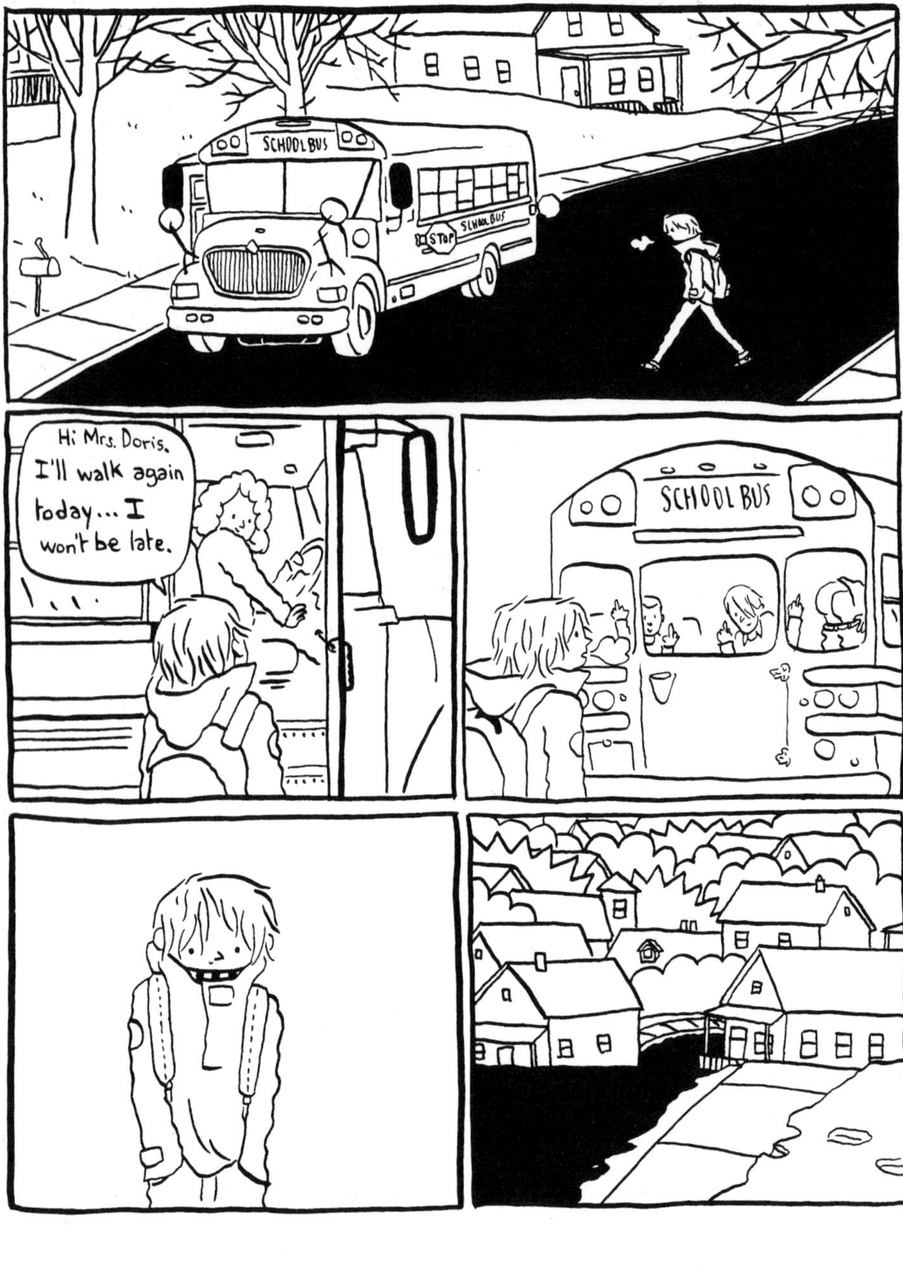
SCHOOL BUS
STOP
SCHOOL BUS
Hi Mrs. Doris. I'll walk again today... I won't be late.
SCHOOL BUS

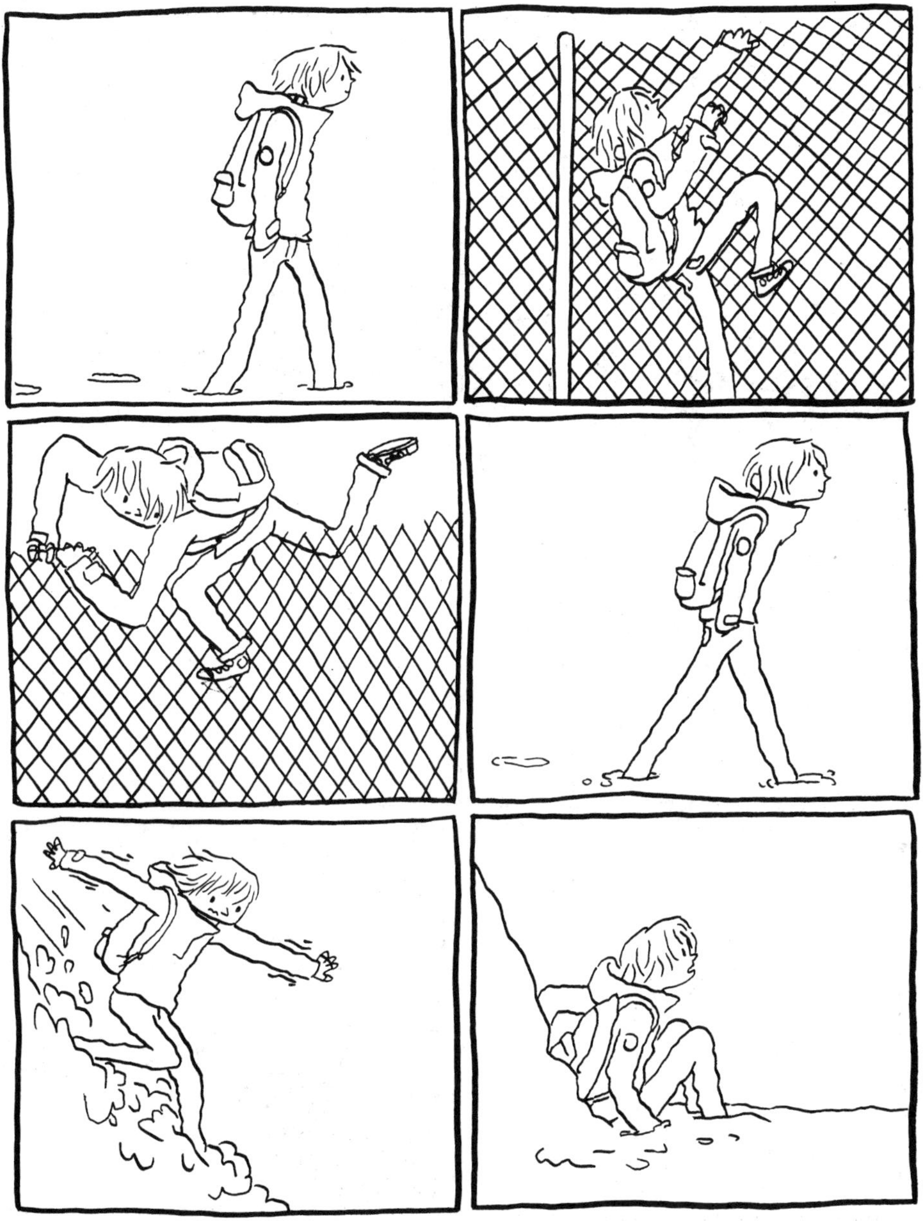

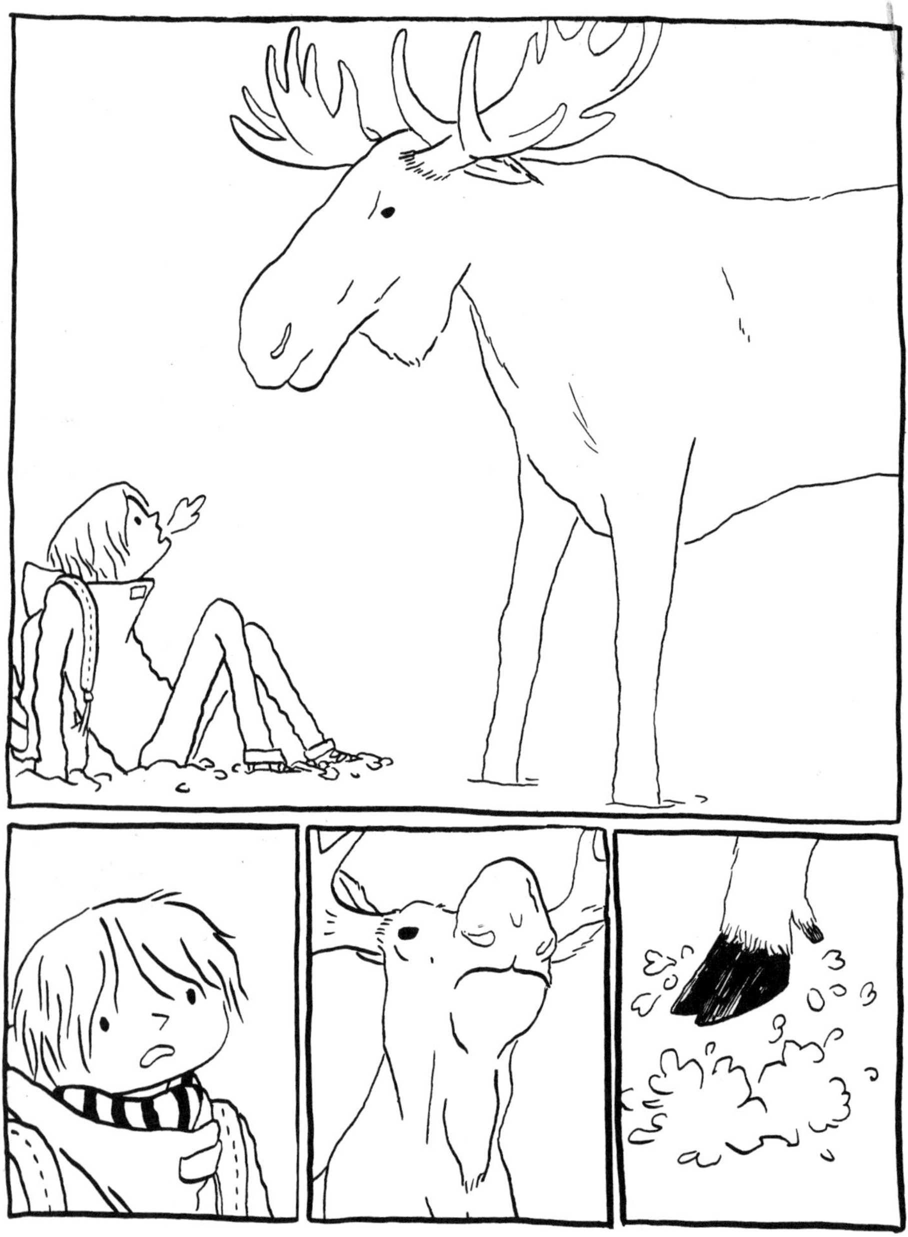

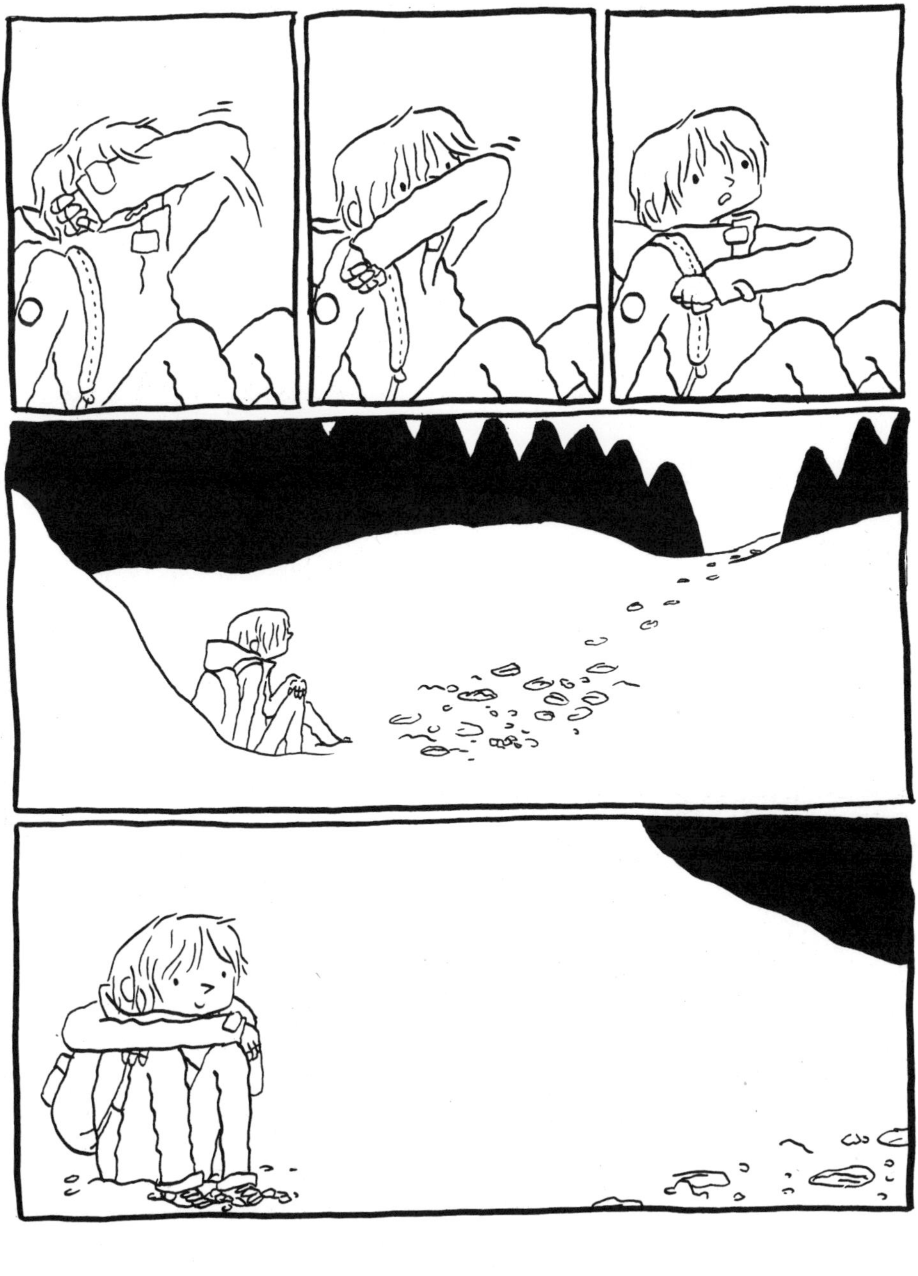

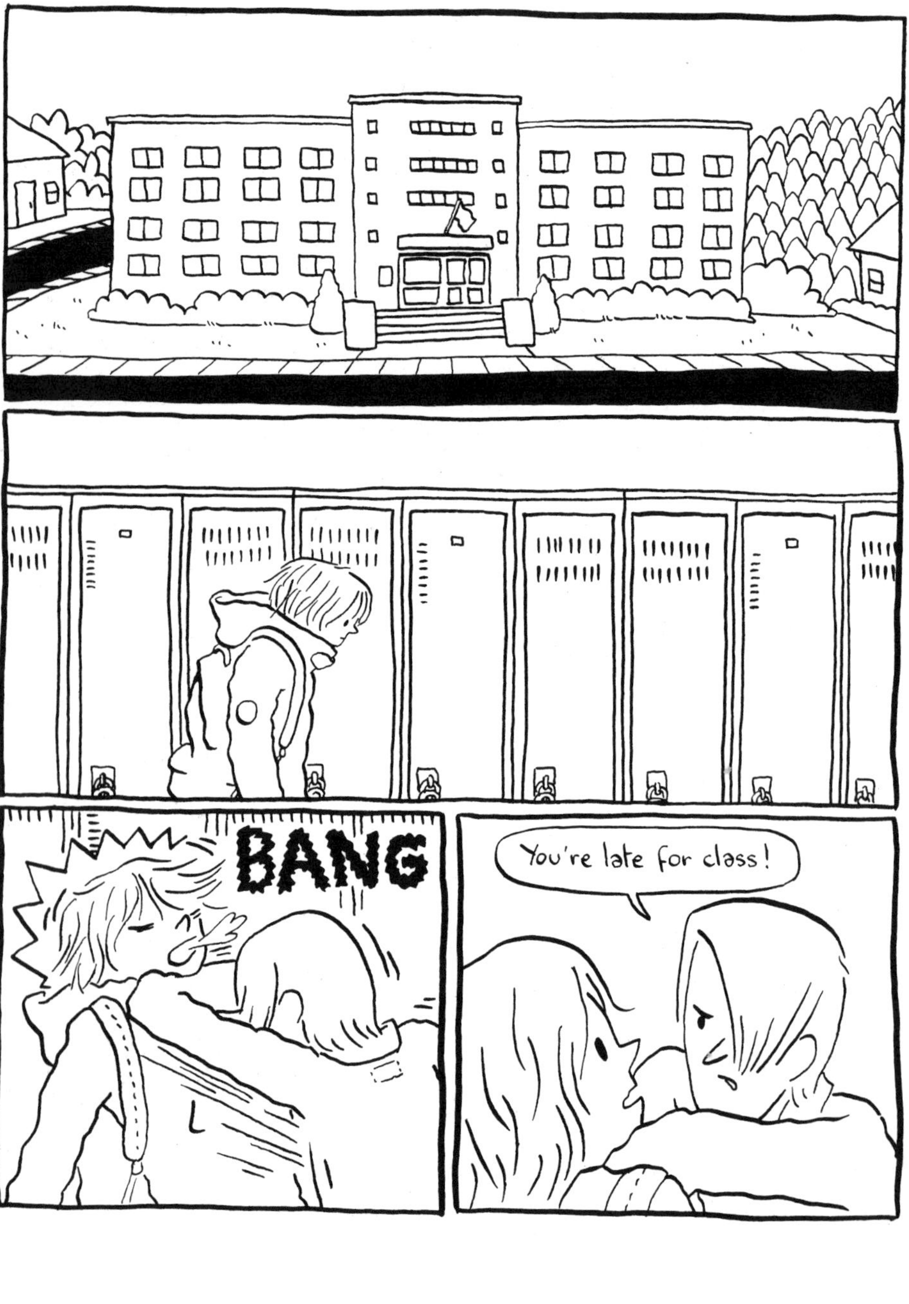
BANG
You're late for class!

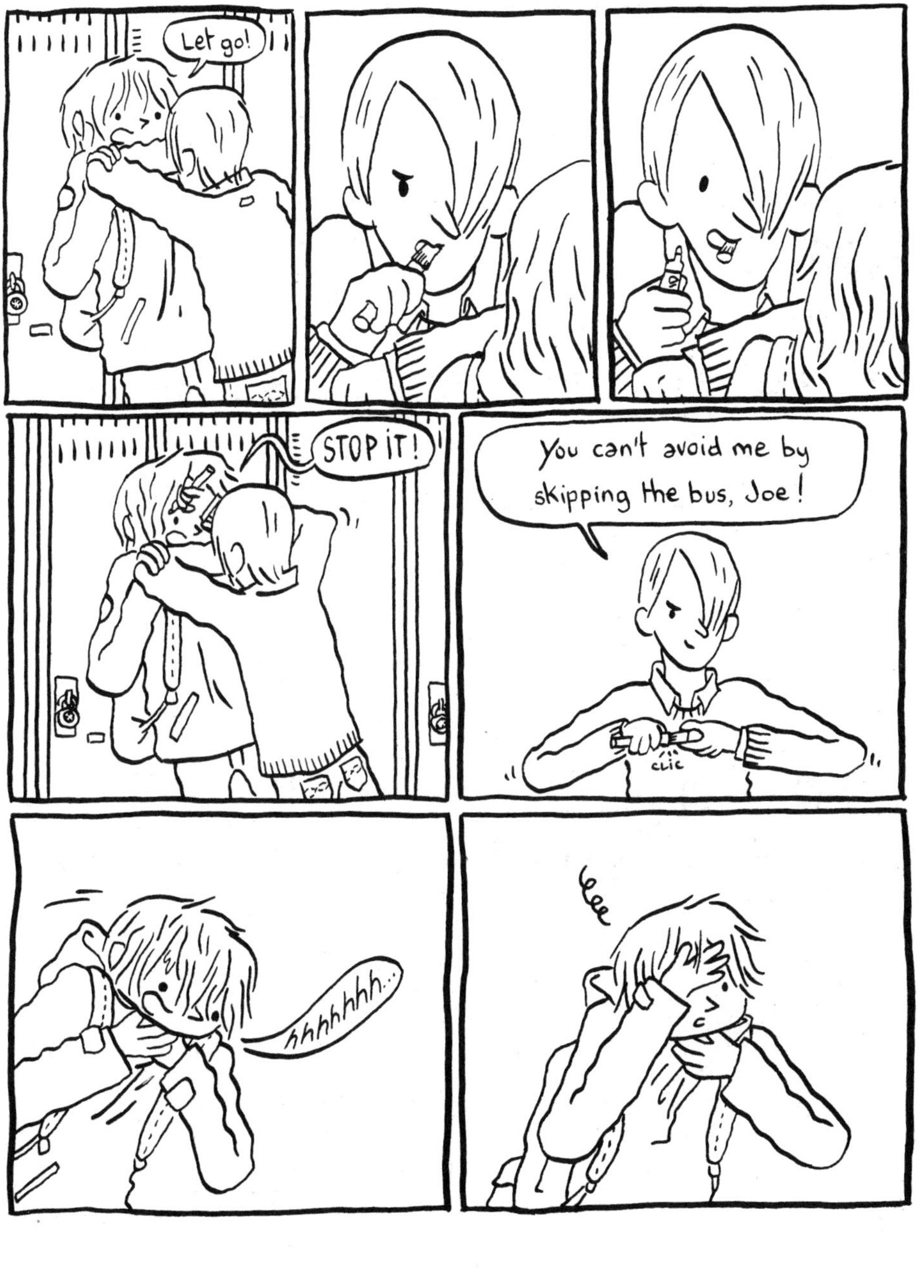
Let go!
STOP IT!
You can't avoid me by skipping the bus, Joe!
clic
hhhhhhh...

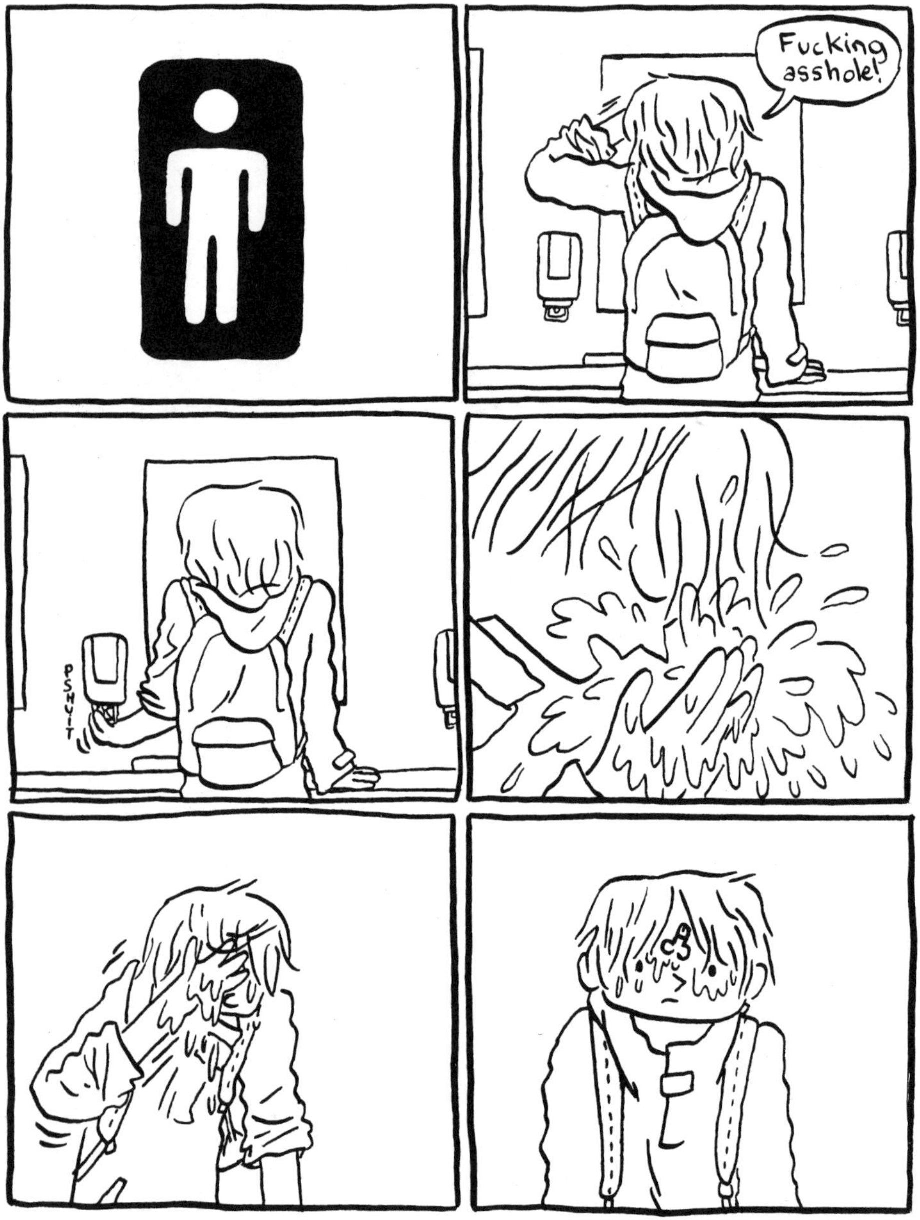
Fucking asshole!
PSHHT

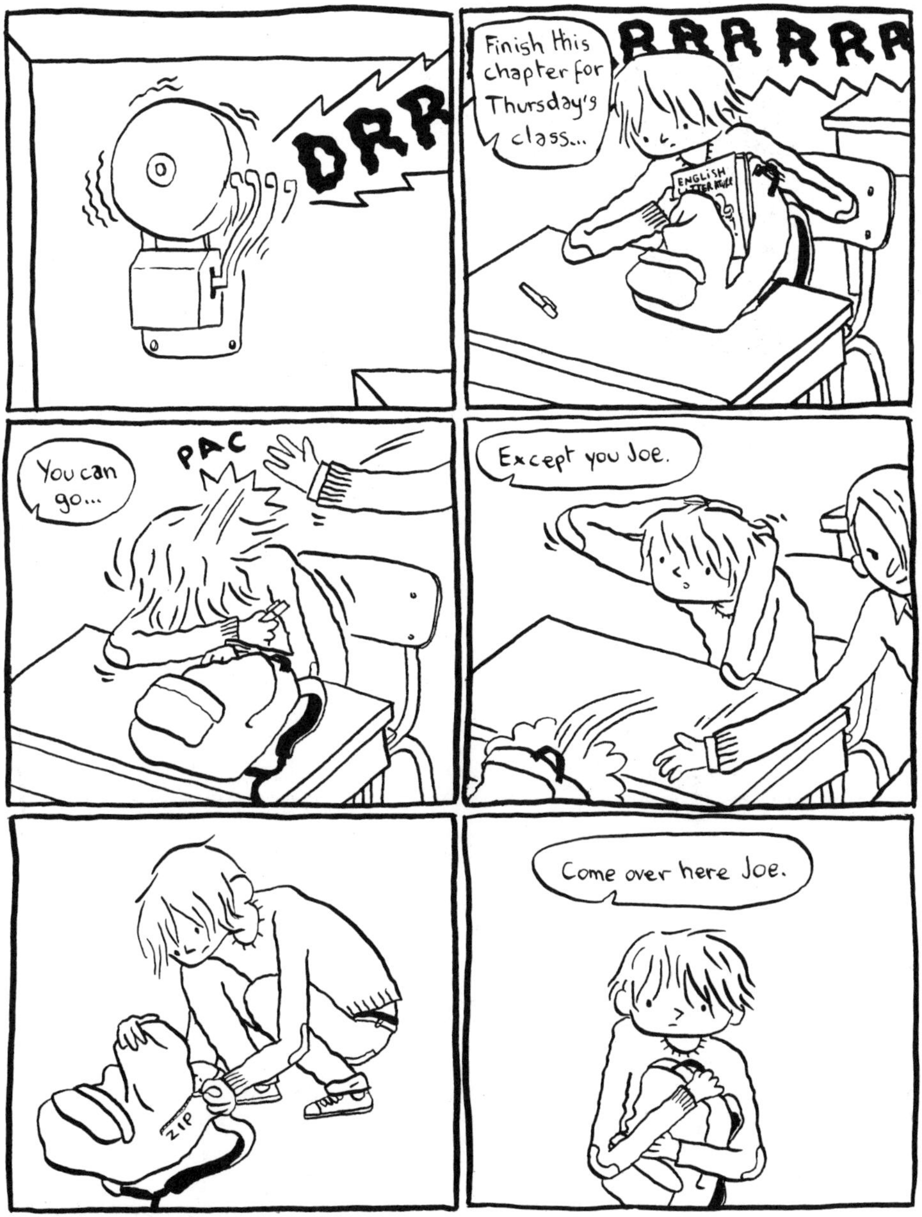
DRR
Finish this chapter for Thursday's class...
RRRRRR
ENGLISH LITTERATURE
You can go...
PAC
Except you Joe.
ZIP
Come over here Joe.

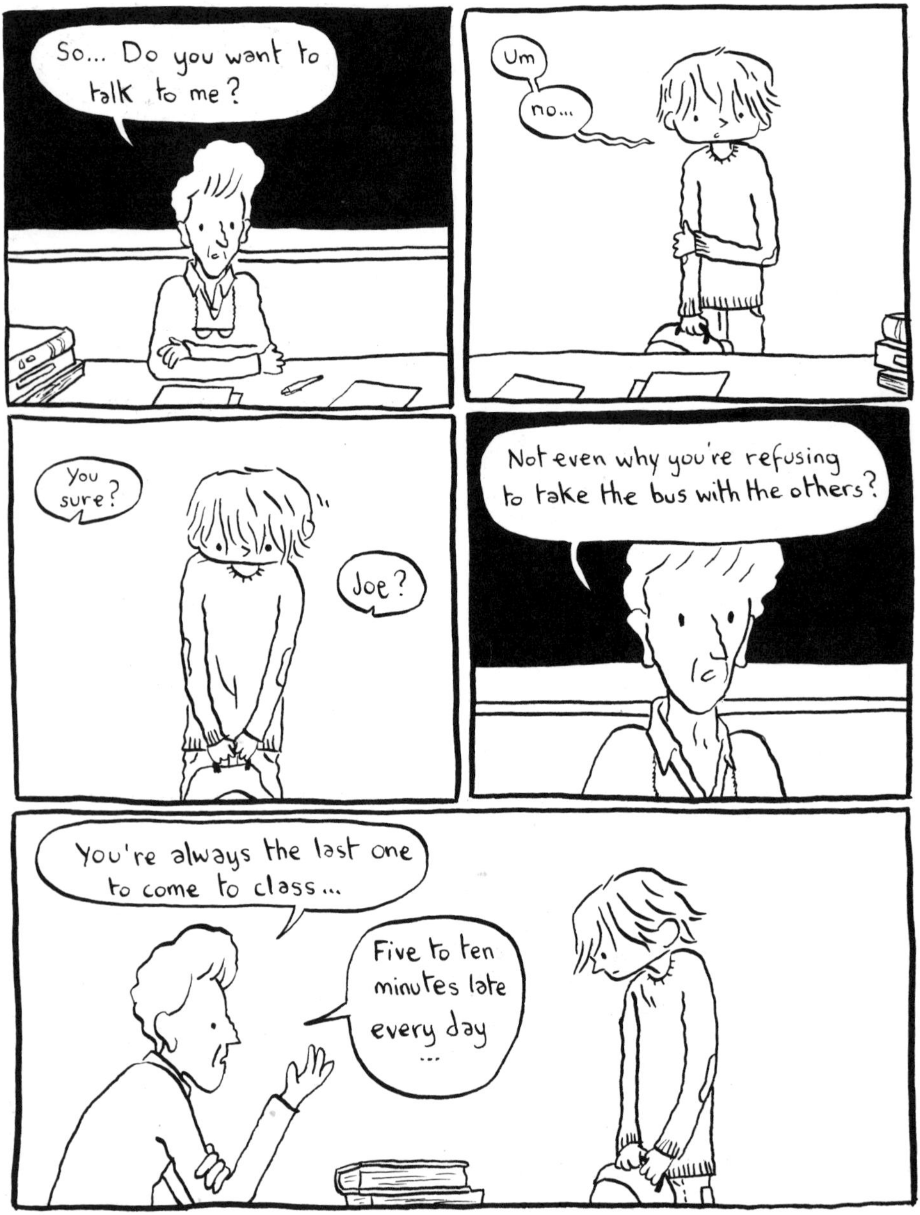

So... Do you want to talk to me?
Um
no...
You sure?
Joe?
Not even why you're refusing to take the bus with the others?
You're always the last one to come to class...
Five to ten minutes late every day ...

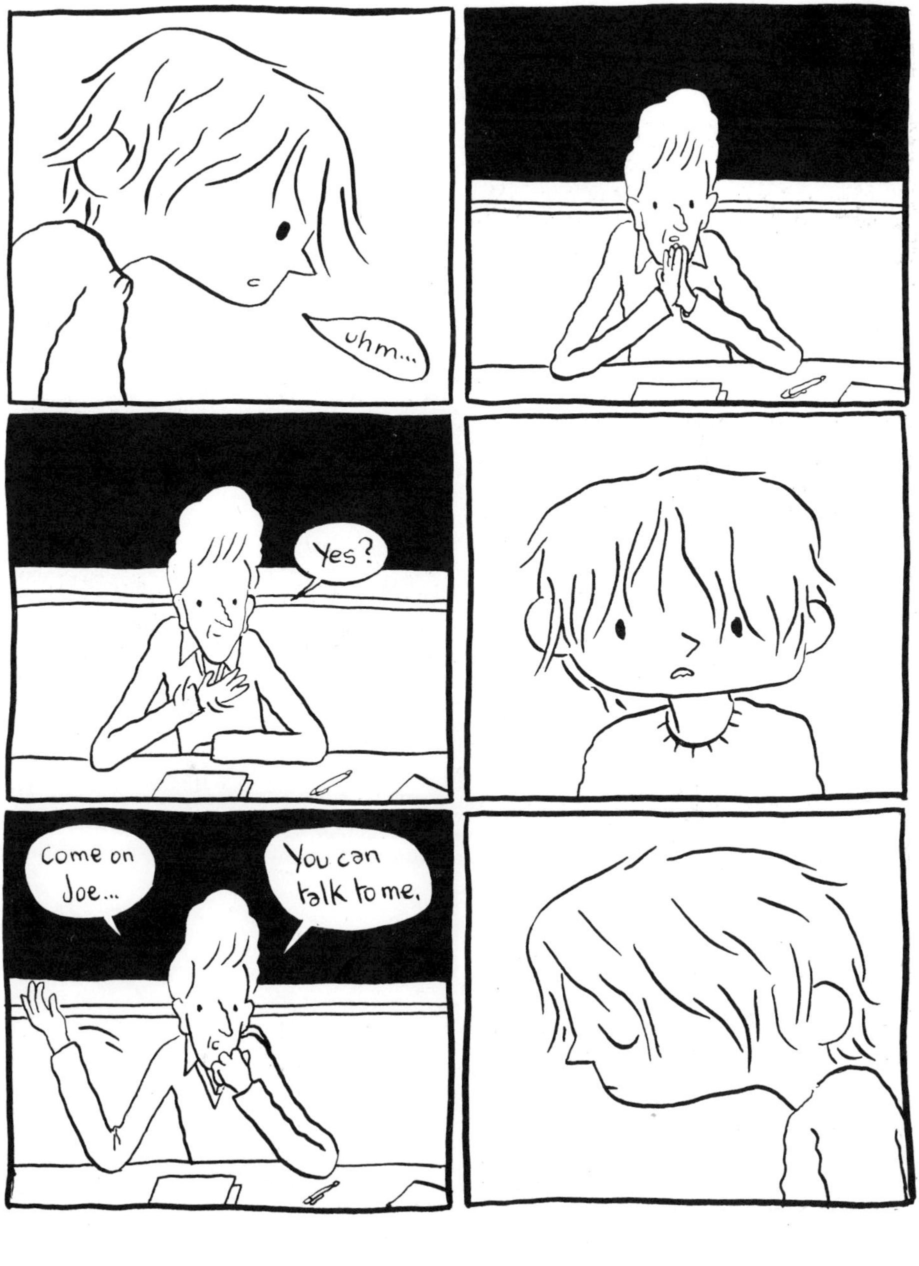
uhm...
Yes?
Come on Joe...
You can talk to me.

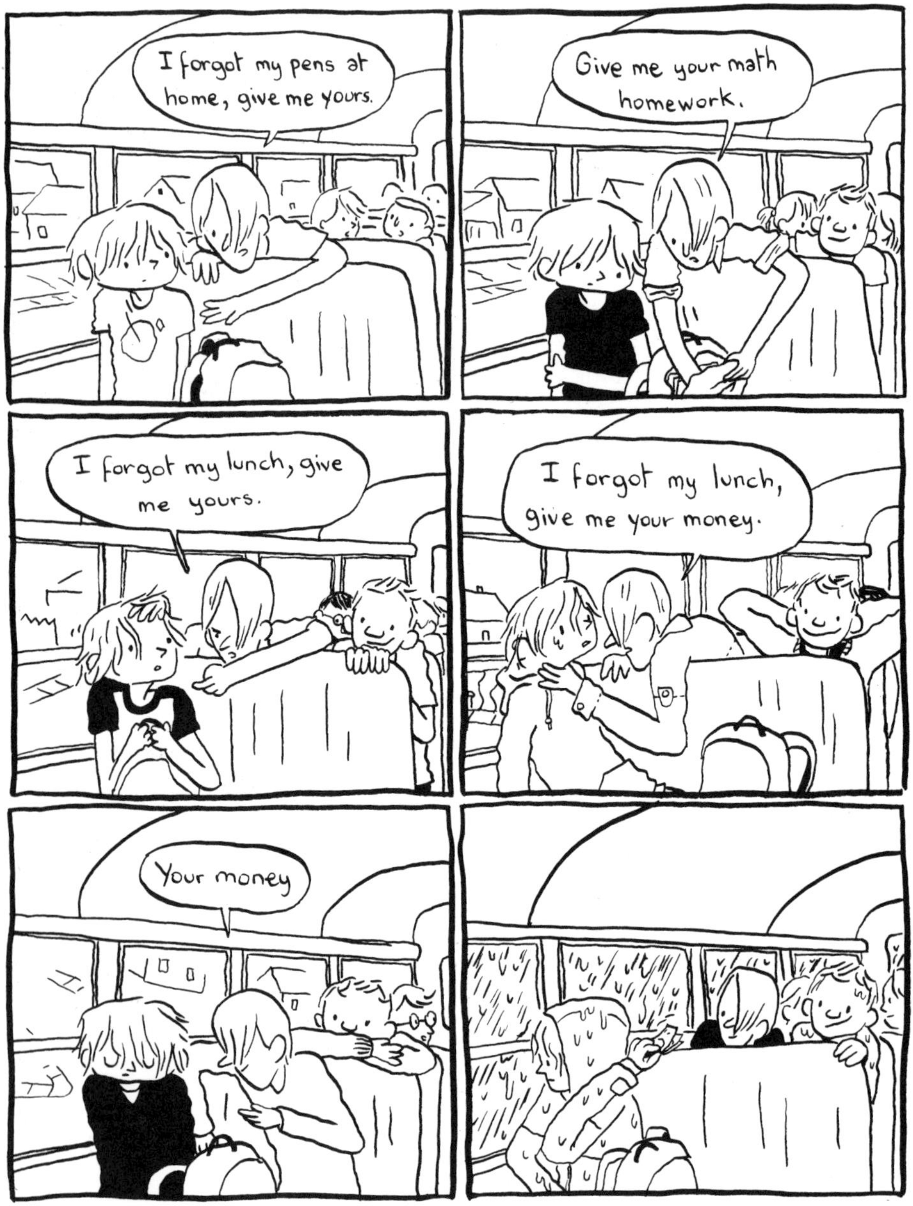
I forgot my pens at home, give me yours.
Give me your math homework.
I forgot my lunch, give me yours.
I forgot my lunch, give me your money.
Your money

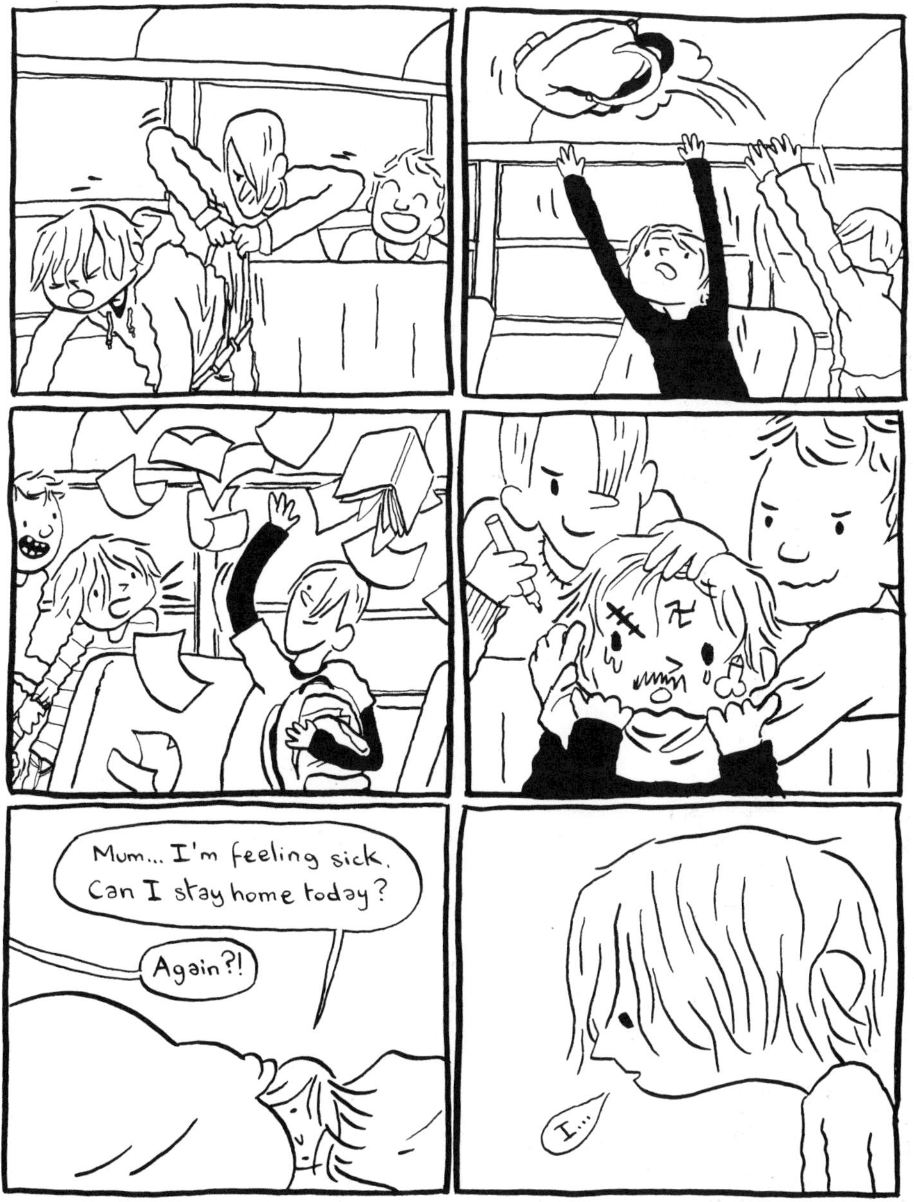
Mum... I'm feeling sick. Can I stay home today?
Again?!
I...

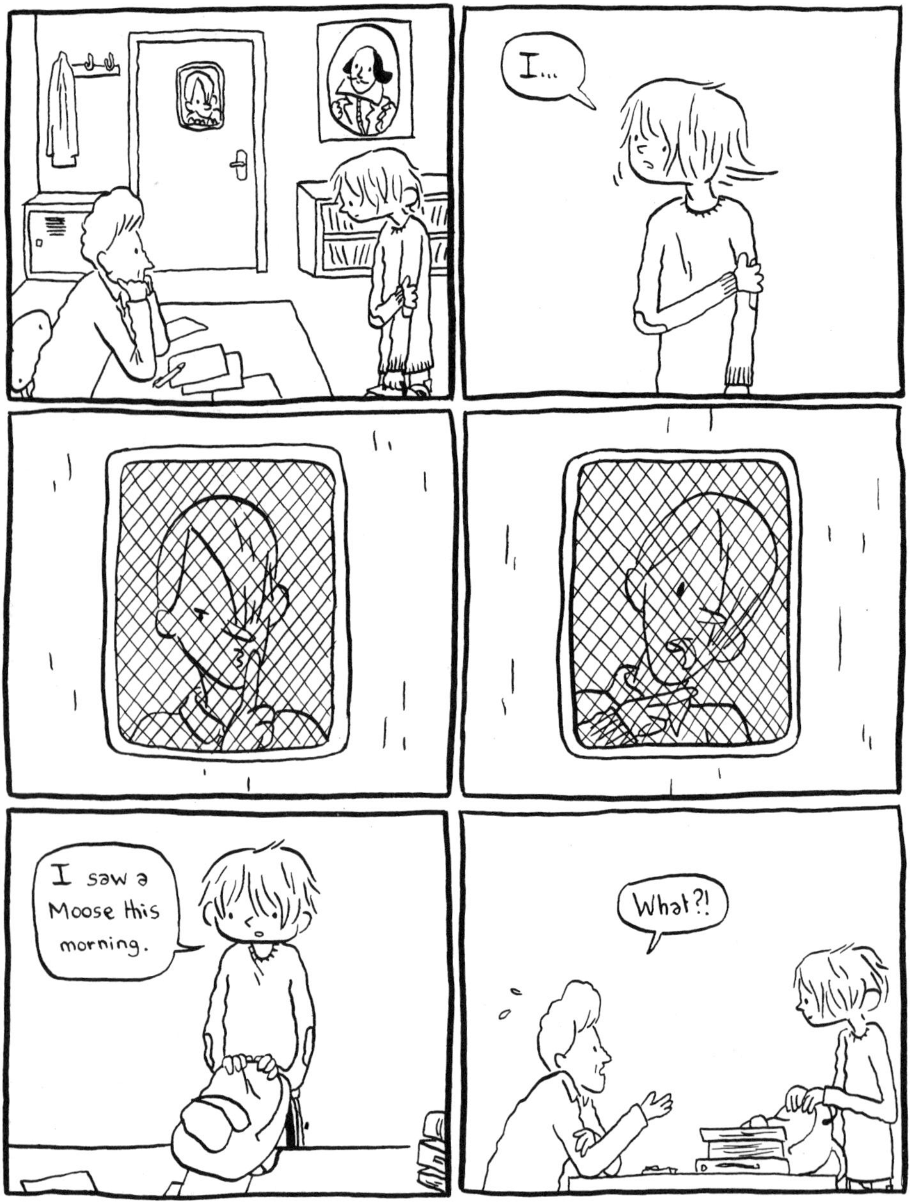
I...
I saw a Moose this morning.
What?!

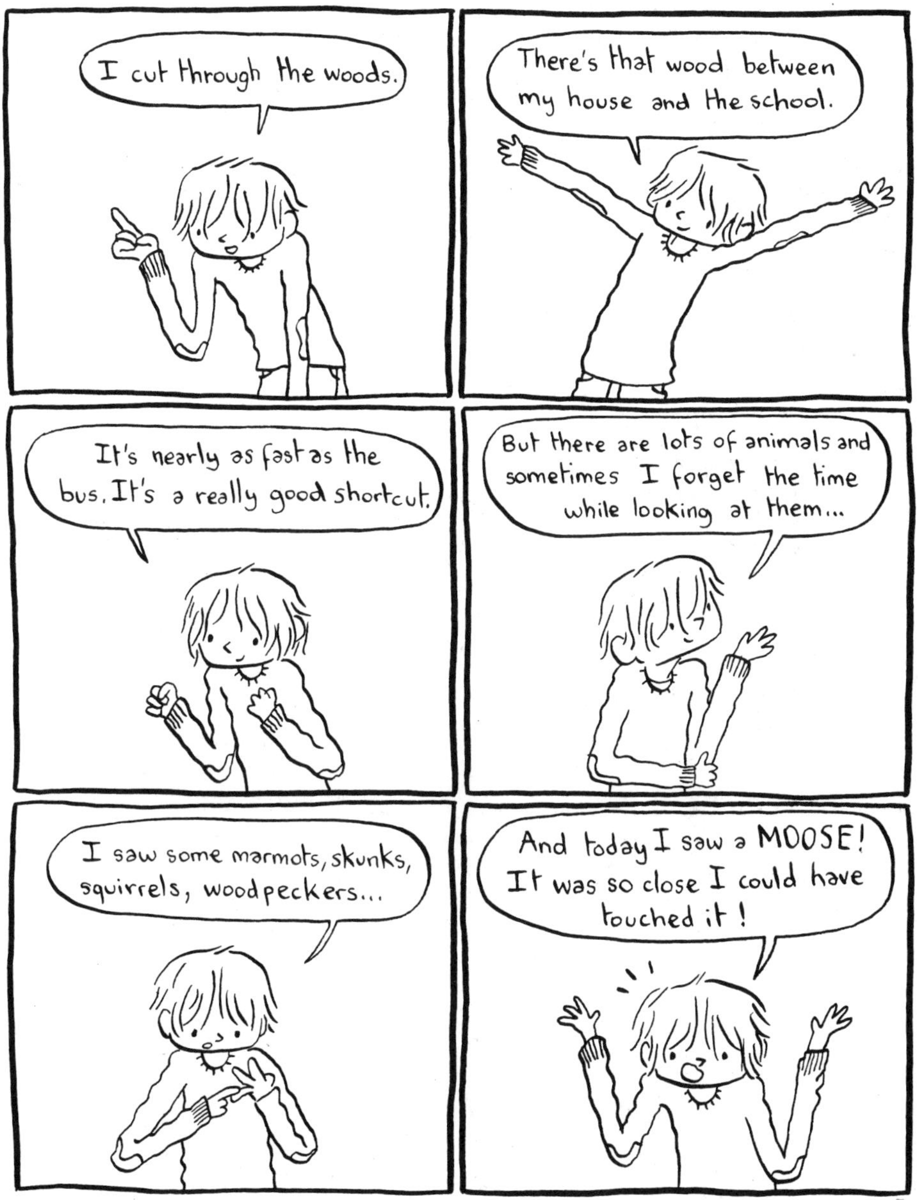
I cut through the woods.
There's that wood between my house and the school.
It's nearly as fast as the bus. It's a really good shortcut.
But there are lots of animals and sometimes I forget the time while looking at them...
I saw some marmots, skunks, squirrels, woodpeckers...
And today I saw a MOOSE! It was so close I could have touched it!

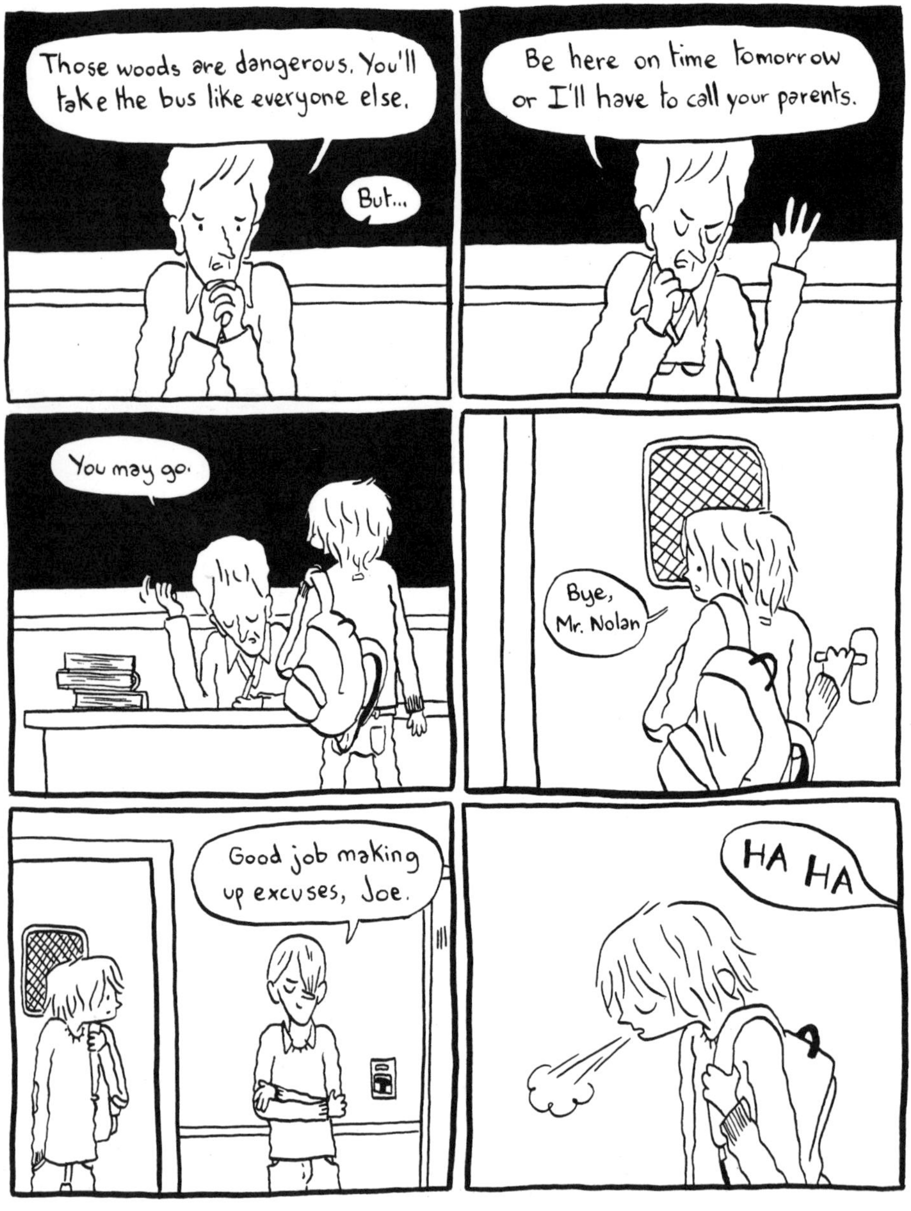
Those woods are dangerous. You'll take the bus like everyone else.
But...
Be here on time tomorrow or I'll have to call your parents.
You may go.
Bye, Mr. Nolan
Good job making up excuses, Joe.
HA HA

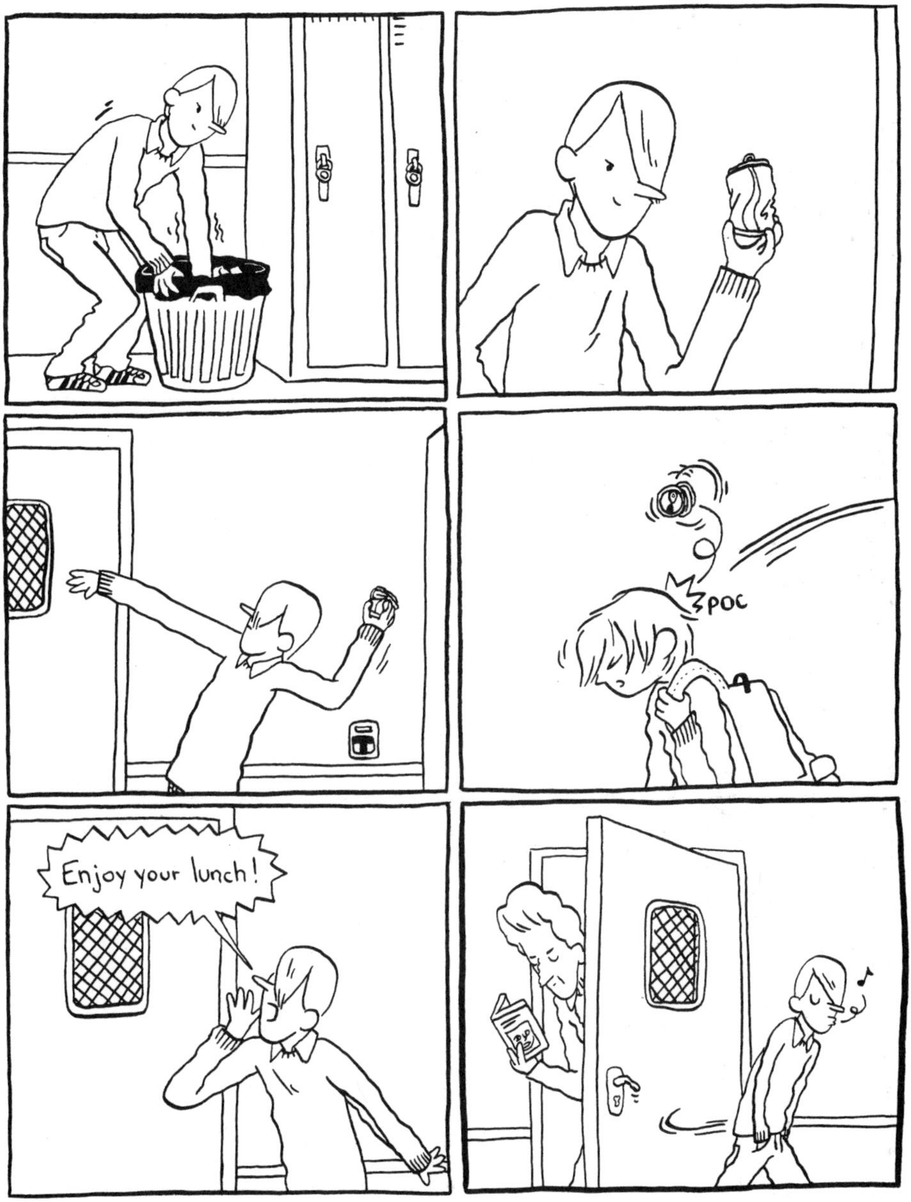
POC
Enjoy your lunch!

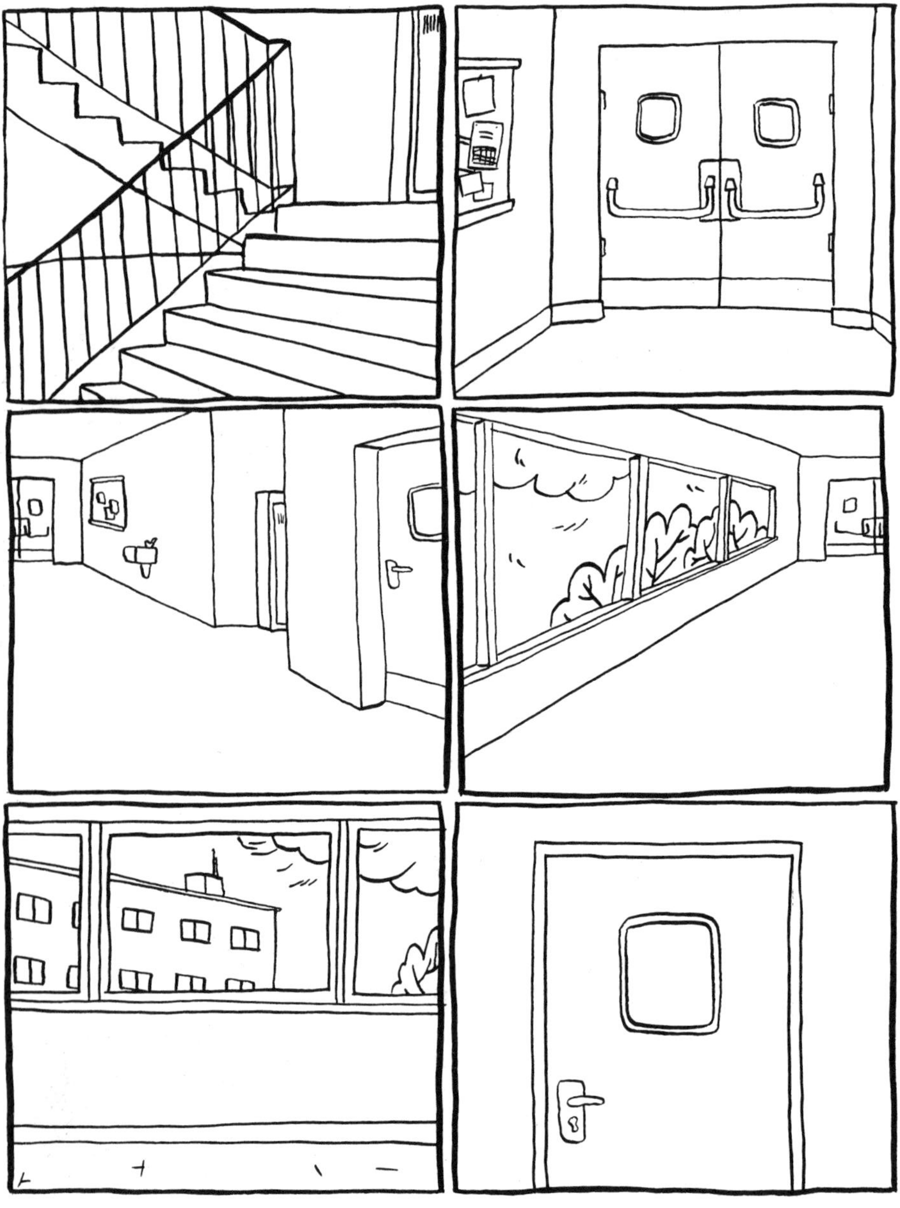

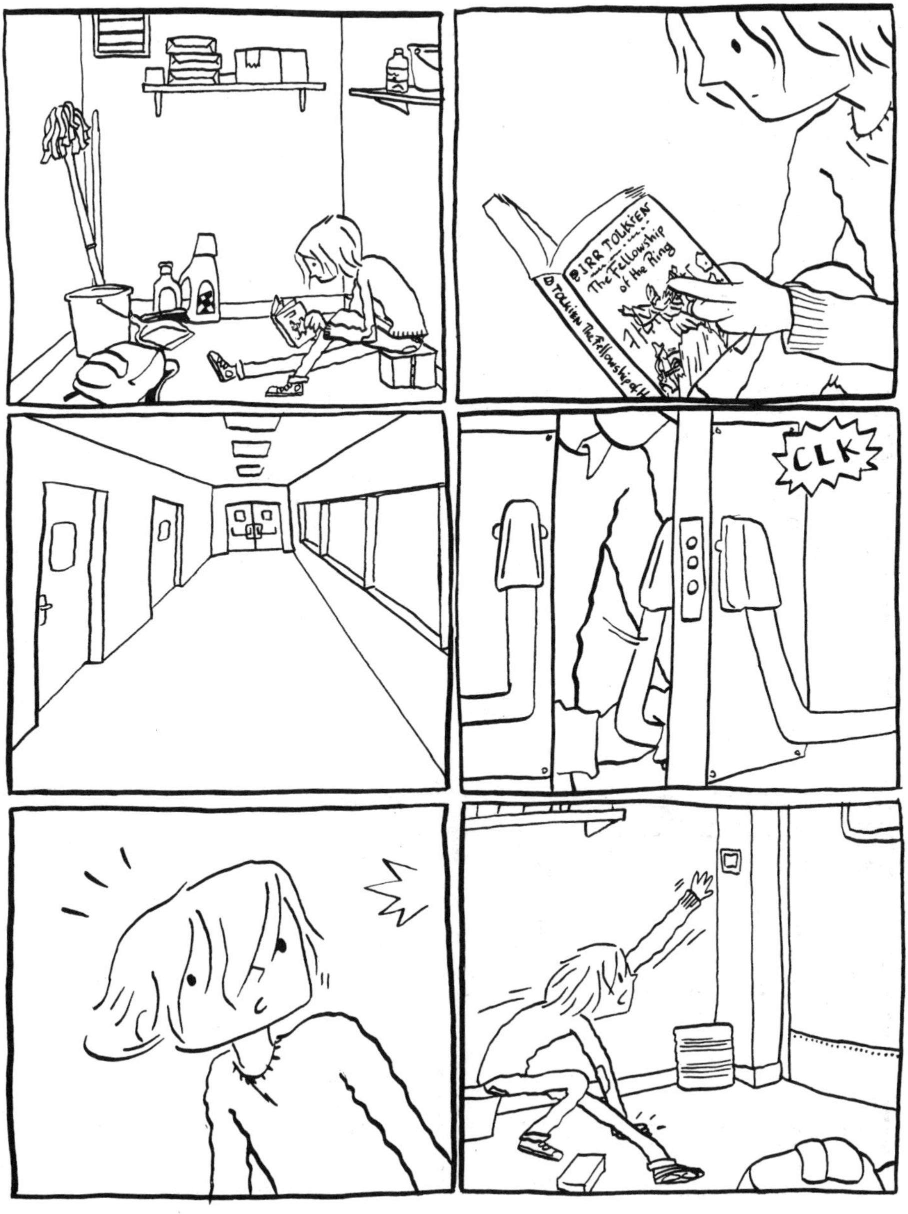

JRR TOLKIEN
The Fellowship of the Ring
TOLKIEN The Fellowship of the
CLK

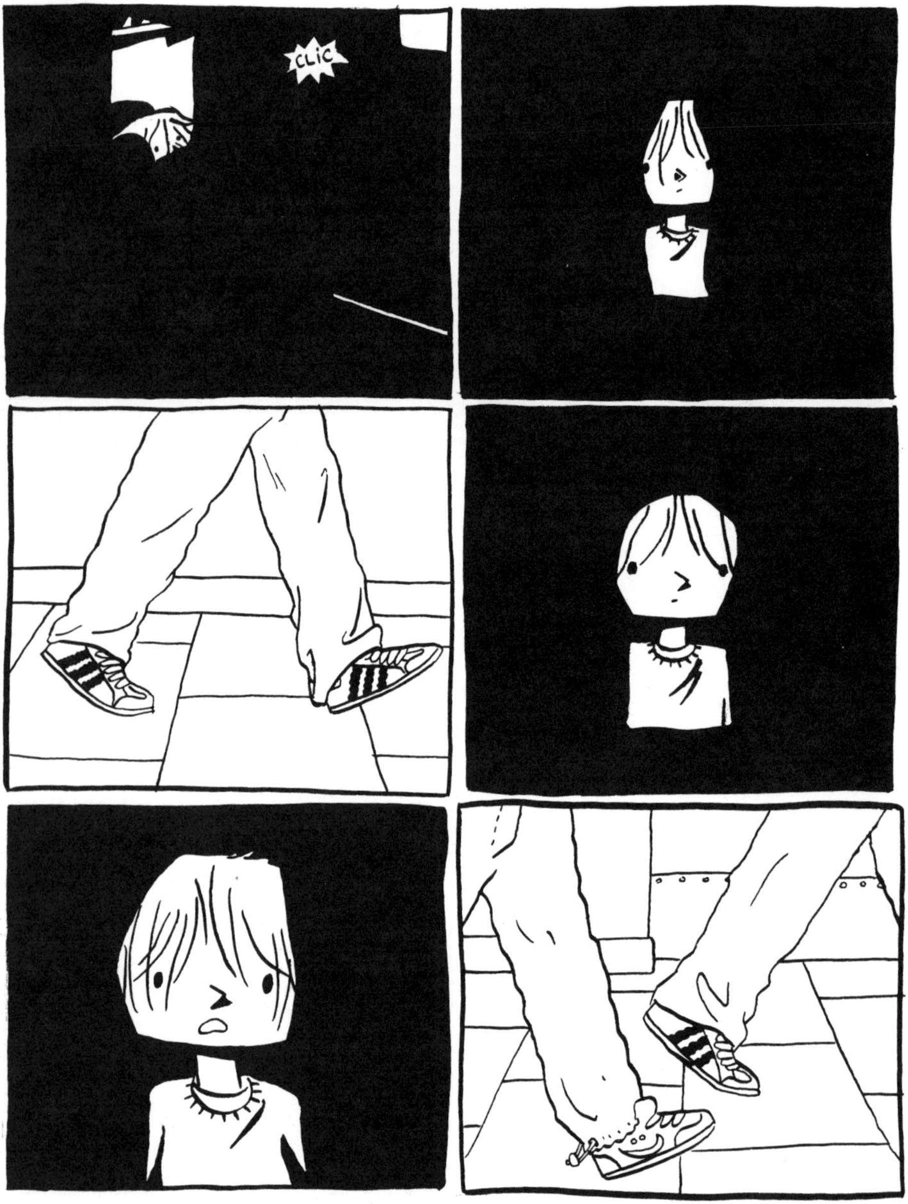
CLIC

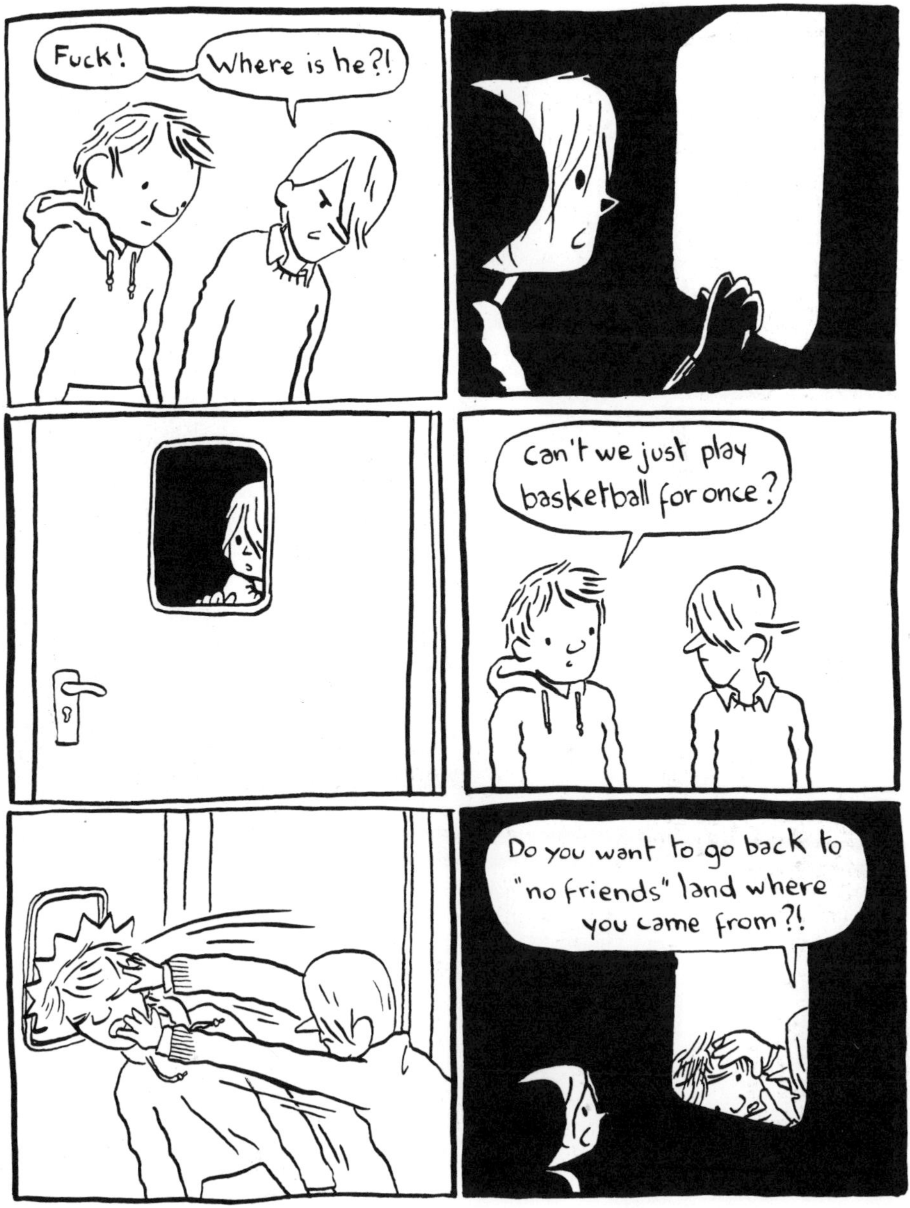
Fuck!
Where is he?!
Can't we just play basketball for once?
Do you want to go back to "no friends" land where you came from?!

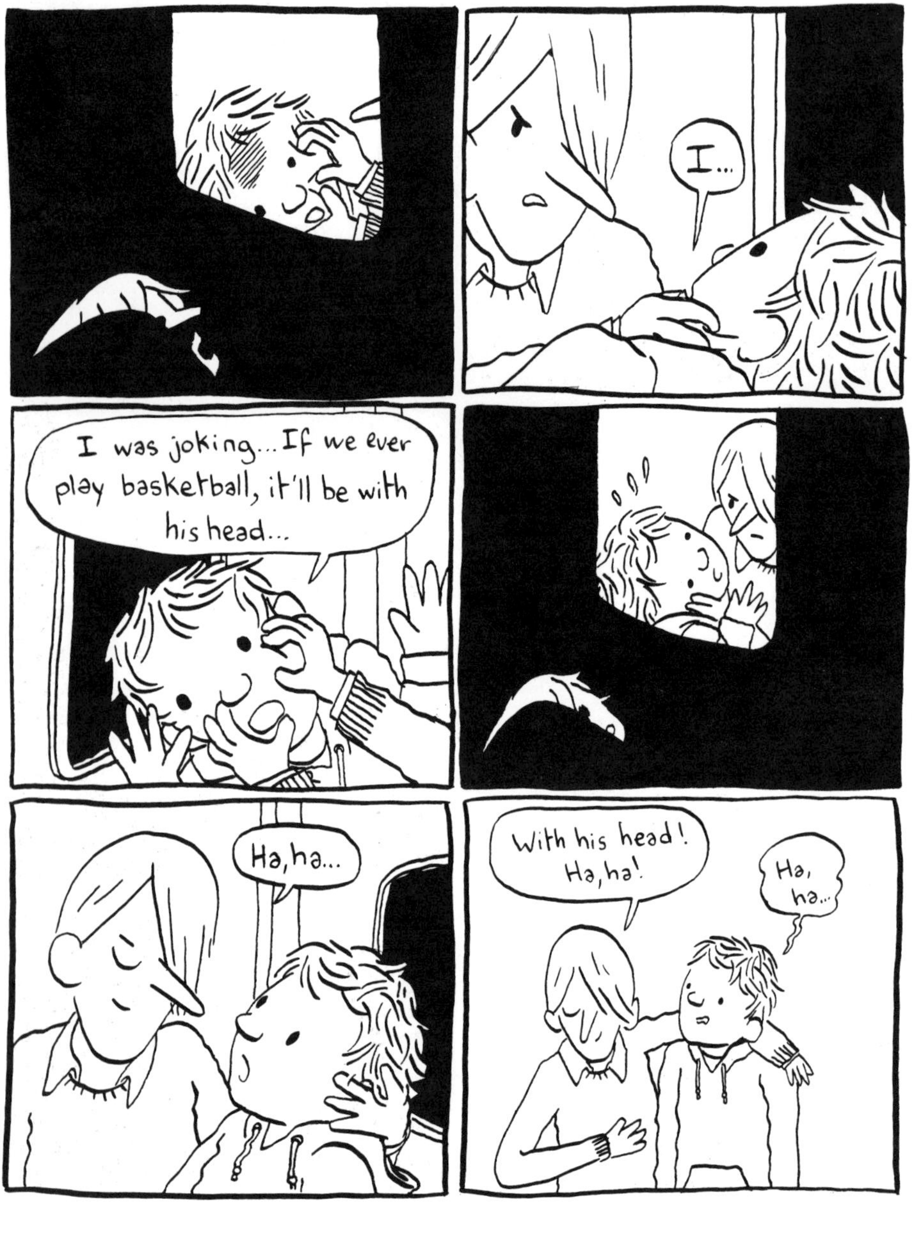
I...
I was joking... If we ever play basketball, it'll be with his head...
Ha, ha...
With his head! Ha, ha!
Ha, ha...

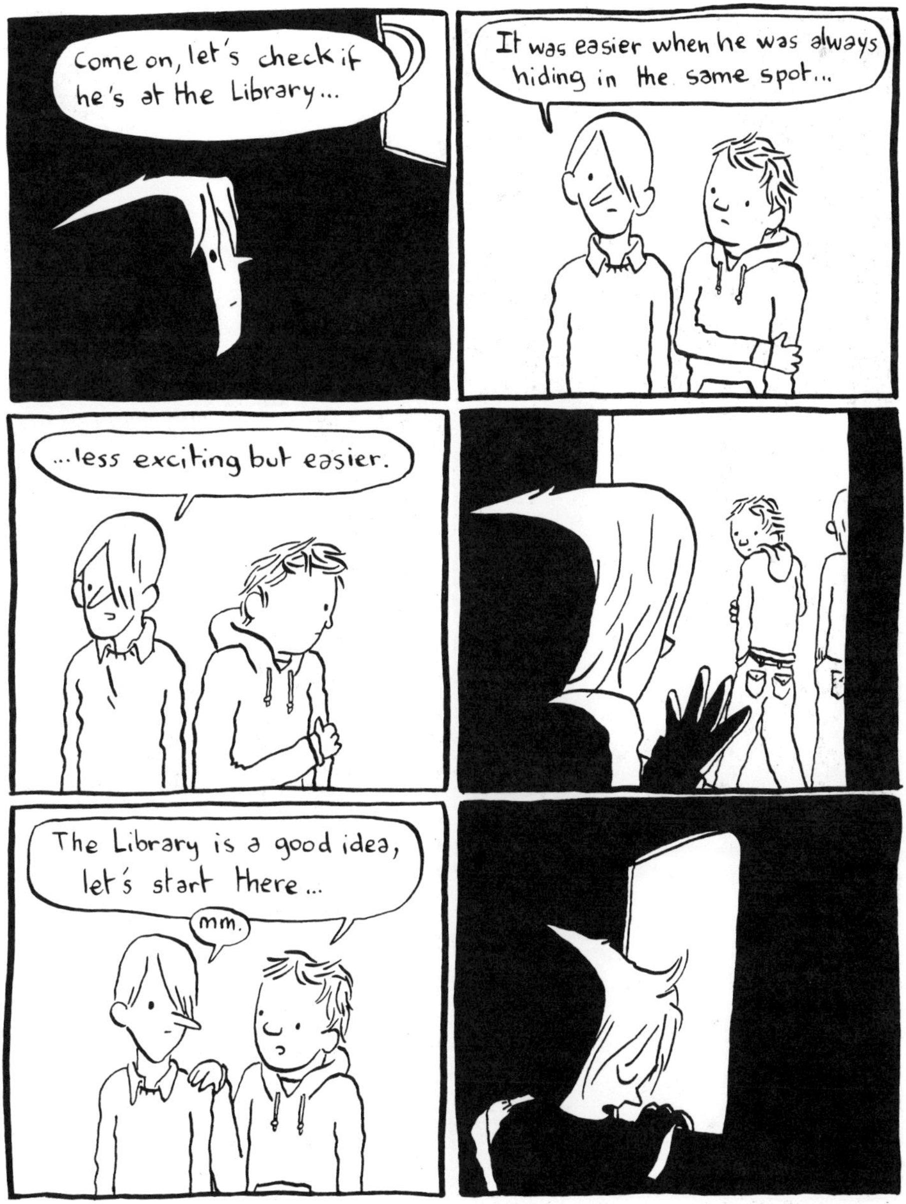
Come on, let's check if he's at the Library...
It was easier when he was always hiding in the same spot...
...less exciting but easier.
The Library is a good idea, let's start there...
mm.

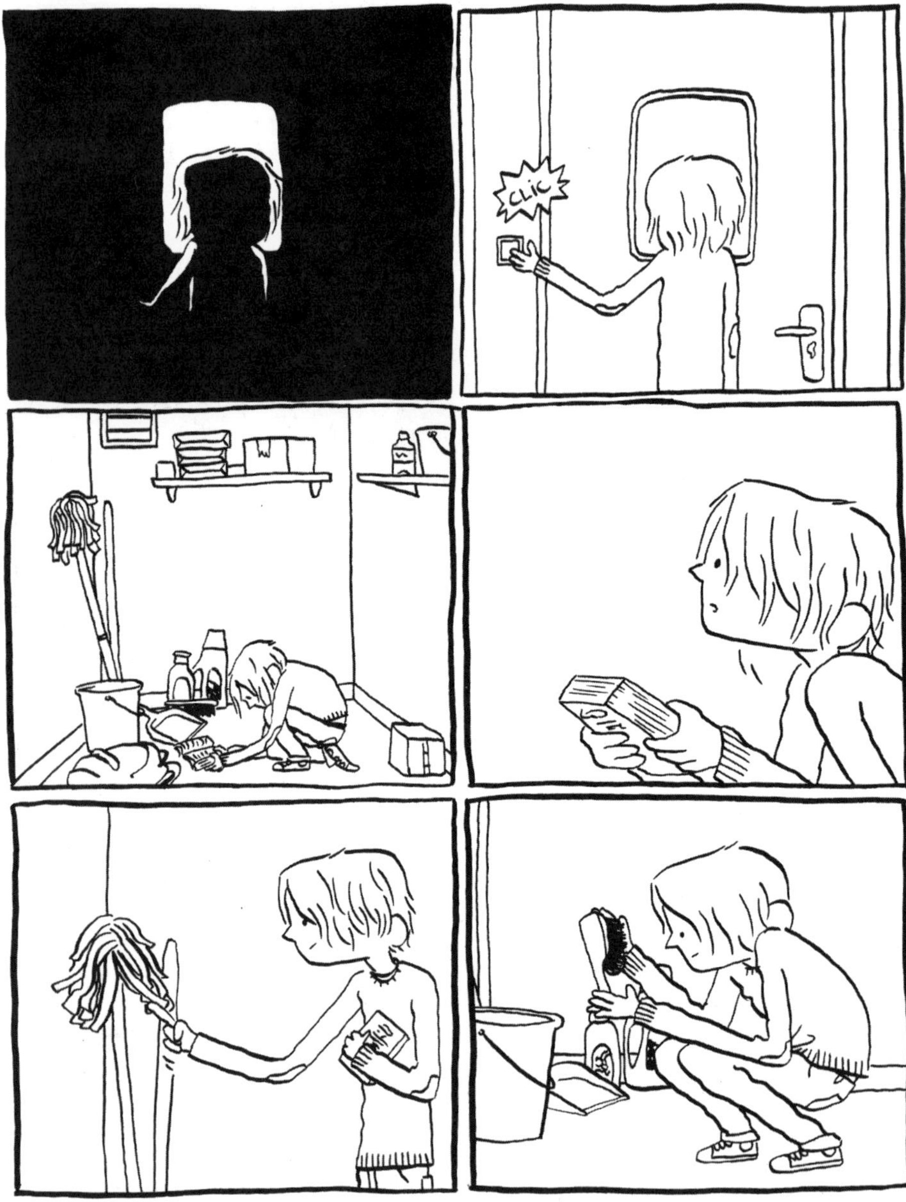
CLIC

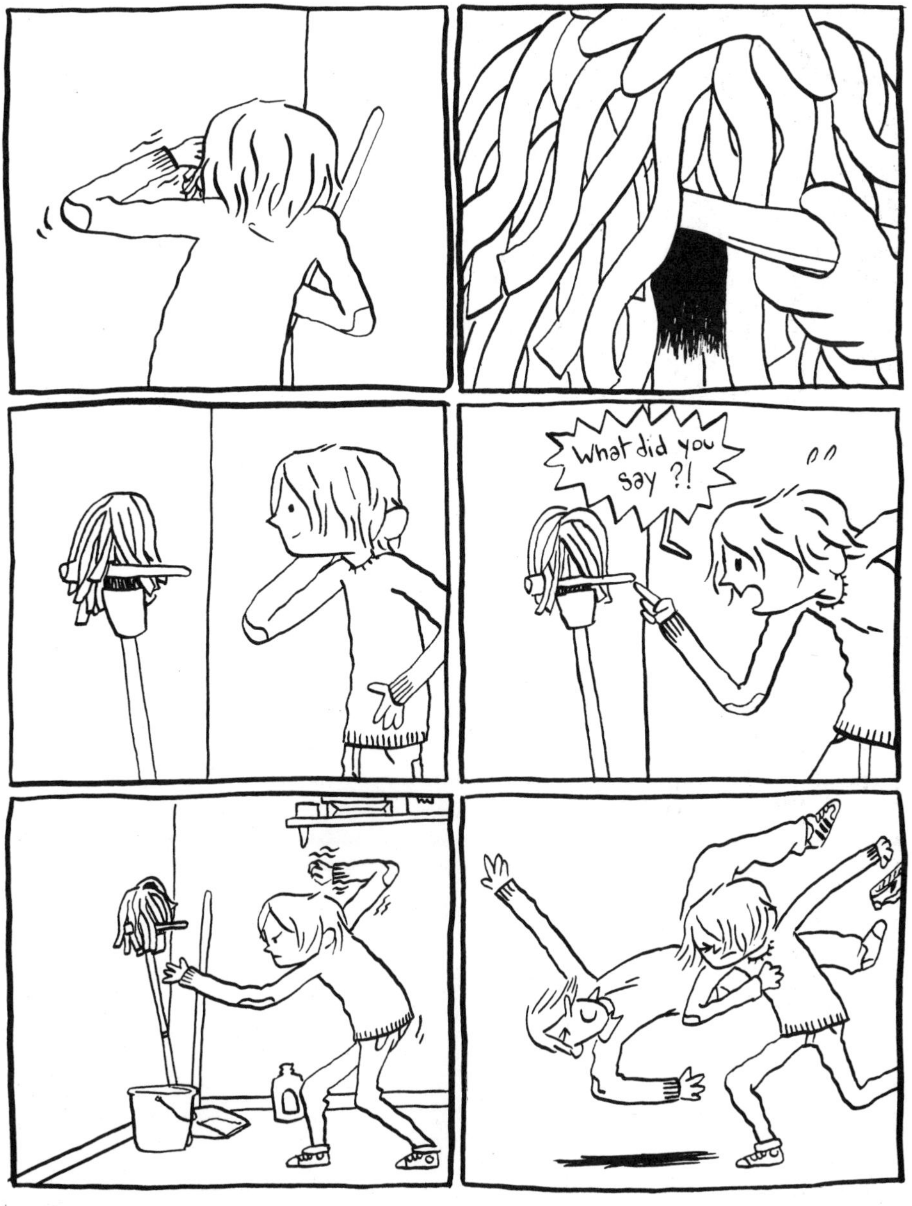
What did you say ?!

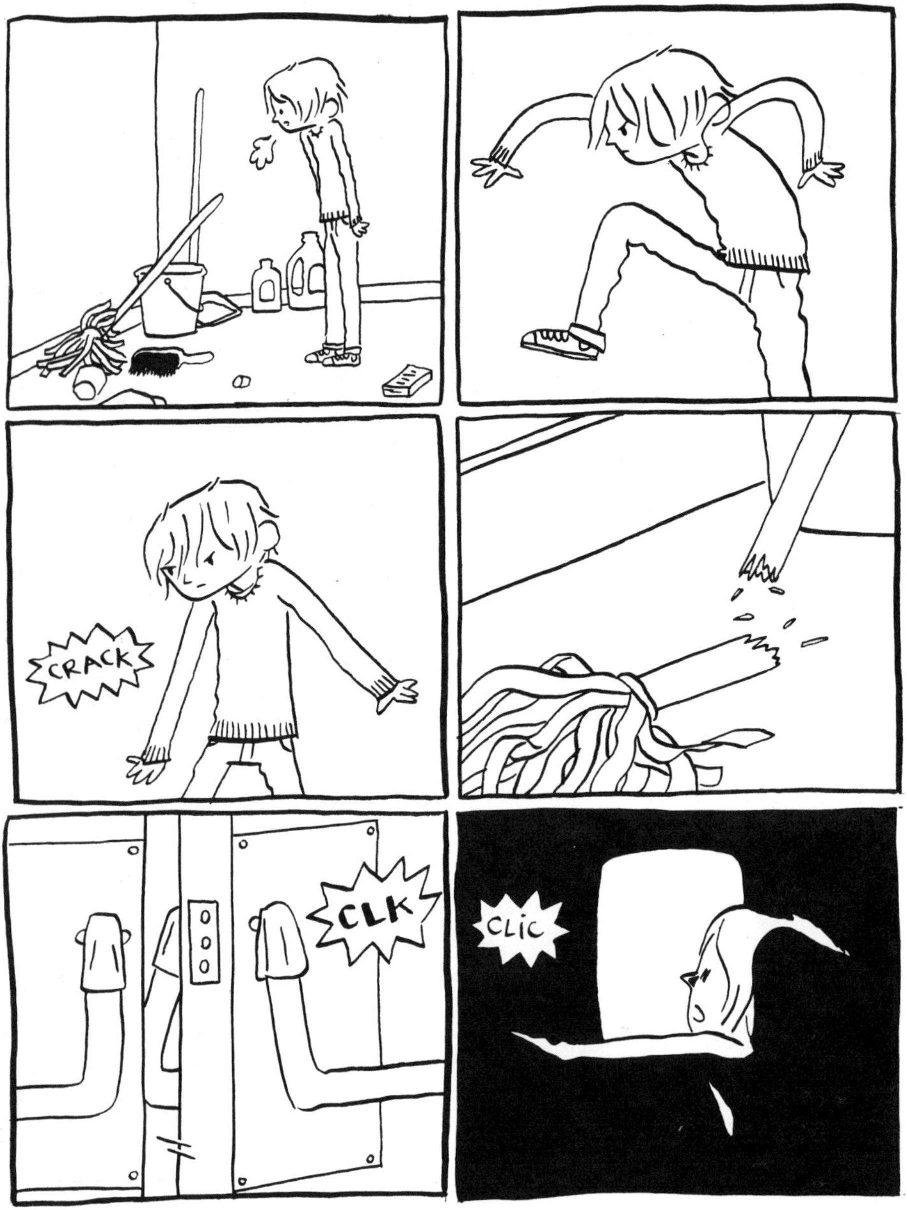
CRACK
CLK
CLIC

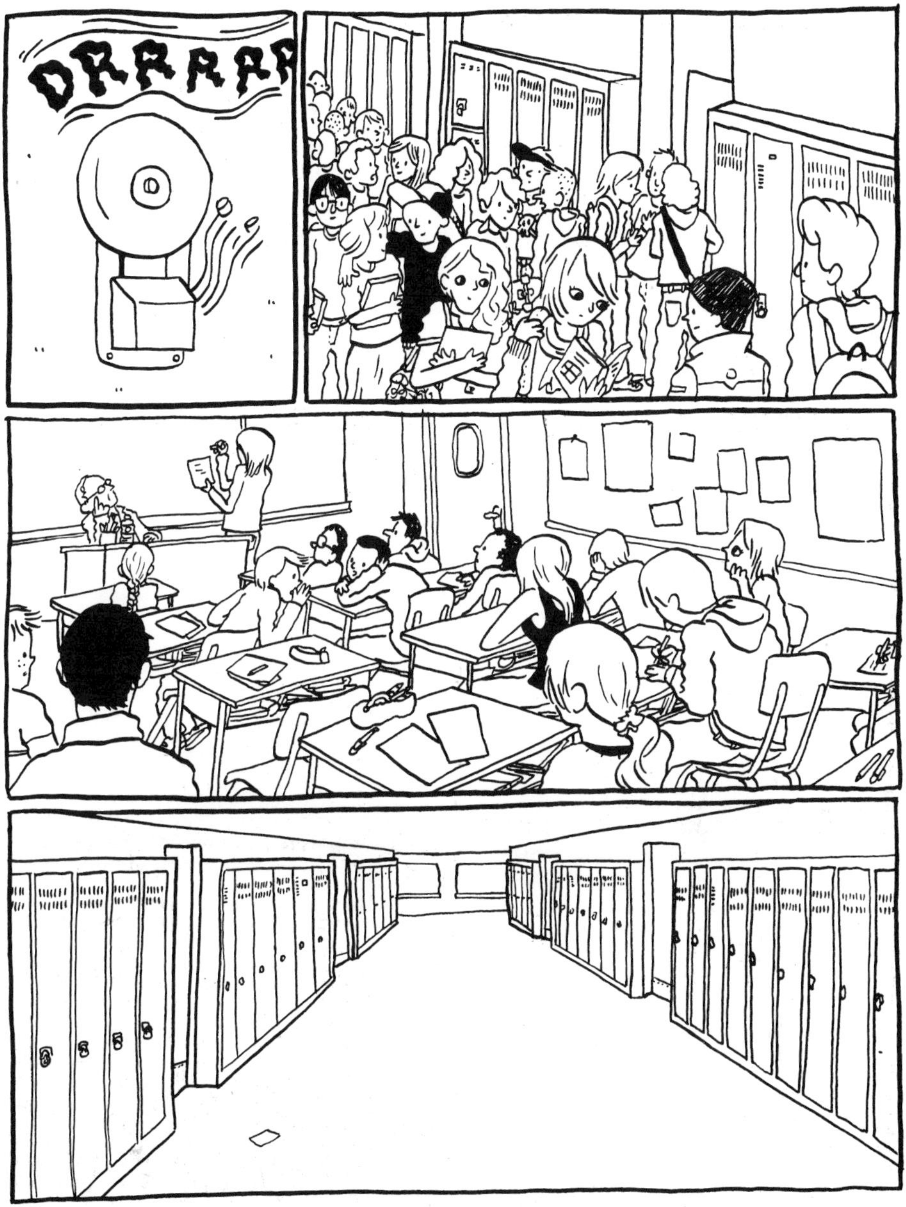
DRRRRR

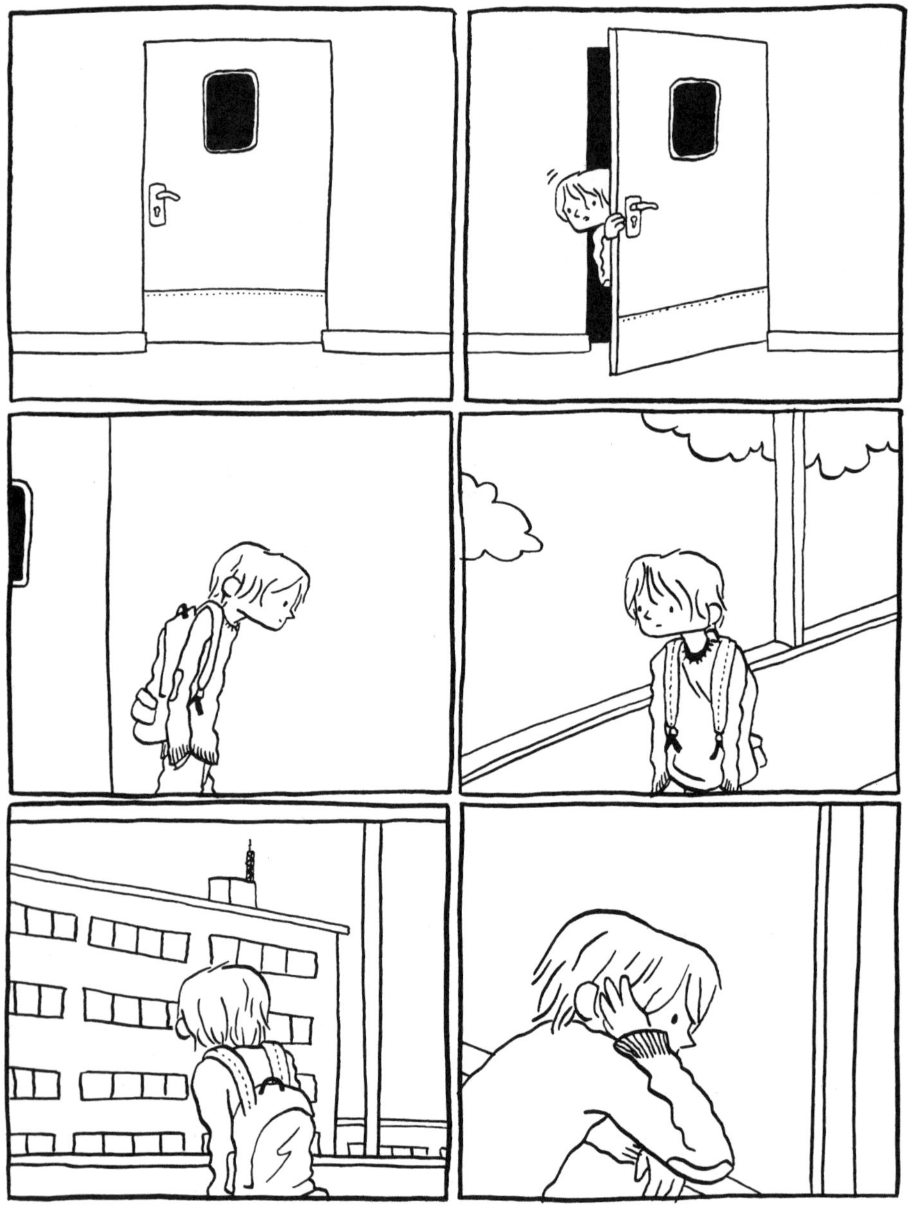

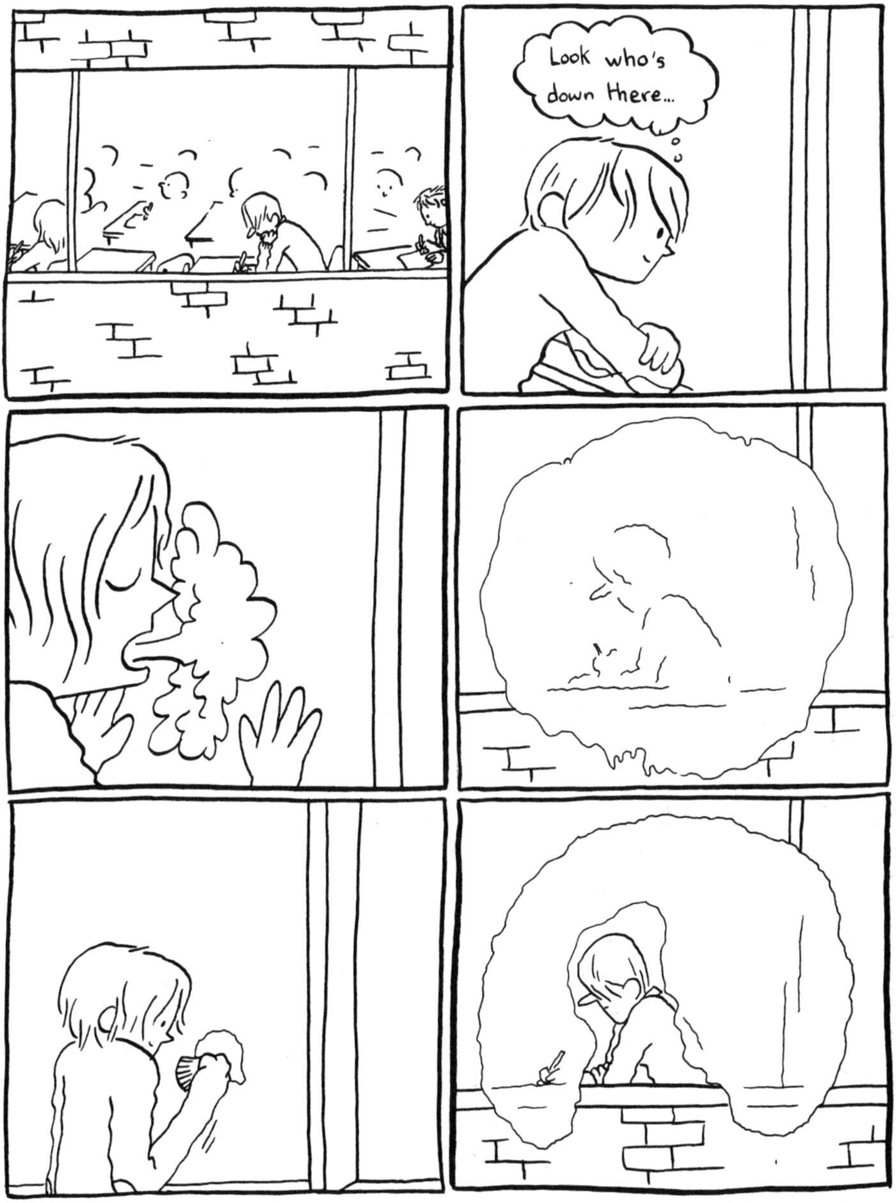
Look who's down there...

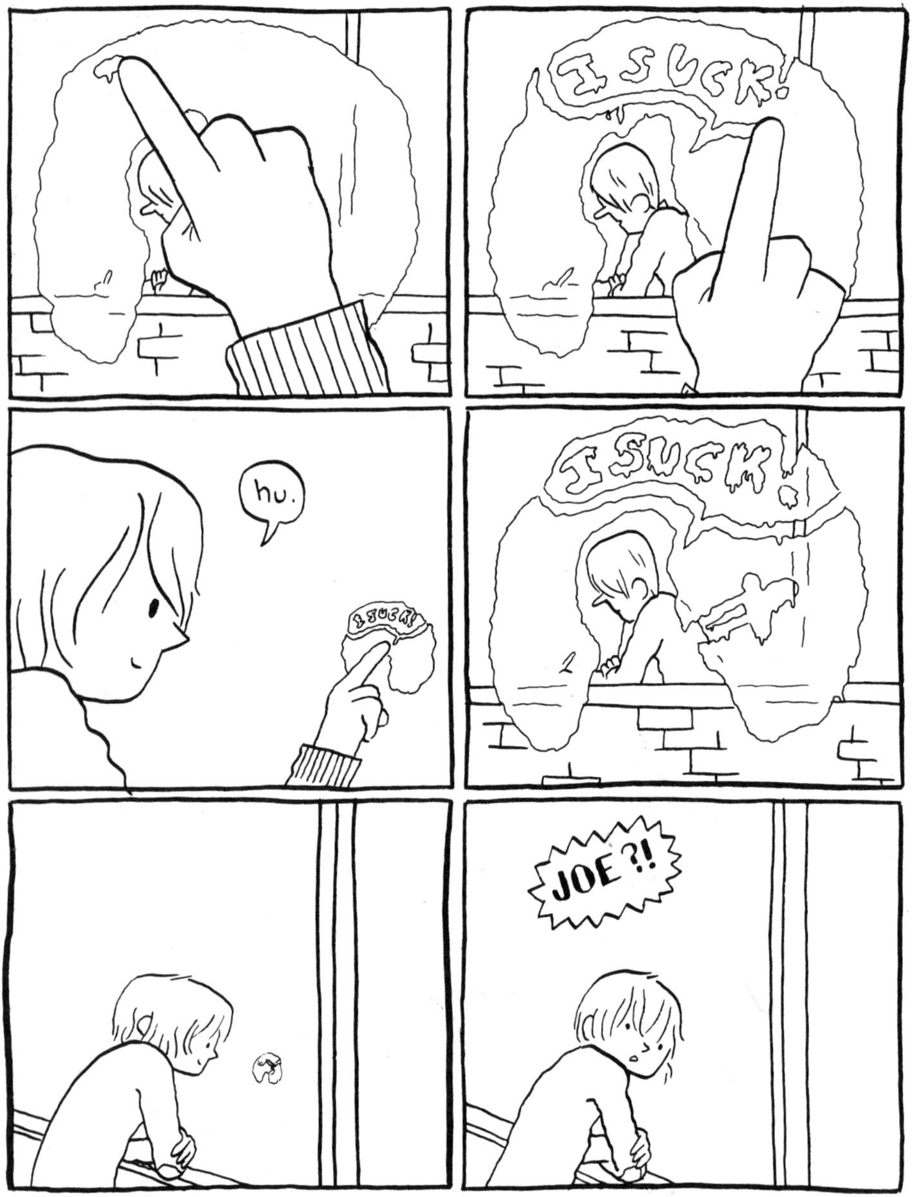
I SUCK!
hu.
I SUCK!
I SUCK!
JOE ?!

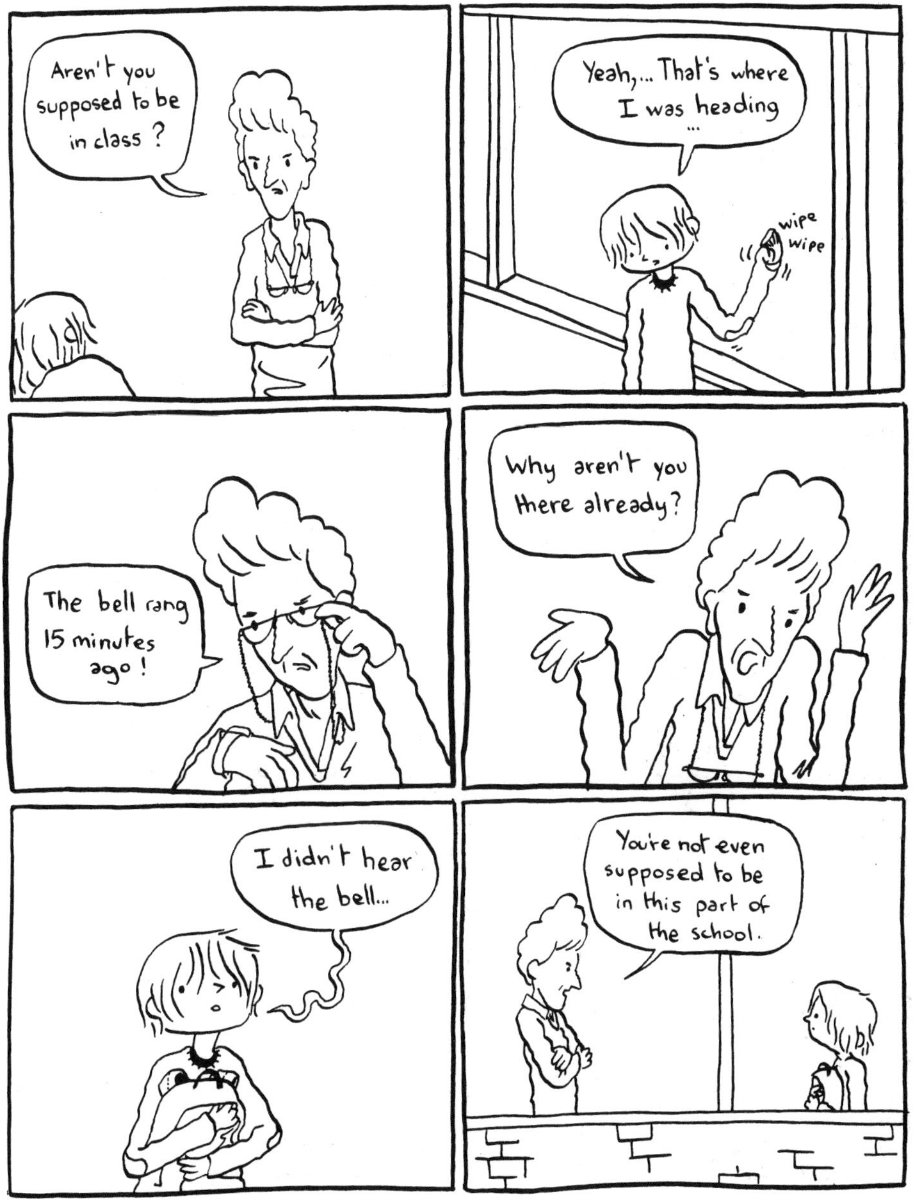
Aren't you supposed to be in class ?
Yeah,... That's where I was heading ...
wipe wipe
The bell rang 15 minutes ago !
Why aren't you there already?
I didn't hear the bell...
You're not even supposed to be in this part of the school.

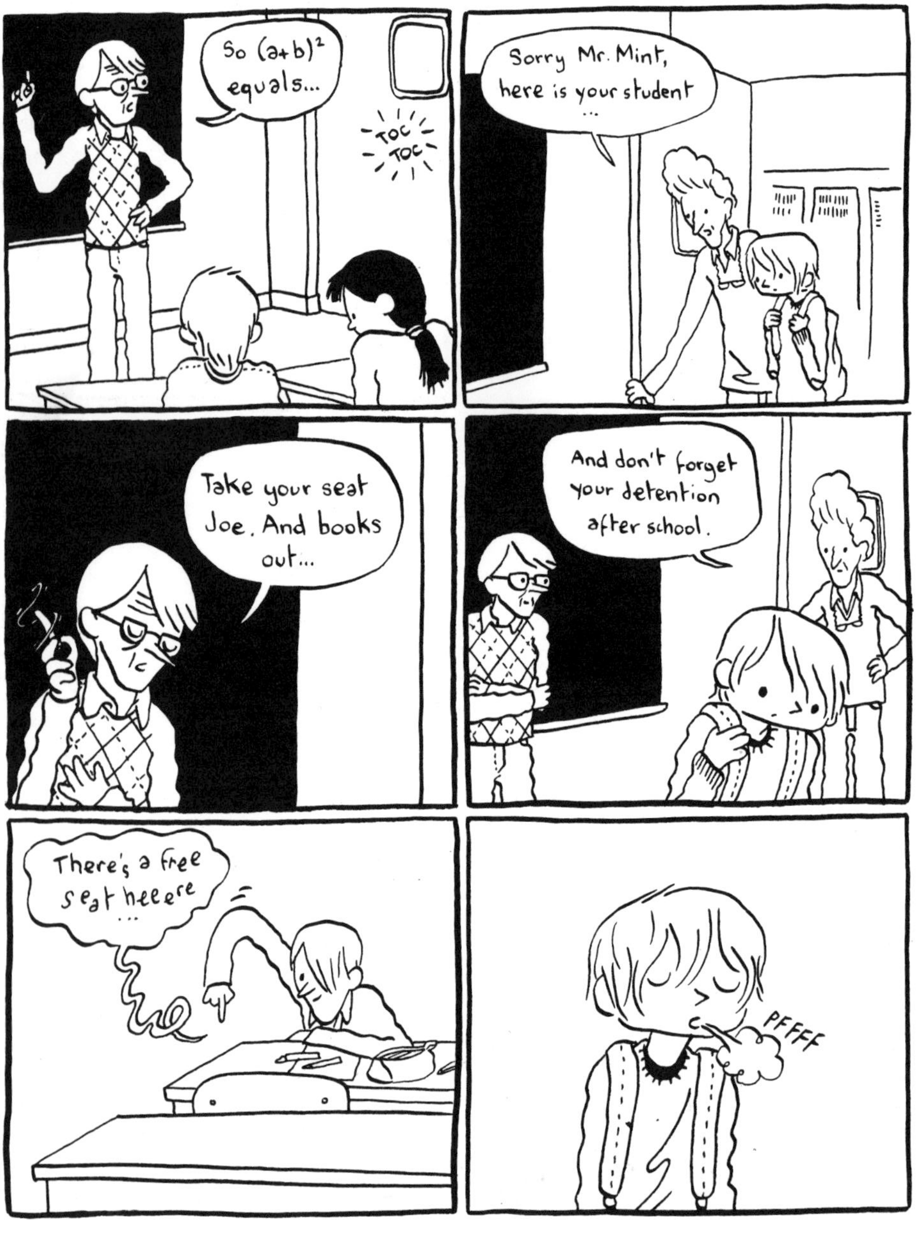
So $(a+b)^2$ equals...
TOC TOC
Sorry Mr. Mint, here is your student ...
Take your seat Joe. And books out...
And don't forget your detention after school.
There's a free seat heeere ...
PFFFF

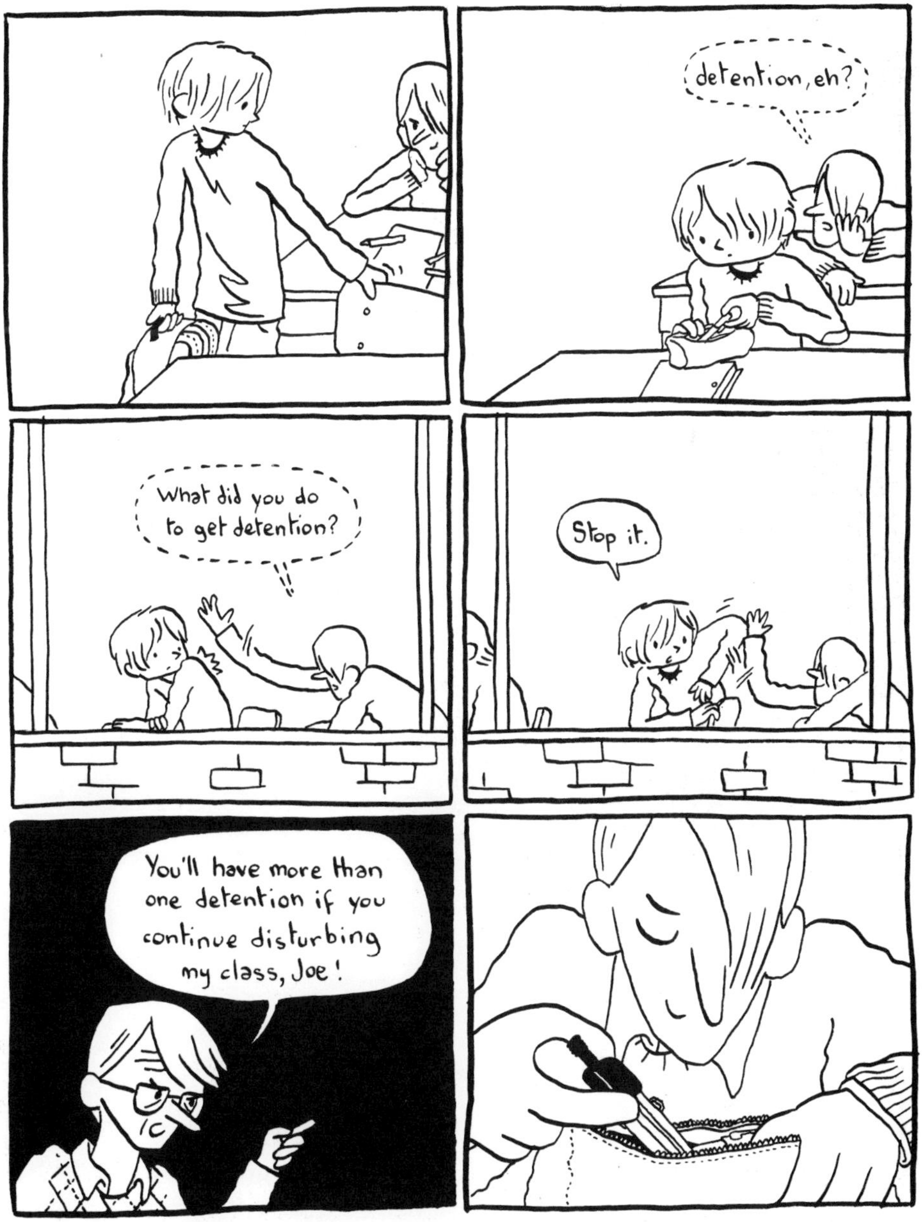
detention, eh?
What did you do to get detention?
Stop it.
You'll have more than one detention if you continue disturbing my class, Joe!

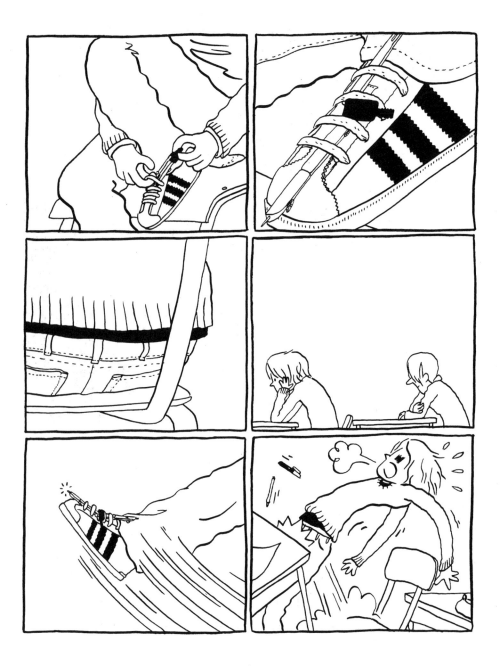

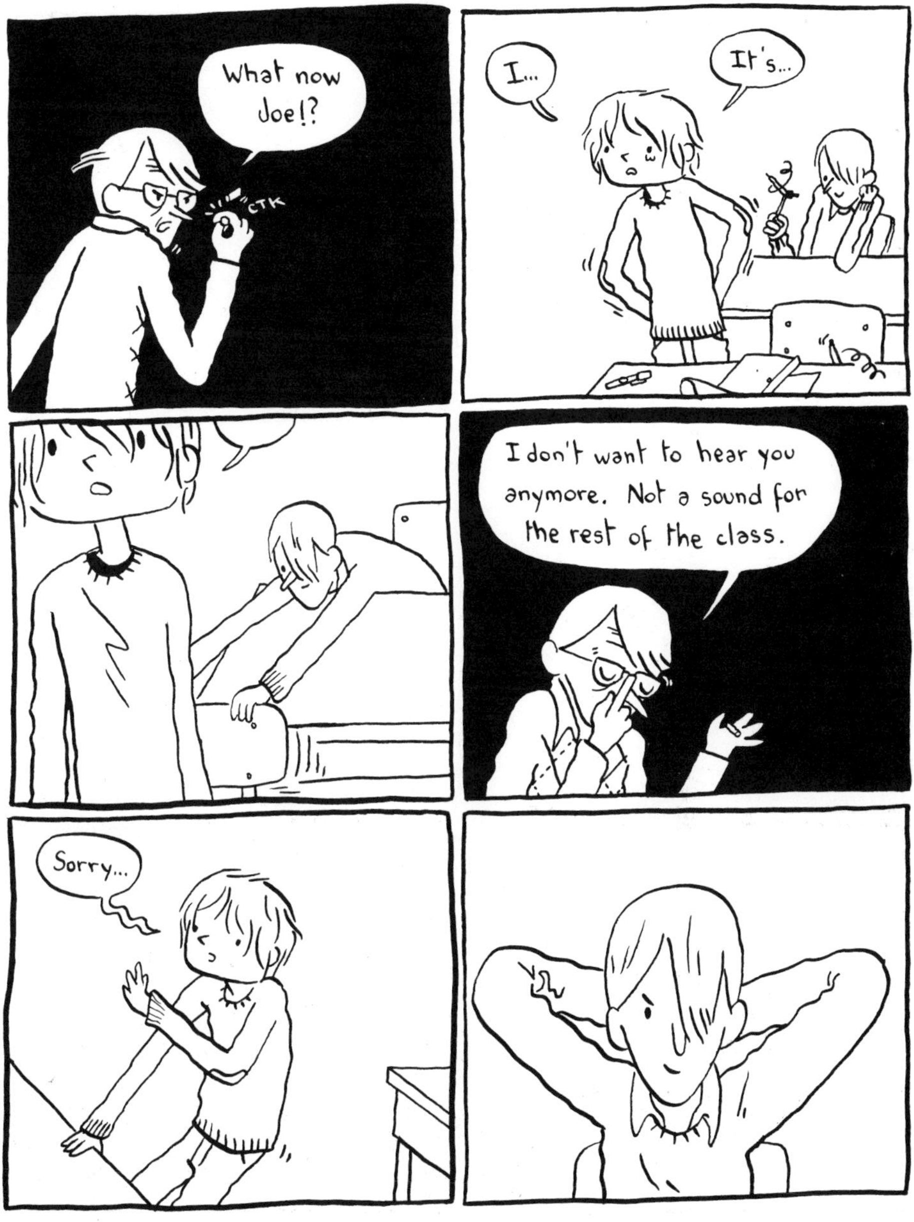
What now Joe!?
CTK
I...
It's...
I don't want to hear you anymore. Not a sound for the rest of the class.
Sorry...

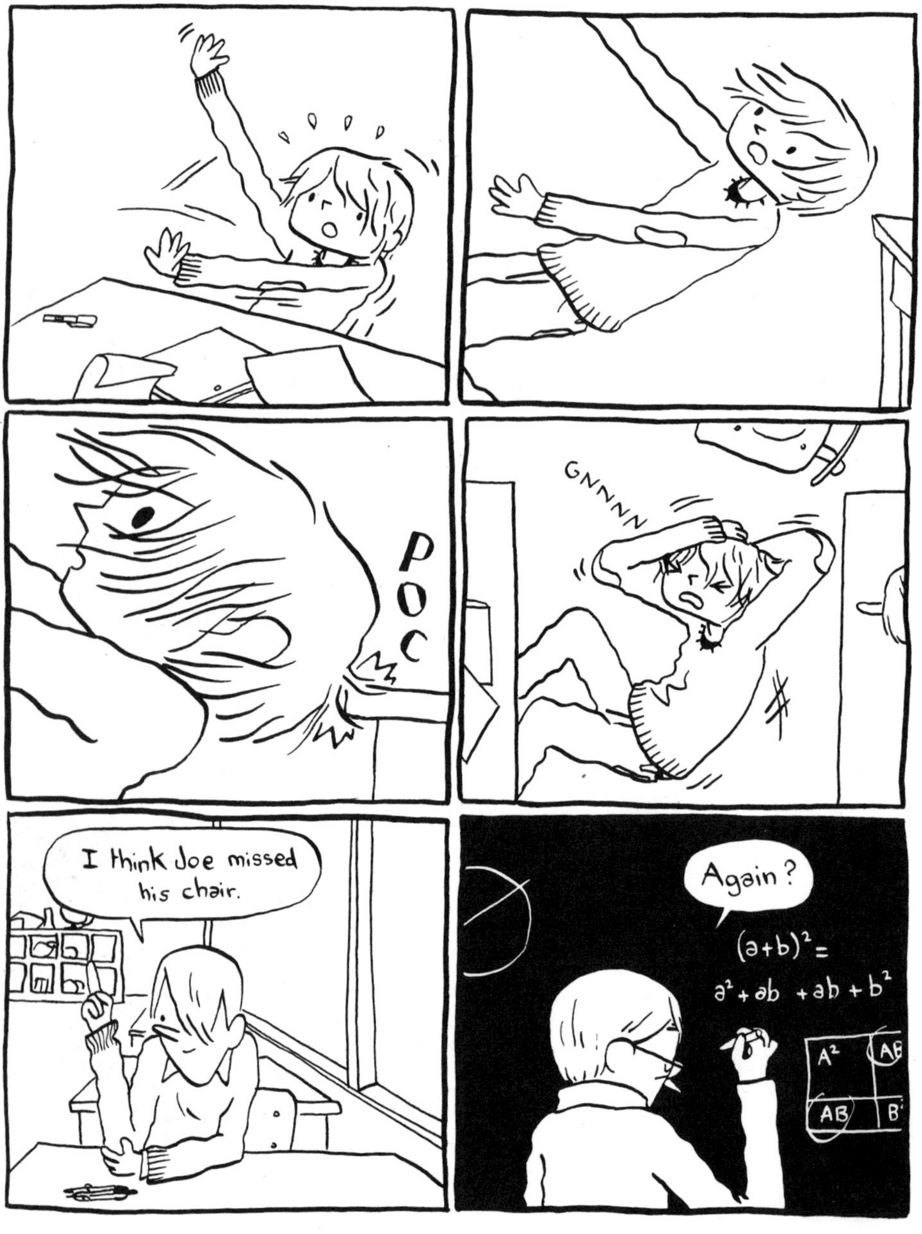
POC
GNNNN
I think Joe missed his chair.
Again?
$(a+b)^2 =$
$a^2 + ab + ab + b^2$
A^2
AB
AB

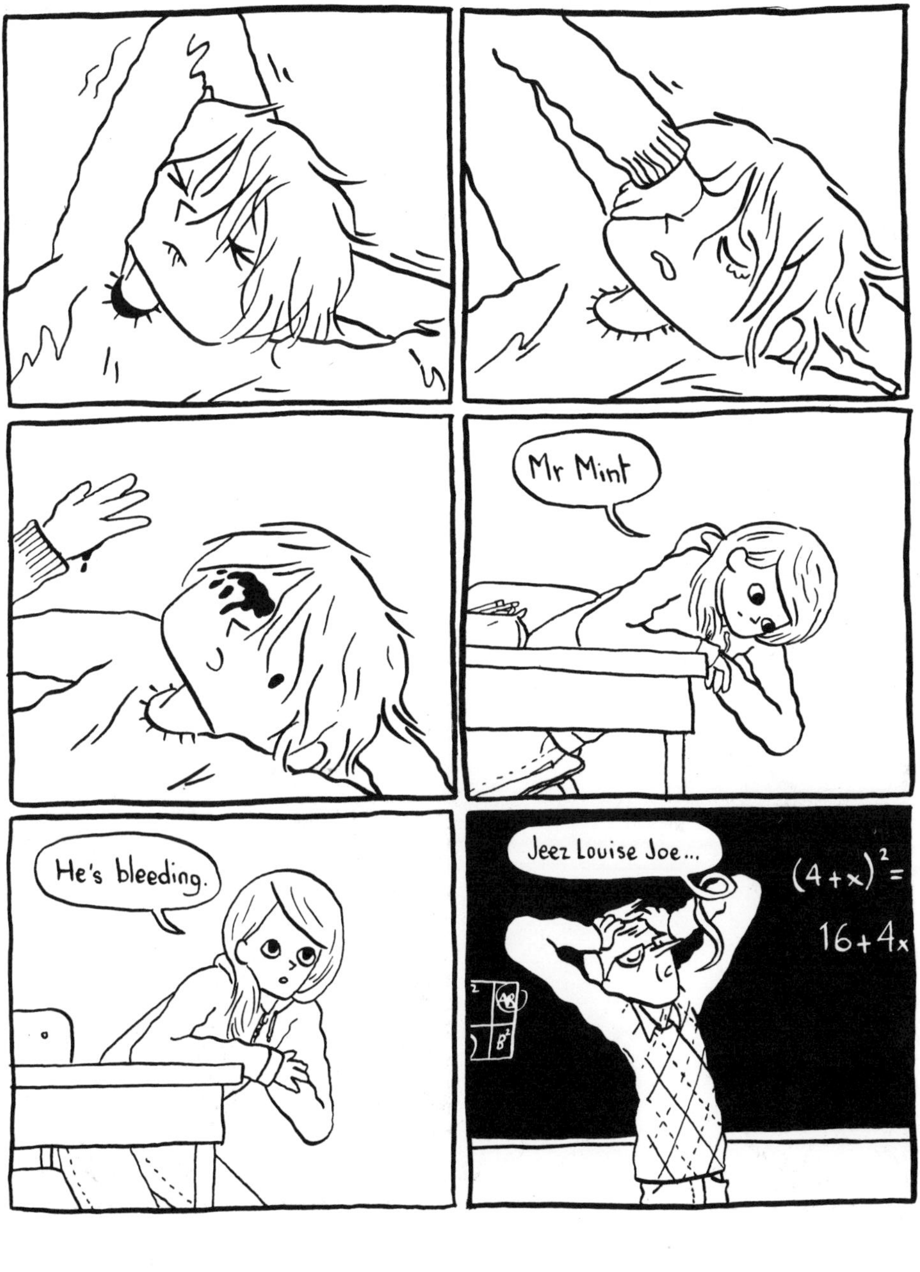
Mr Mint
He's bleeding.
Jeez Louise Joe...
(4+x)² =
16+4x

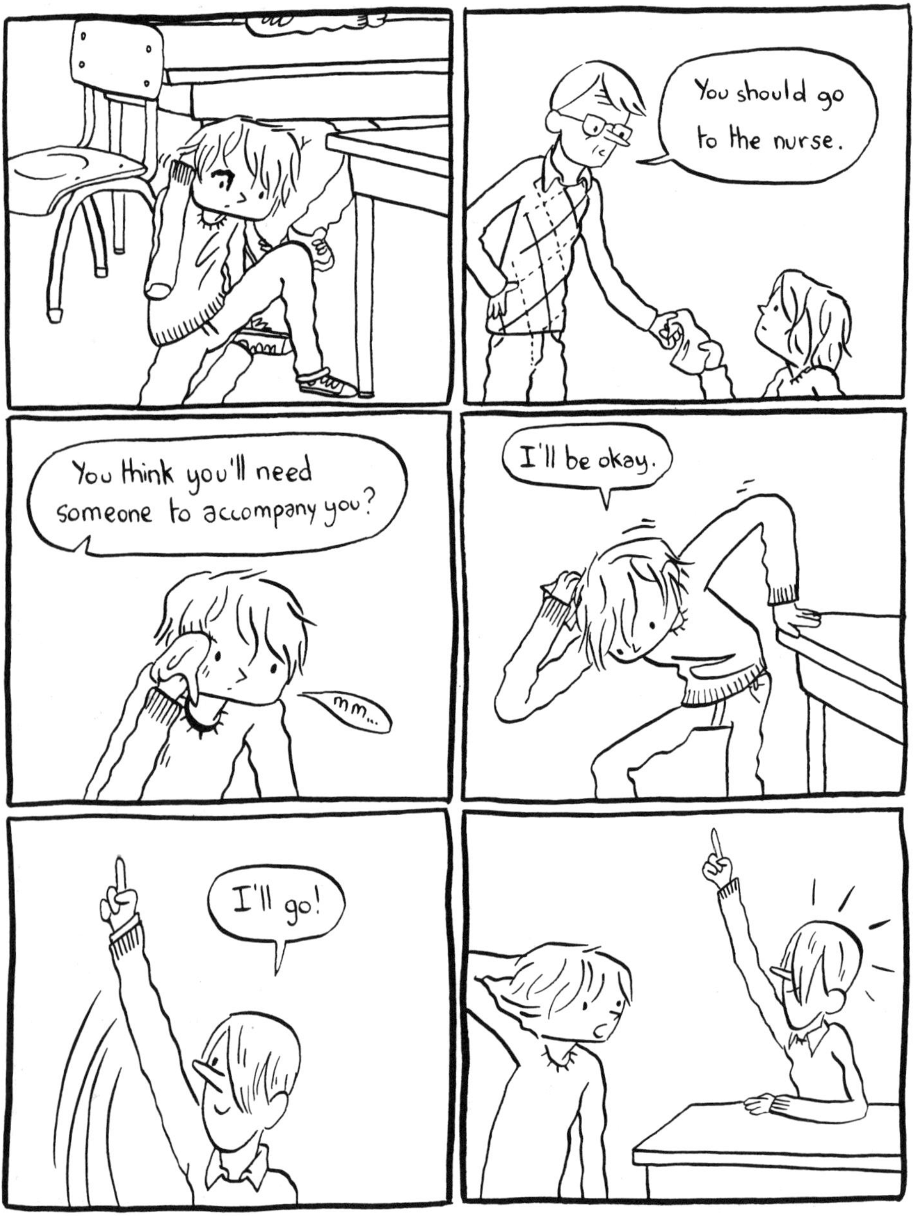
You should go to the nurse.
You think you'll need someone to accompany you?
mm...
I'll be okay.
I'll go!

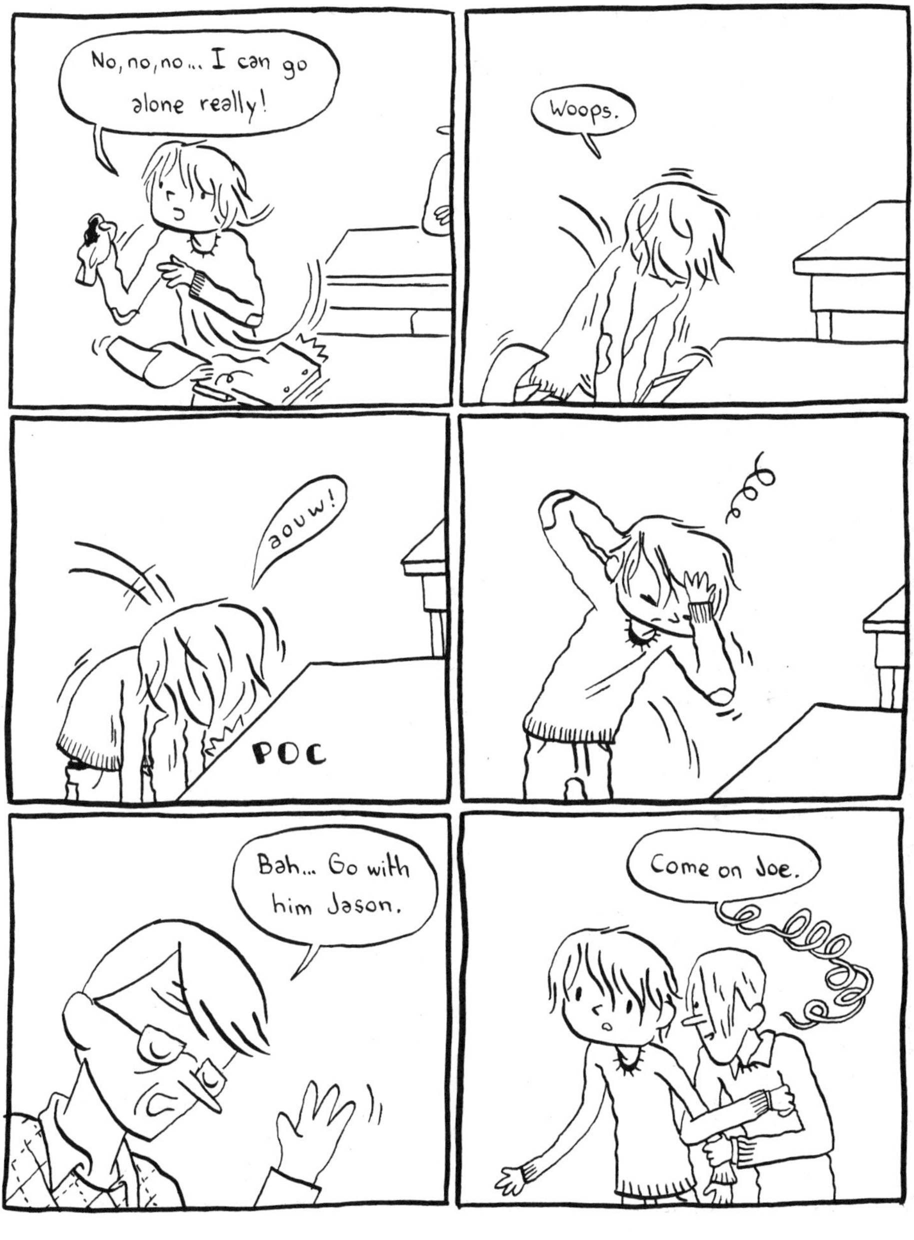
No, no, no... I can go alone really!
Woops.
aouw!
POC
Bah... Go with him Jason.
Come on Joe.

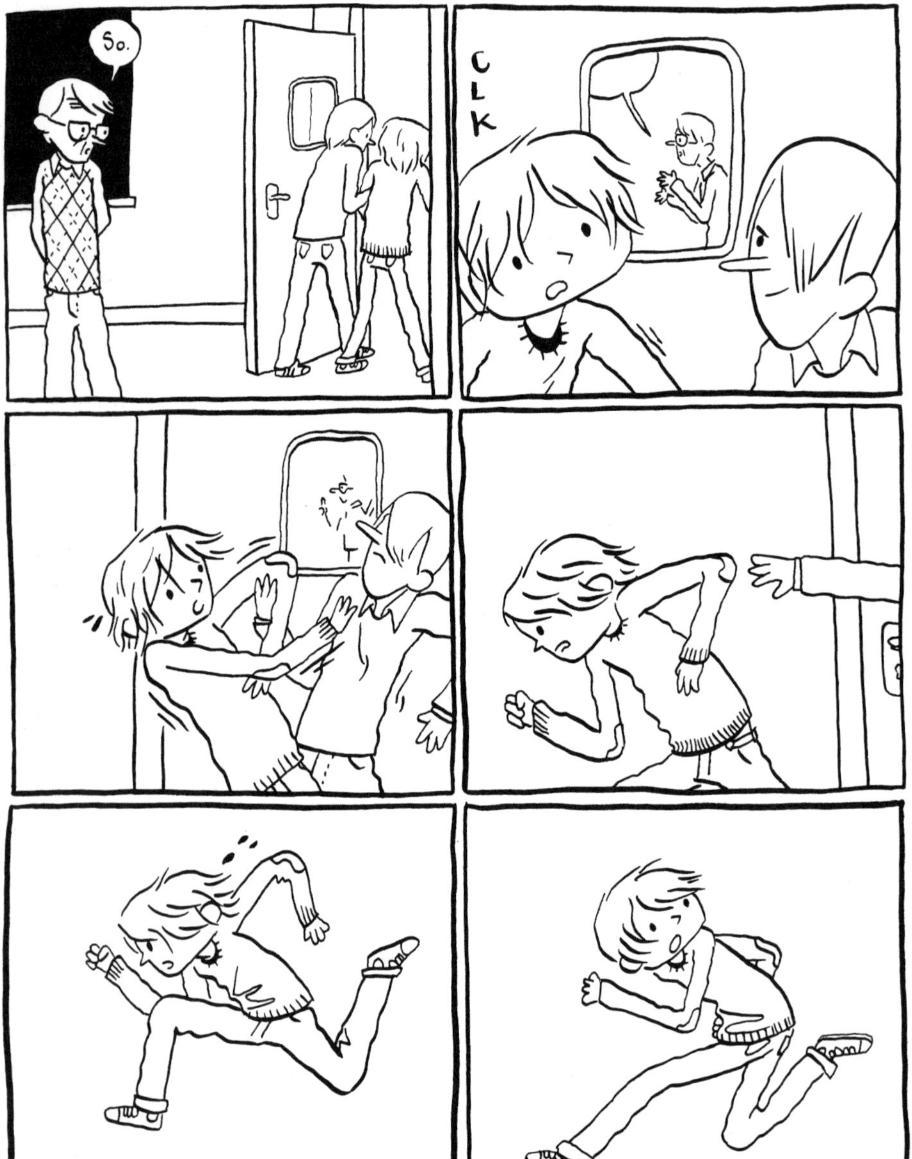
So.
CLK

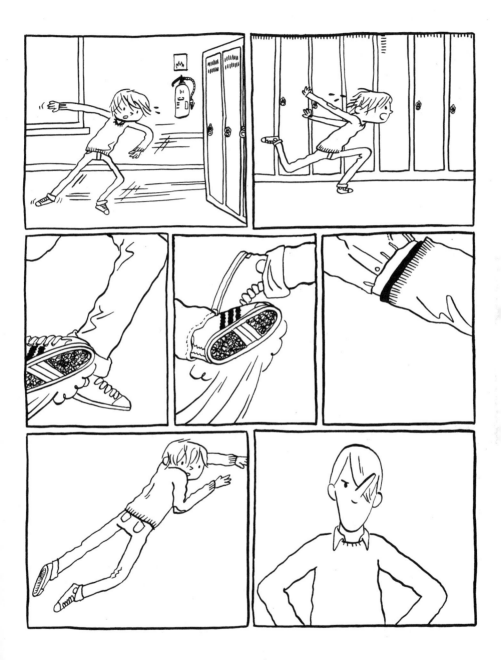

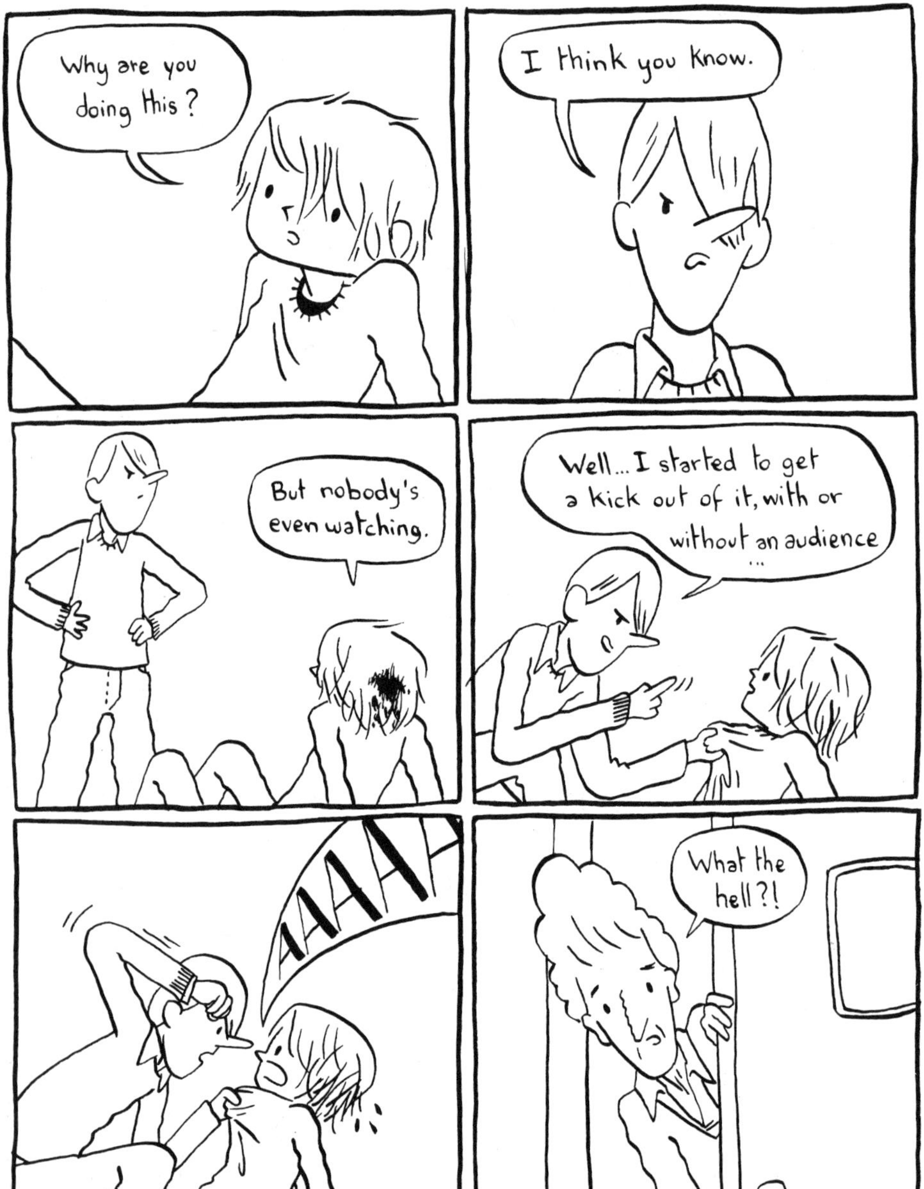
Why are you doing this?
I think you know.
But nobody's even watching.
Well... I started to get a kick out of it, with or without an audience...
AAAA
What the hell?!

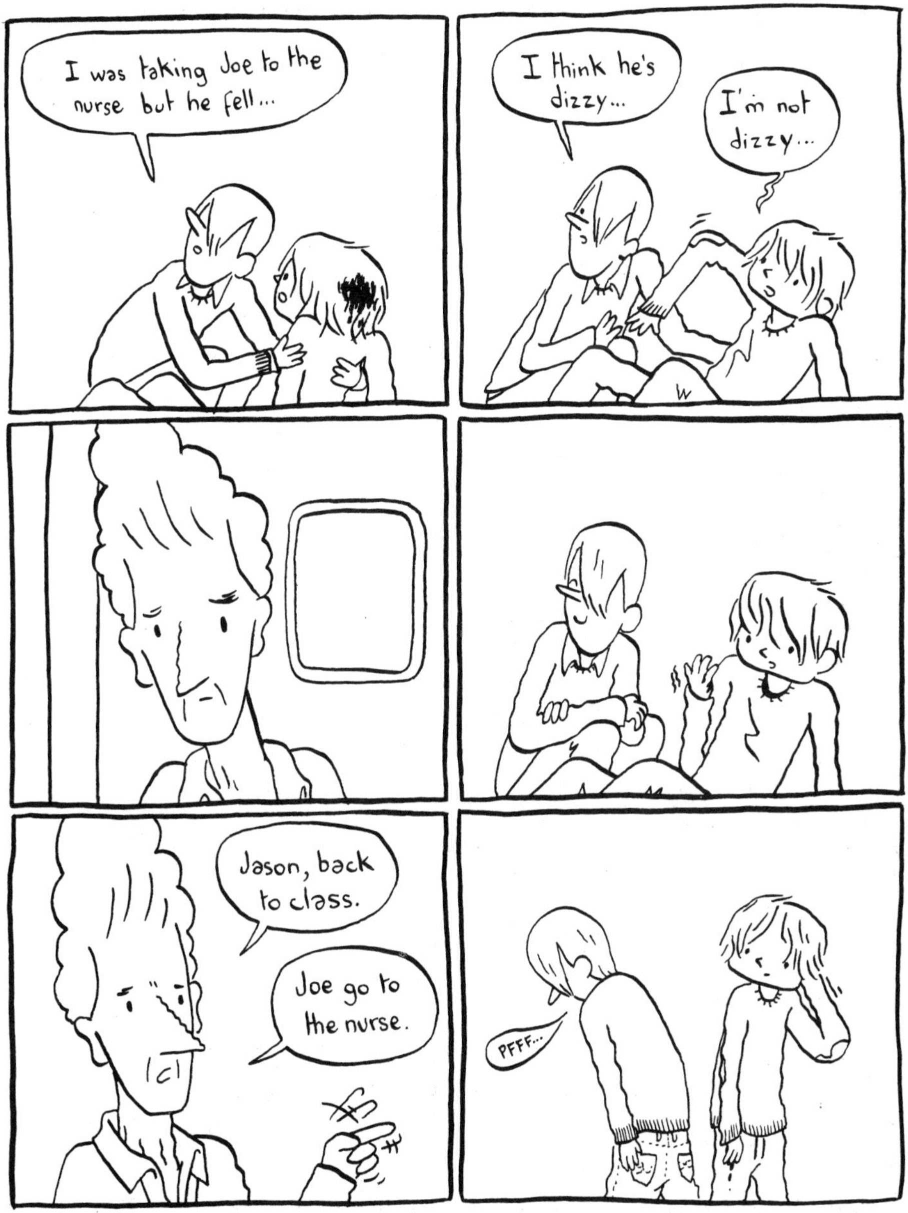
I was taking Joe to the nurse but he fell...
I think he's dizzy...
I'm not dizzy...
Jason, back to class.
Joe go to the nurse.
PFFF...

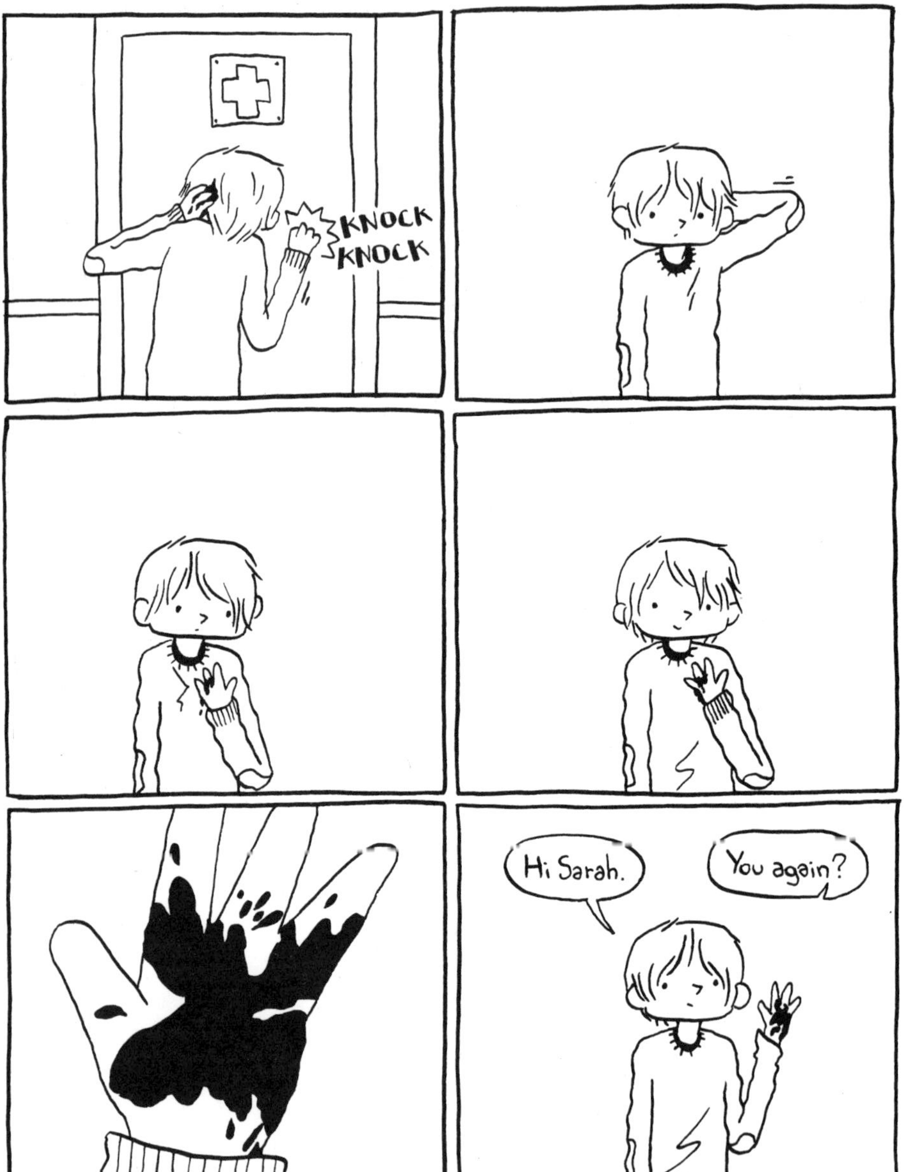
KNOCK
KNOCK
Hi Sarah.
You again?

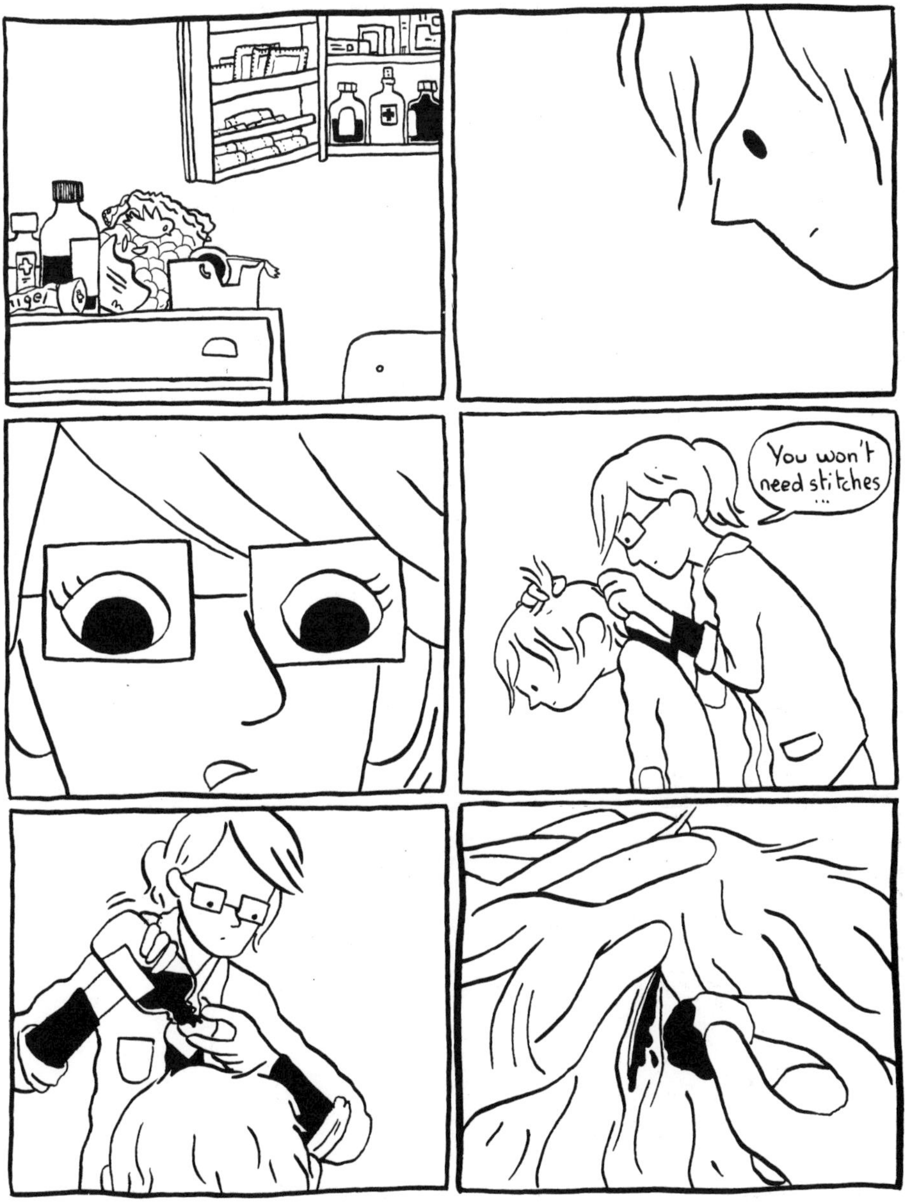
You won't need stitches ...

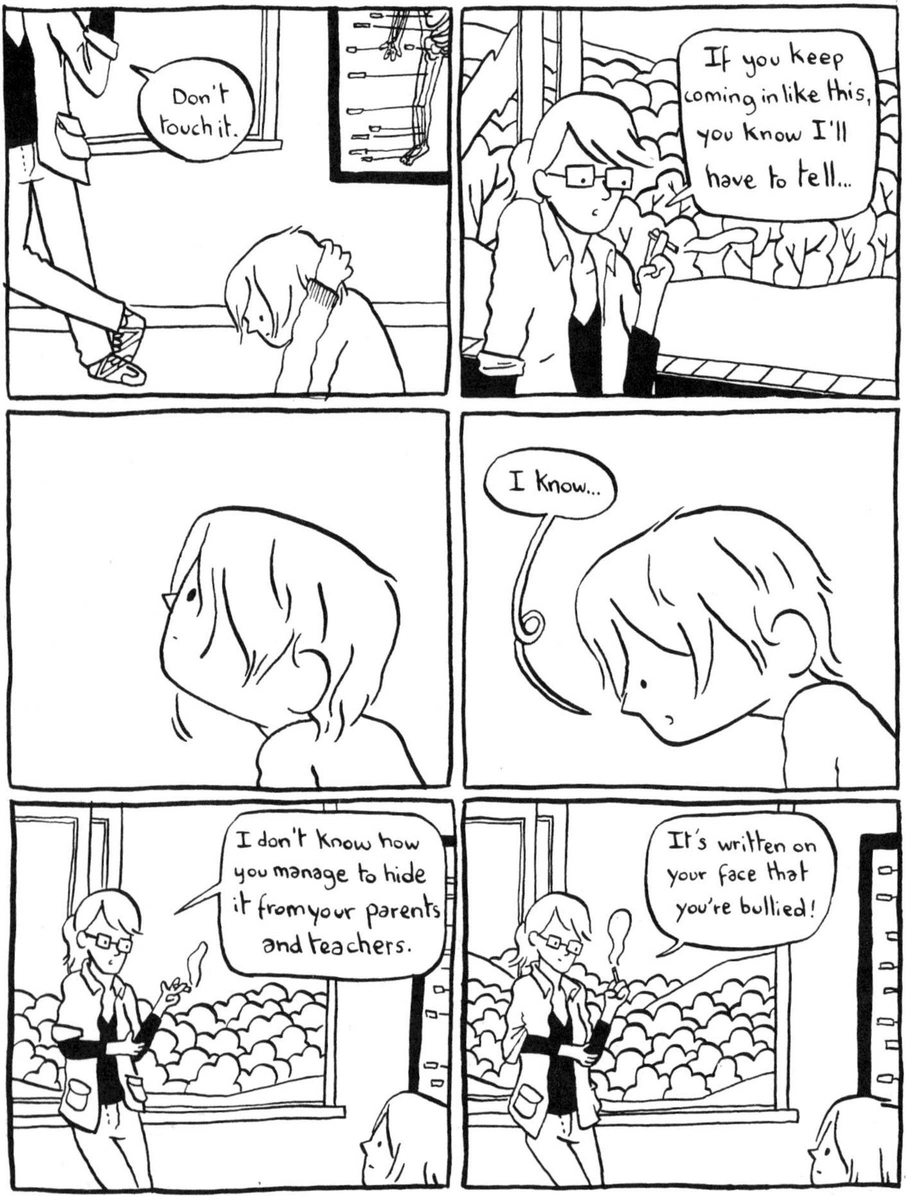
Don't touch it.
If you keep coming in like this, you know I'll have to tell...
I know...
I don't know how you manage to hide it from your parents and teachers.
It's written on your face that you're bullied!

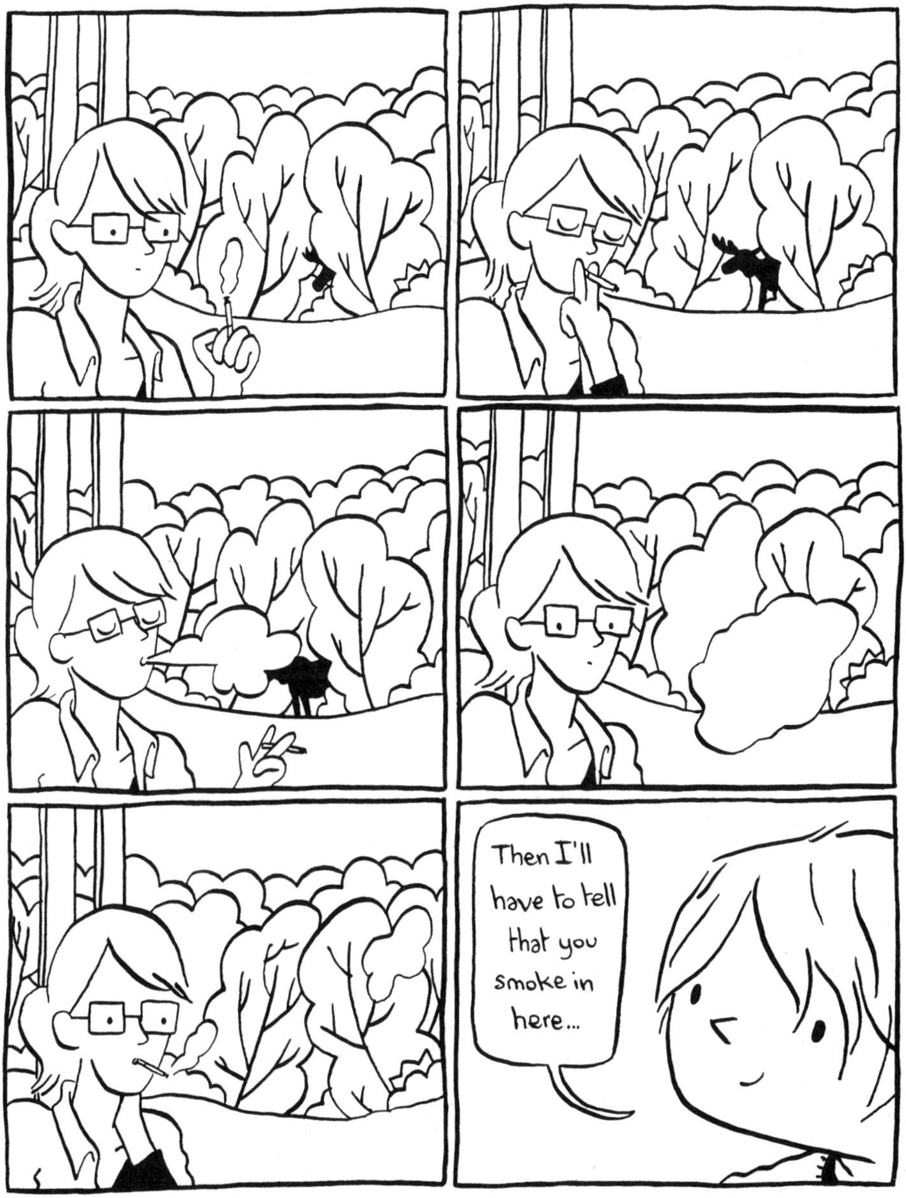
Then I'll have to tell that you smoke in here...

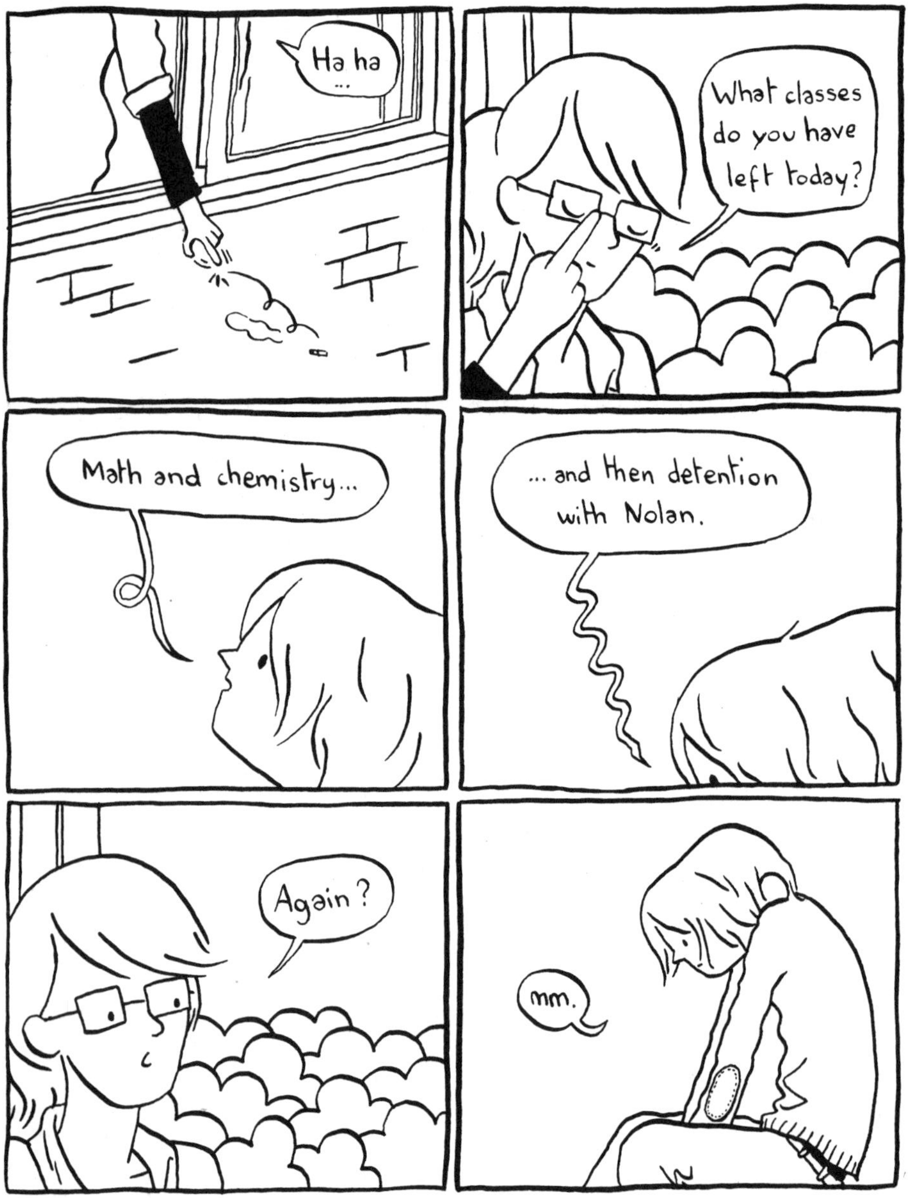
Ha ha
...
What classes do you have left today?
Math and chemistry...
... and then detention with Nolan.
Again?
mm.

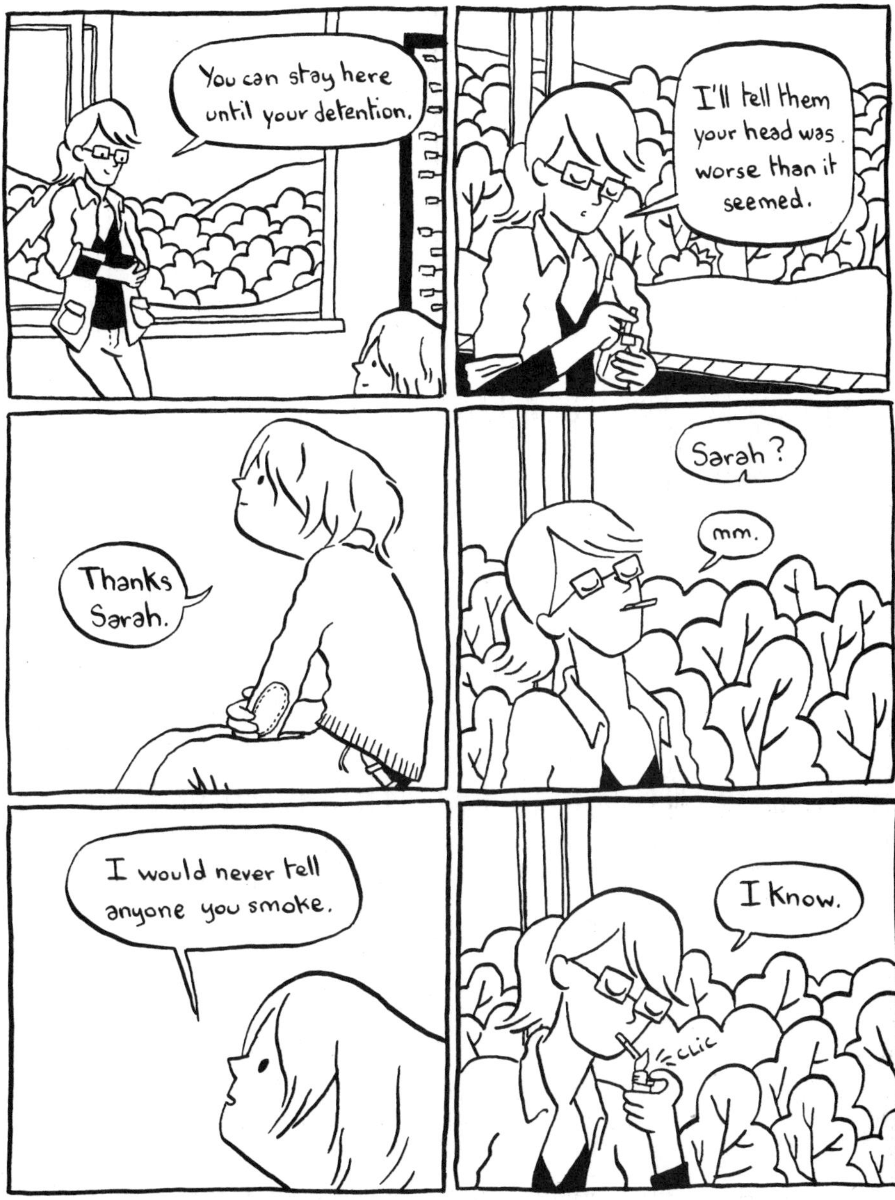
You can stay here until your detention.
I'll tell them your head was worse than it seemed.
Thanks Sarah.
Sarah?
mm.
I would never tell anyone you smoke.
I know.
CLIC

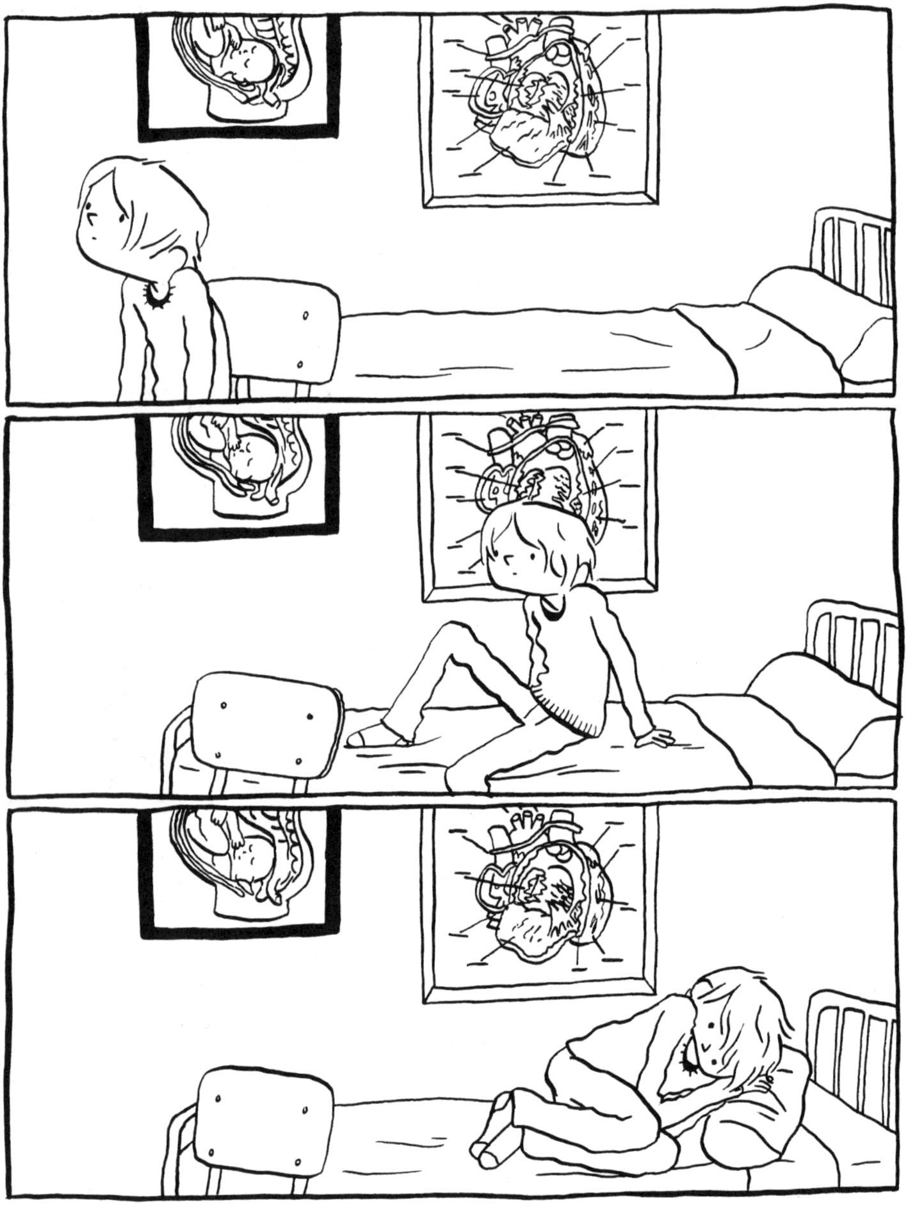

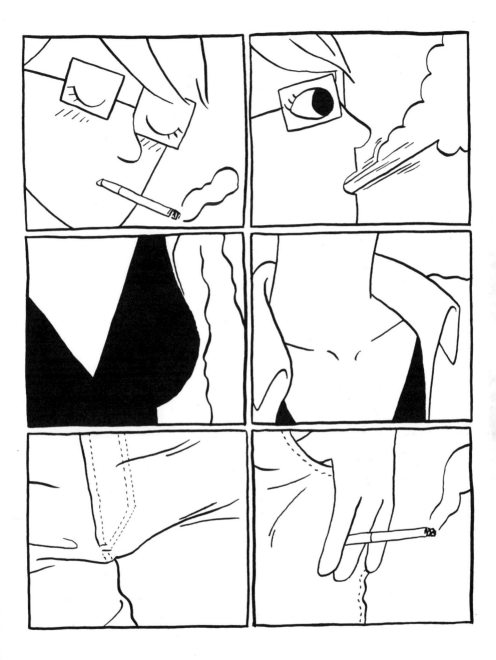

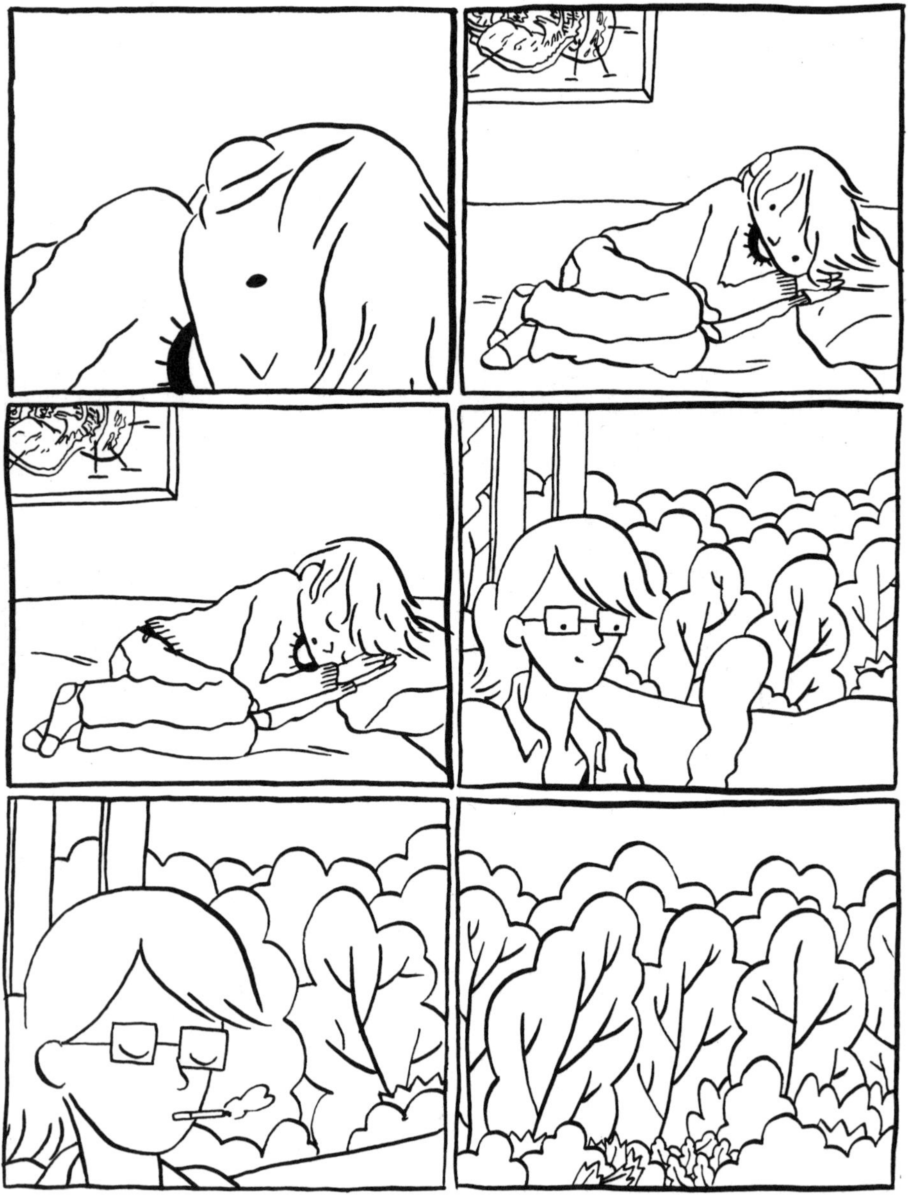

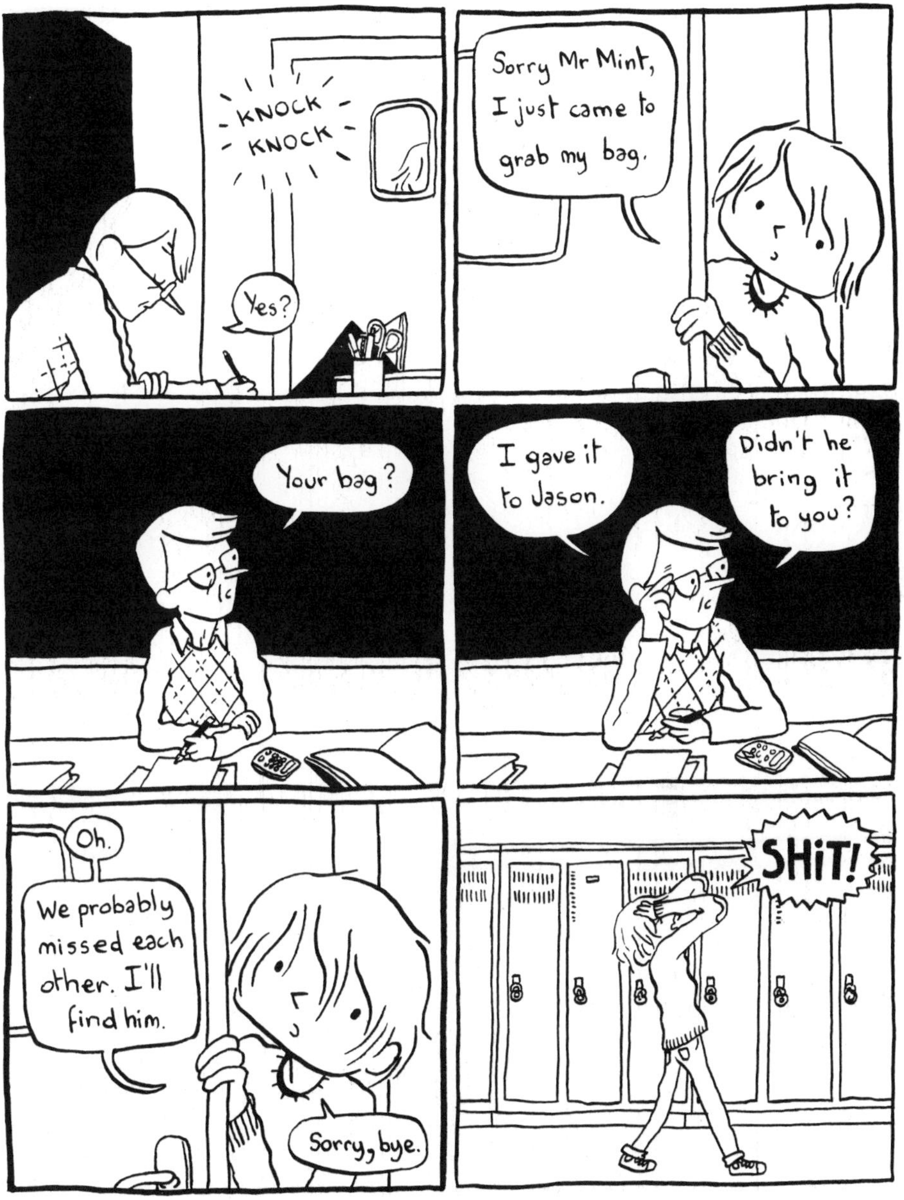
KNOCK KNOCK
Yes?
Sorry Mr Mint, I just came to grab my bag.
Your bag?
I gave it to Jason.
Didn't he bring it to you?
Oh.
We probably missed each other. I'll find him.
Sorry, bye.
SHiT!

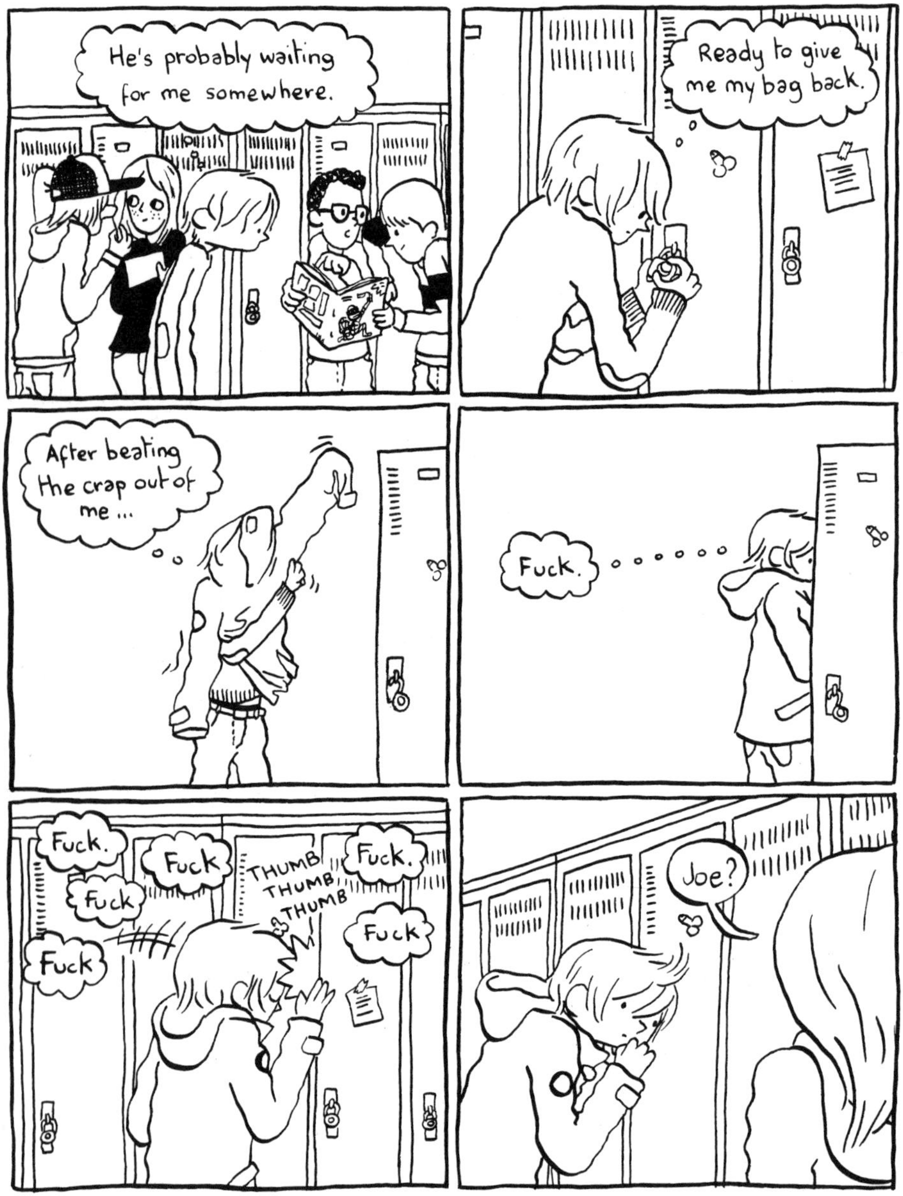
He's probably waiting for me somewhere.
Ready to give me my bag back.
After beating the crap out of me...
Fuck.
Fuck.
Fuck
Fuck
Fuck
THUMB THUMB THUMB
Fuck.
Fuck
Joe?

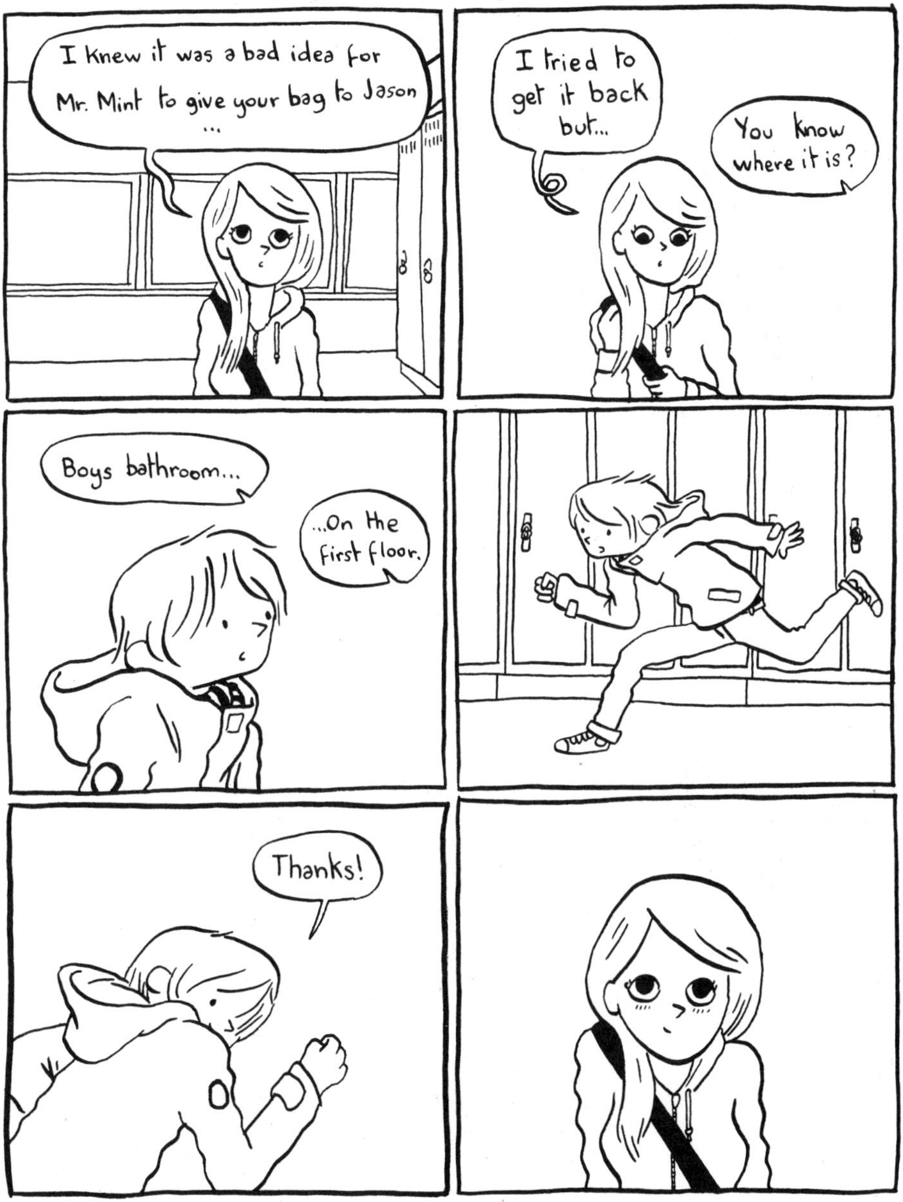
I knew it was a bad idea for Mr. Mint to give your bag to Jason ...
I tried to get it back but...
You know where it is?
Boys bathroom...
...On the first floor.
Thanks!

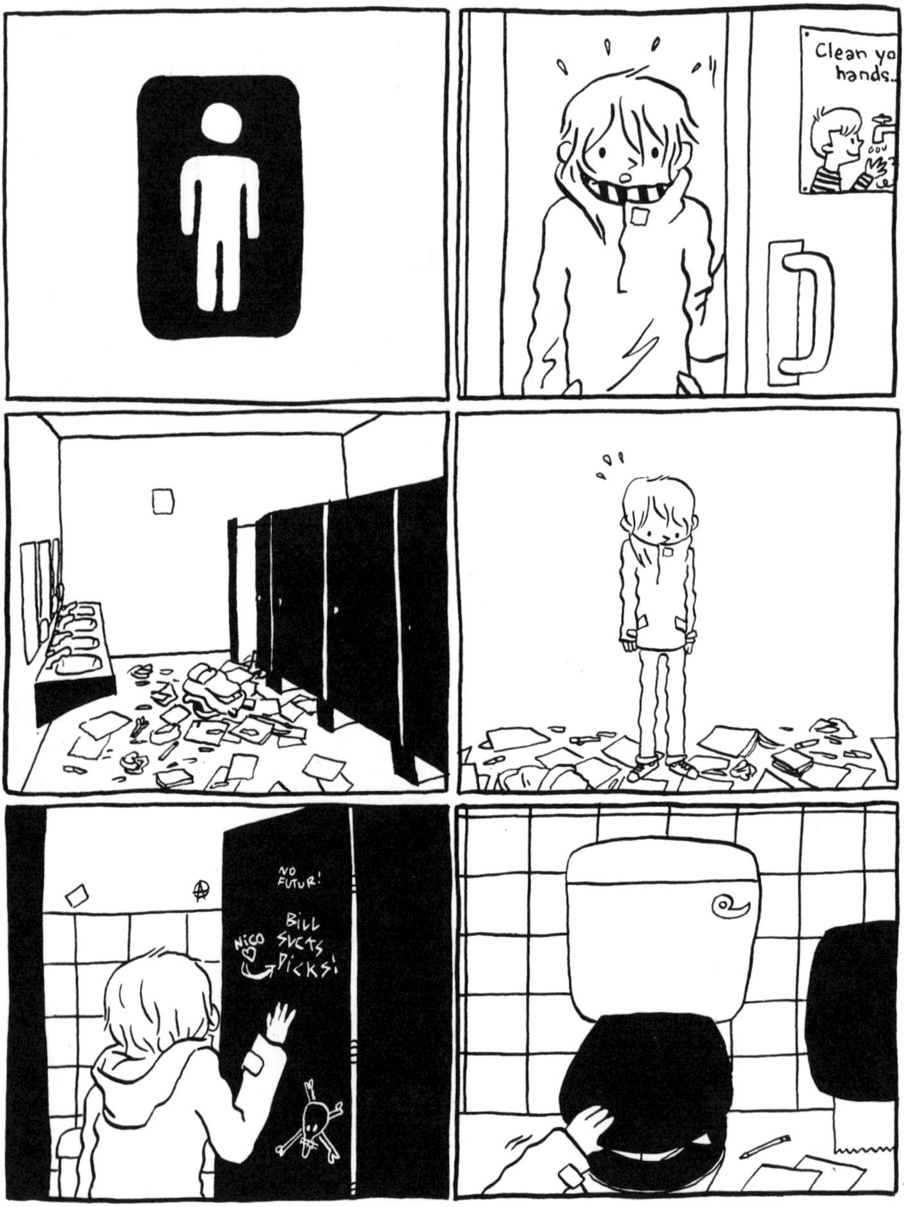

Clean yo
hands..
NO
FUTUR!
BILL
SUCKS
DICKS!
NICO

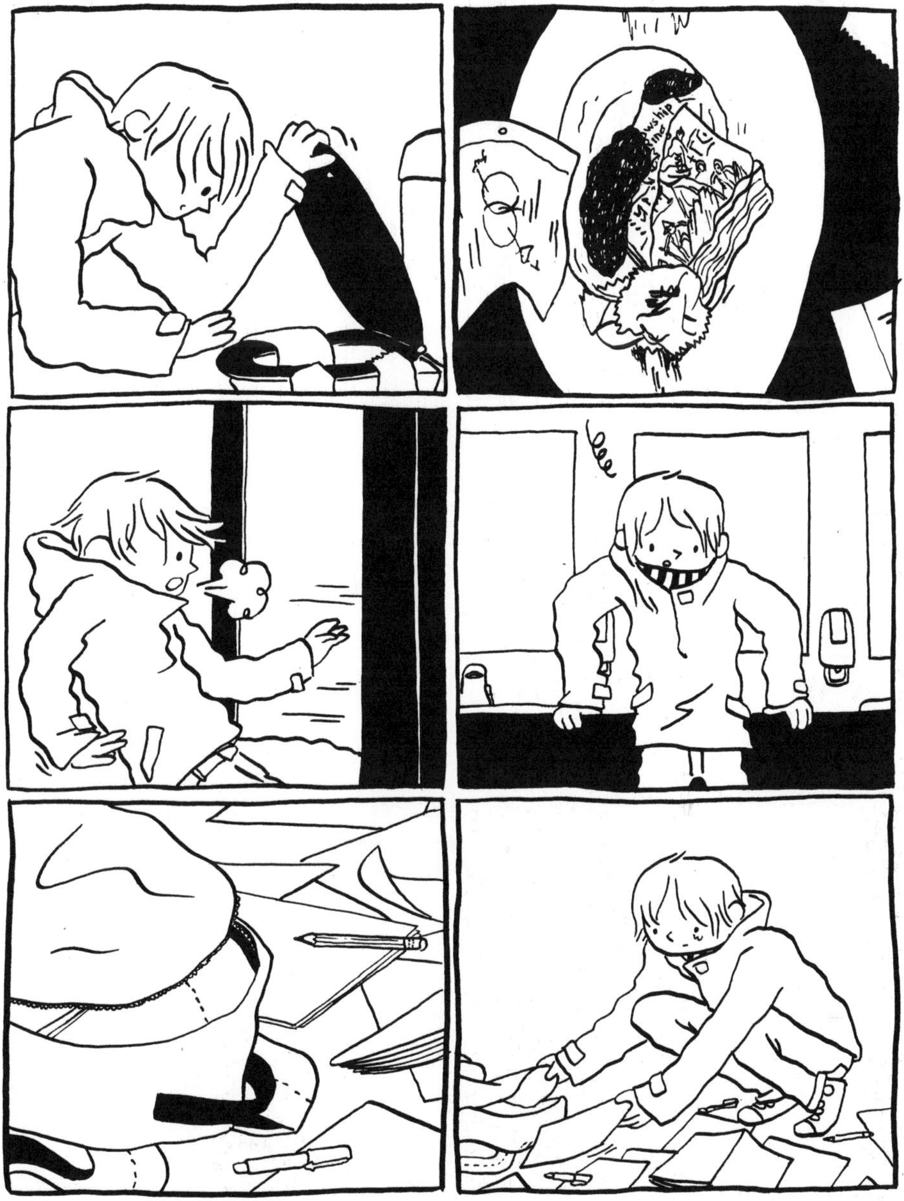

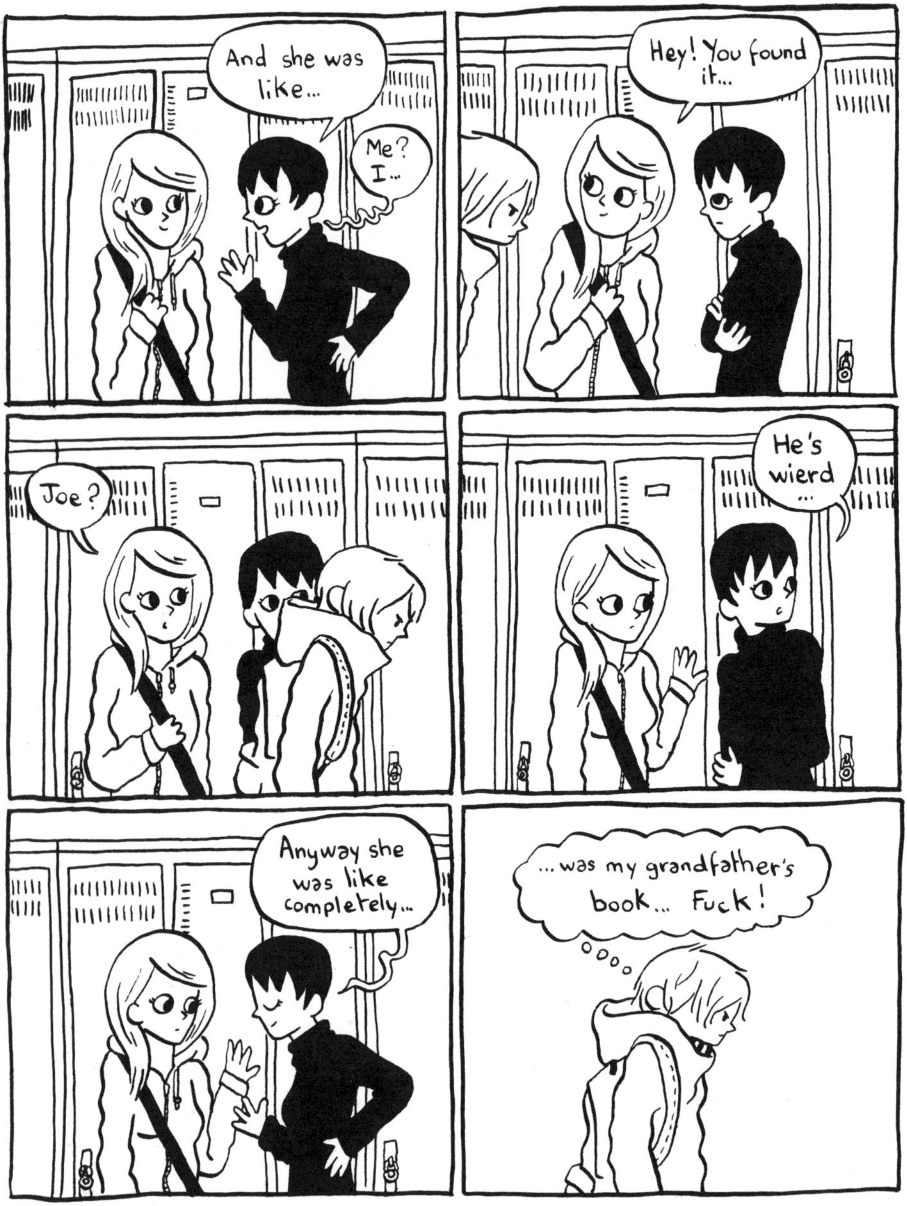
And she was like...
Me? I...
Hey! You found it...
Joe?
He's wierd ...
Anyway she was like completely...
... was my grandfather's book... Fuck!

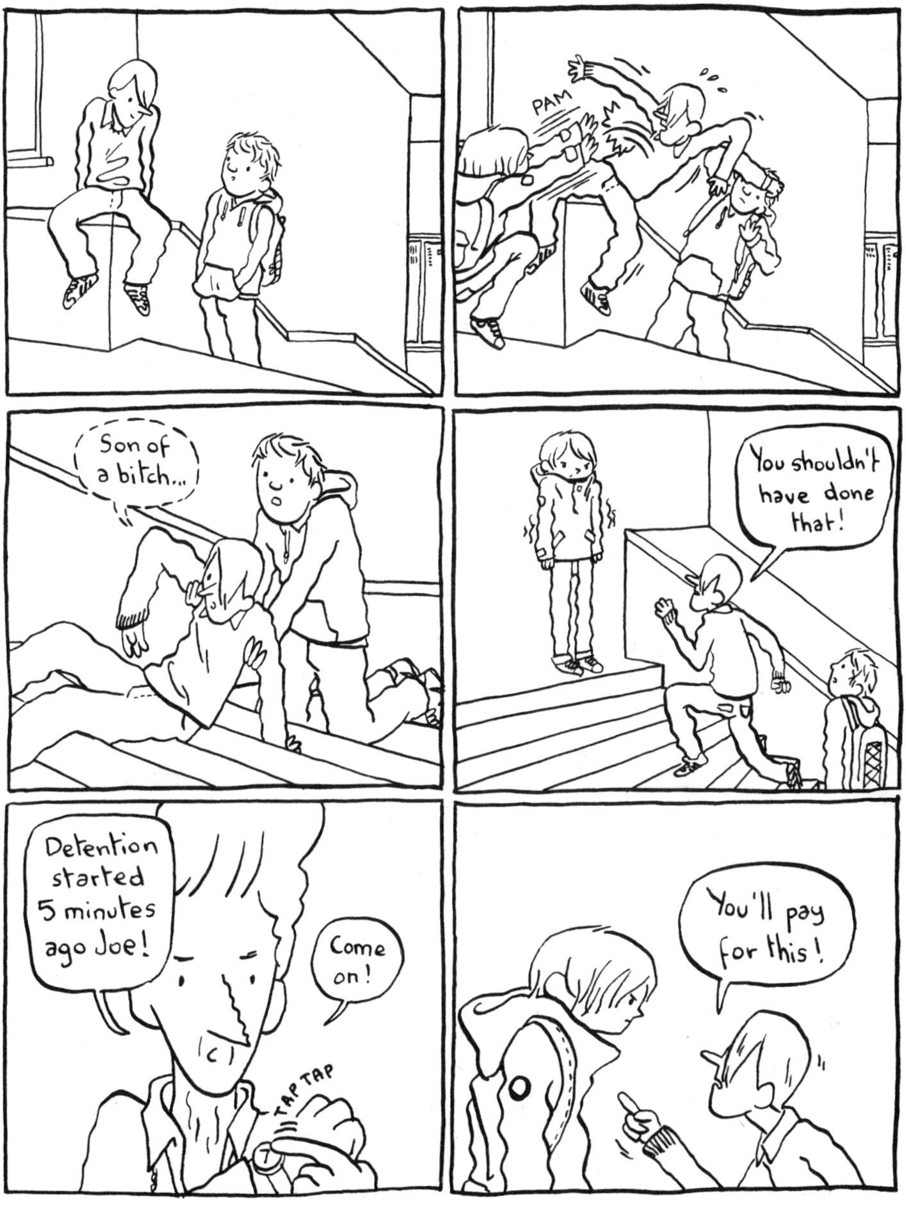
PAM
Son of a bitch...
You shouldn't have done that!
Detention started 5 minutes ago Joe!
Come on!
TAP TAP
You'll pay for this!

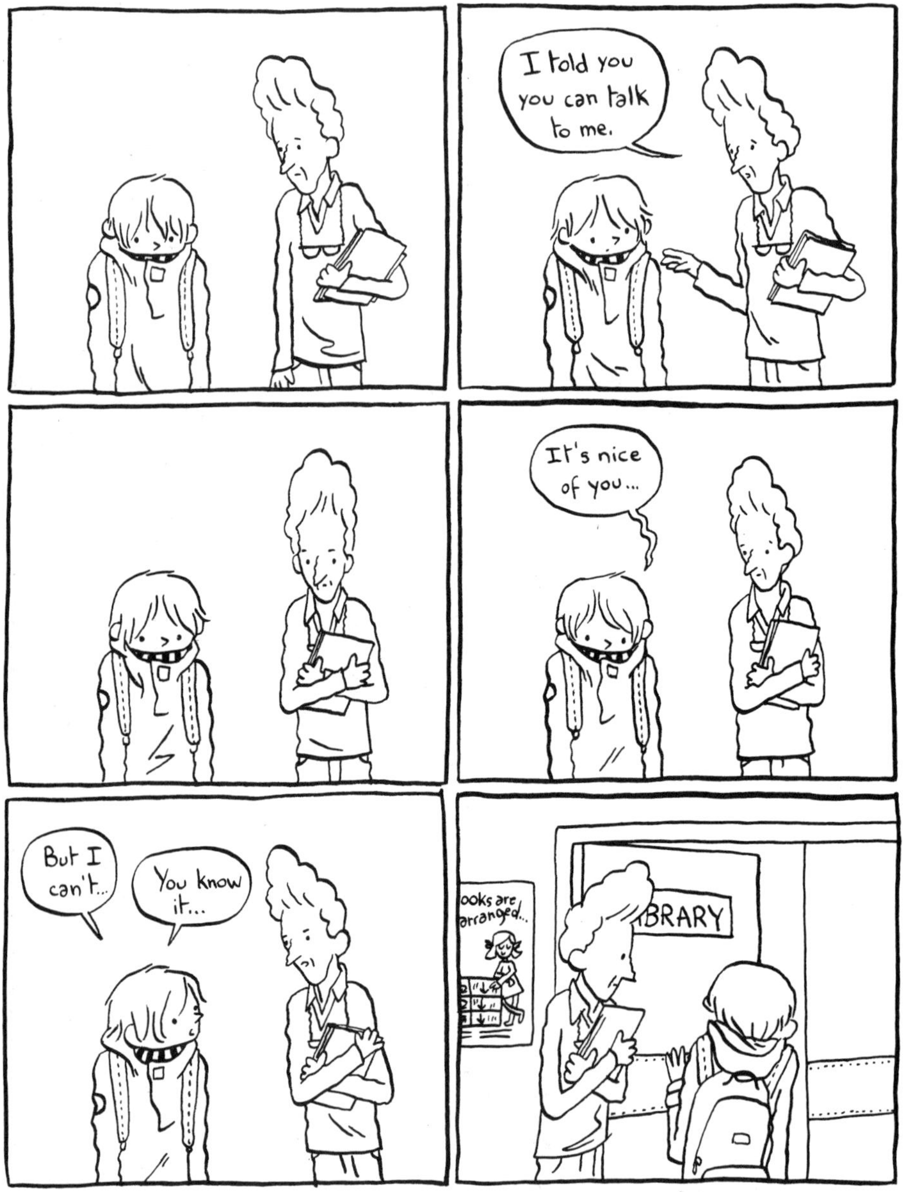

I told you you can talk to me.
It's nice of you...
But I can't...
You know it...
ooks are arranged...
BRARY

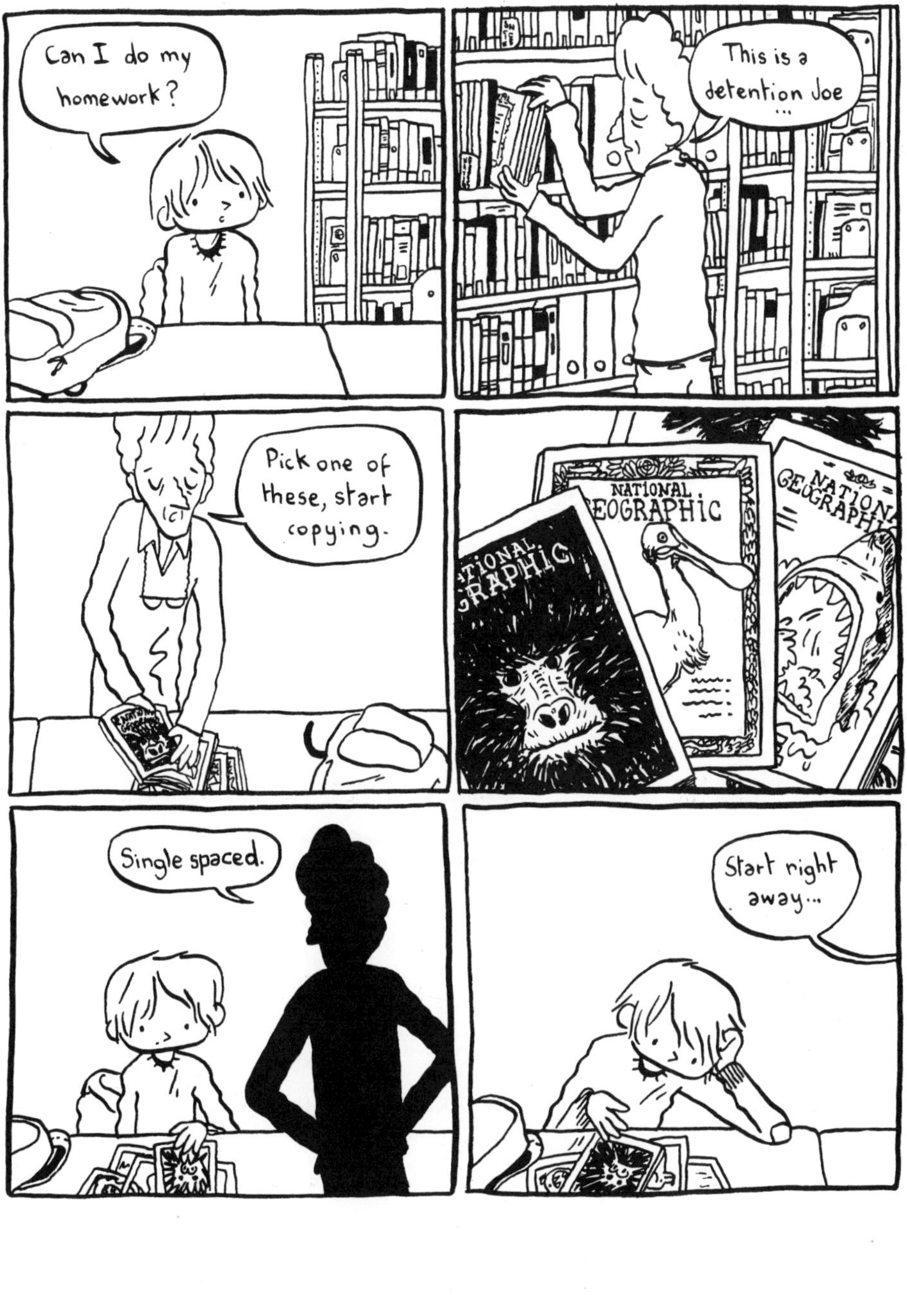
Can I do my homework?
This is a detention Joe...
Pick one of these, start copying.
NATIONAL GEOGRAPHIC
NATIONAL GEOGRAPHIC
NATIONAL GEOGRAPHIC
Single spaced.
Start right away...

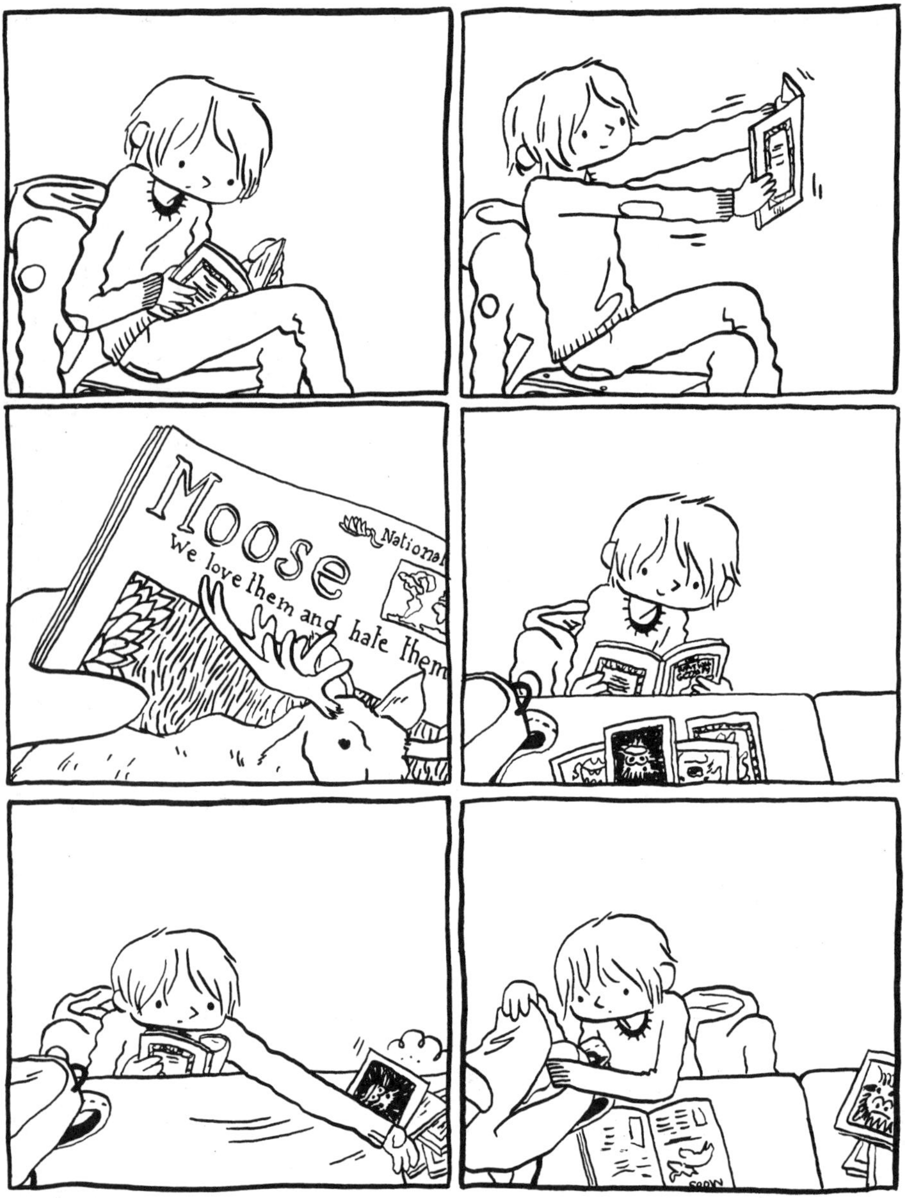
Moose
National
We love them and hate them

Within the magazine page shown:

oose

ove them and hate them.

National Geographic

☐ Moose Range

⊕ Fast Facts

Type: Mammal

Diet: Herbivore

Average life span in the wild: 15 to 20 years

Size: Height at shoulder, 5 to 6,5 feet (1.5 to 2 m)

Weight: 1,800 lbs (820 kg)

Group name: Herd

Size to a 6 ft (2m) man

oo many moose?

In winter they eat shrubs and pinecones, but they also scrape snow with their large hooves to clear areas for browsing on moss and lichen. These hooves act as snowshoes

far more plenti
northern regions
America, Europe, a
ice melts, moose a
lakes, rivers or wet
plant

all the
s are
eir

Moose are so t
to brow
shr

Males, called bulls, bellow
loudly to attract mates each
September and October.
The usually solitary bulls
together
me
battle
supremacy.
two sexes go
llowing year.
in the
they
ignore
Females
in the
some 30
These calves
Males, called bulls
September and Oct
bulls may come
antlers for mating
their separate

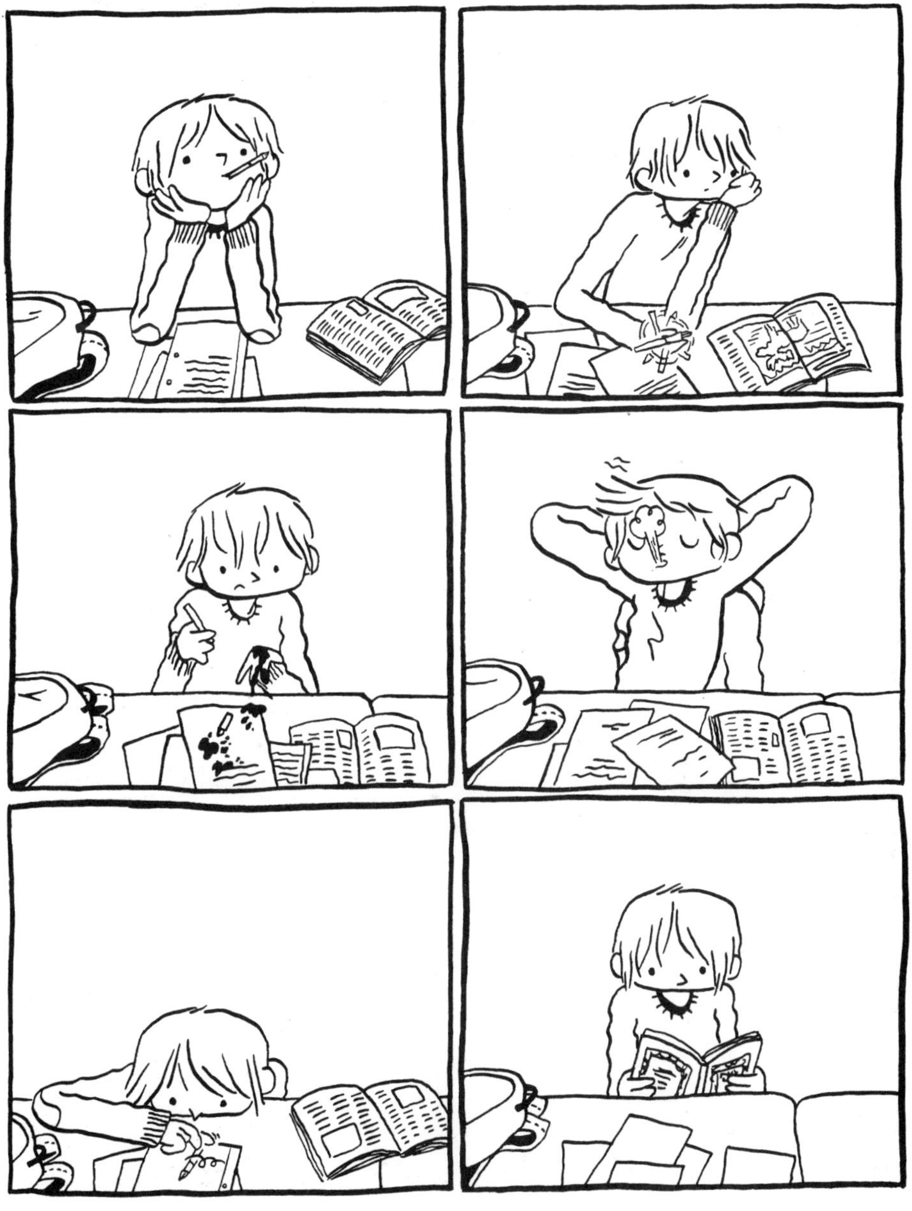

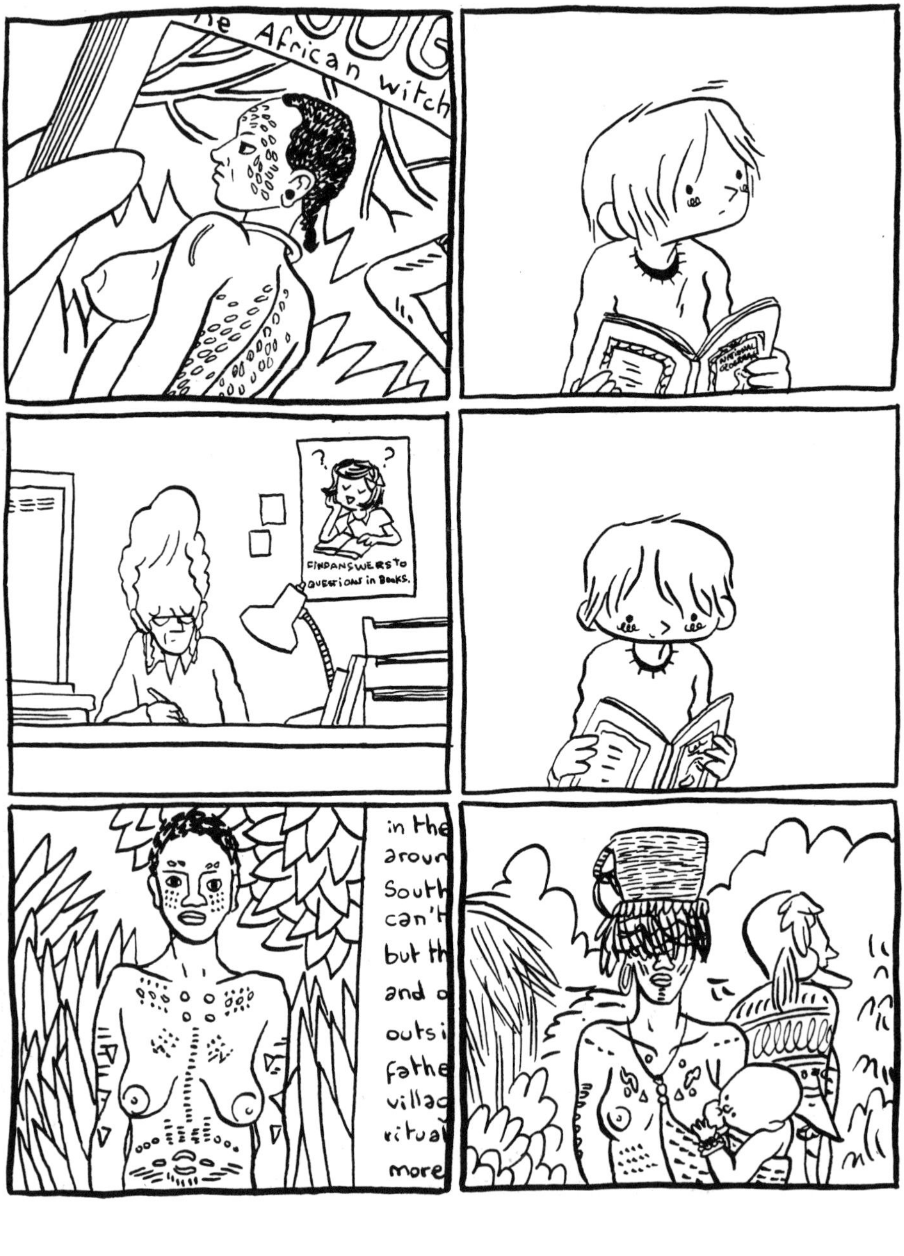

he African witch
FIND ANSWERS TO QUESTIONS in BOOKS.
in the
aroun
South
can't
but th
and o
outsi
fathe
villag
ritua
more

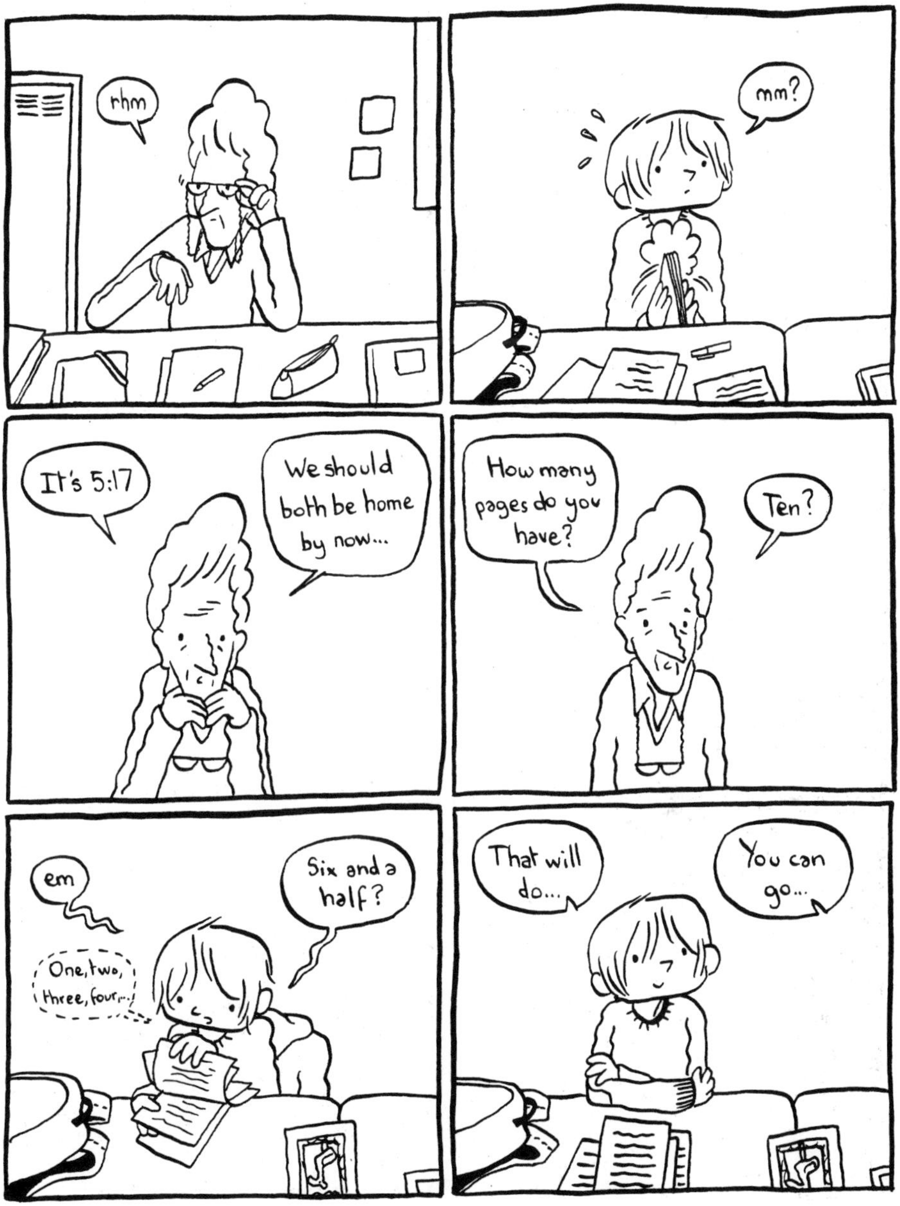
rhm
mm?
It's 5:17
We should both be home by now...
How many pages do you have?
Ten?
em
Six and a half?
One, two, three, four,...
That will do...
You can go...

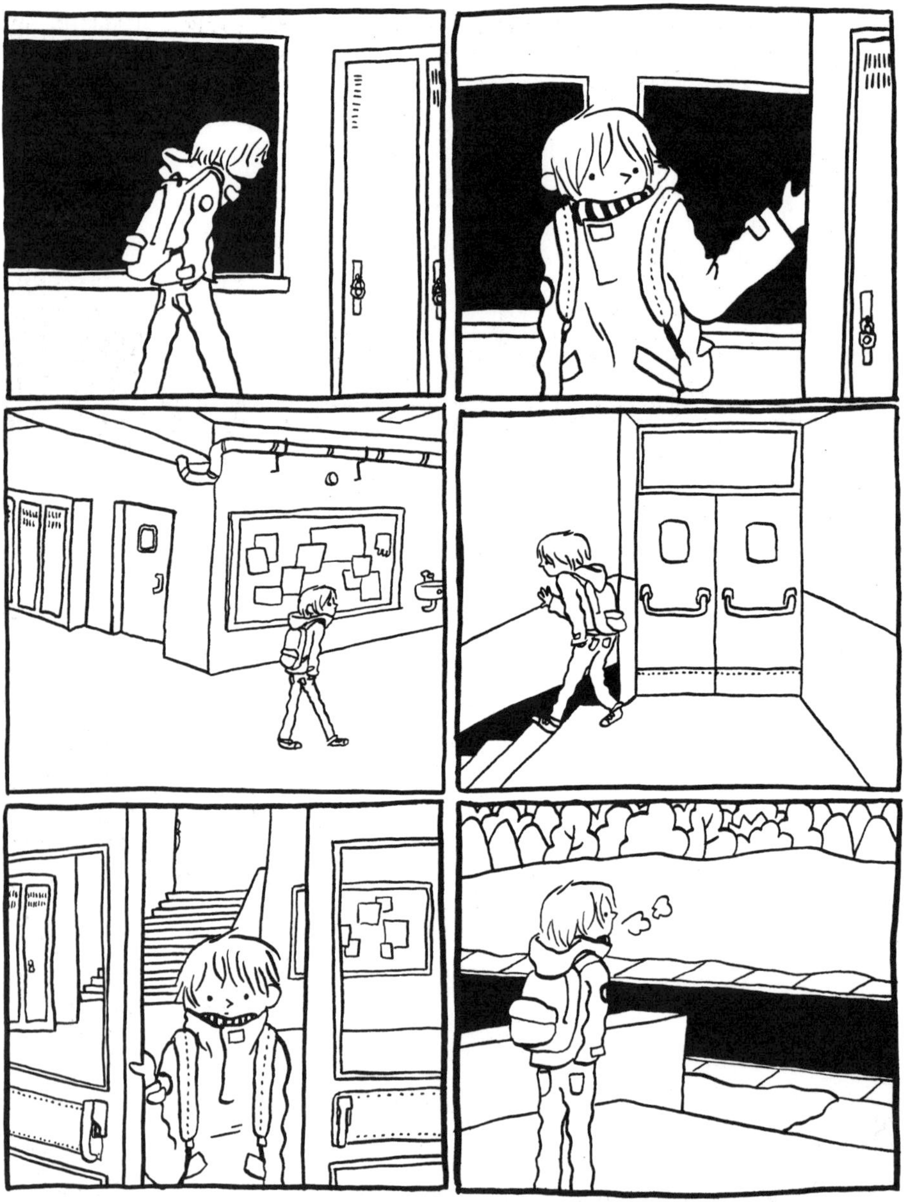

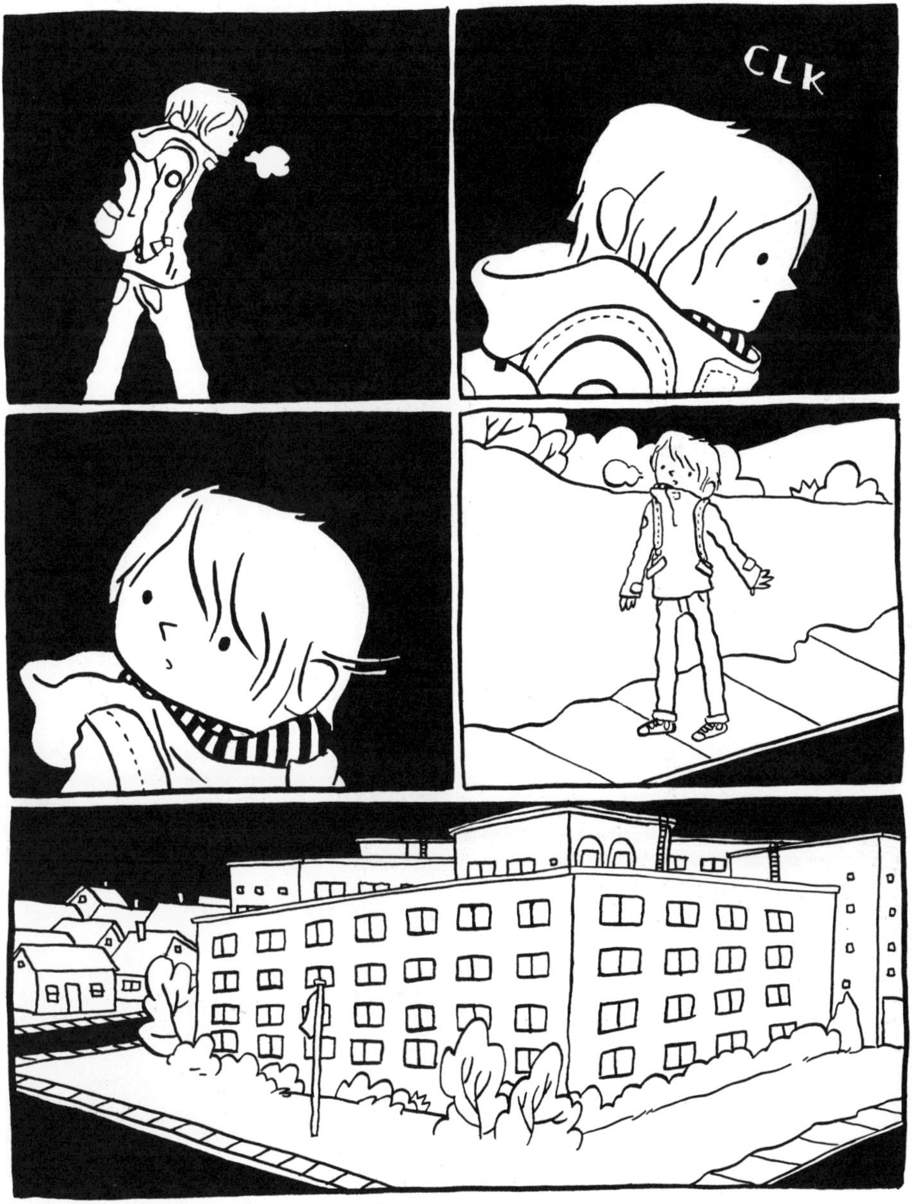
CLK

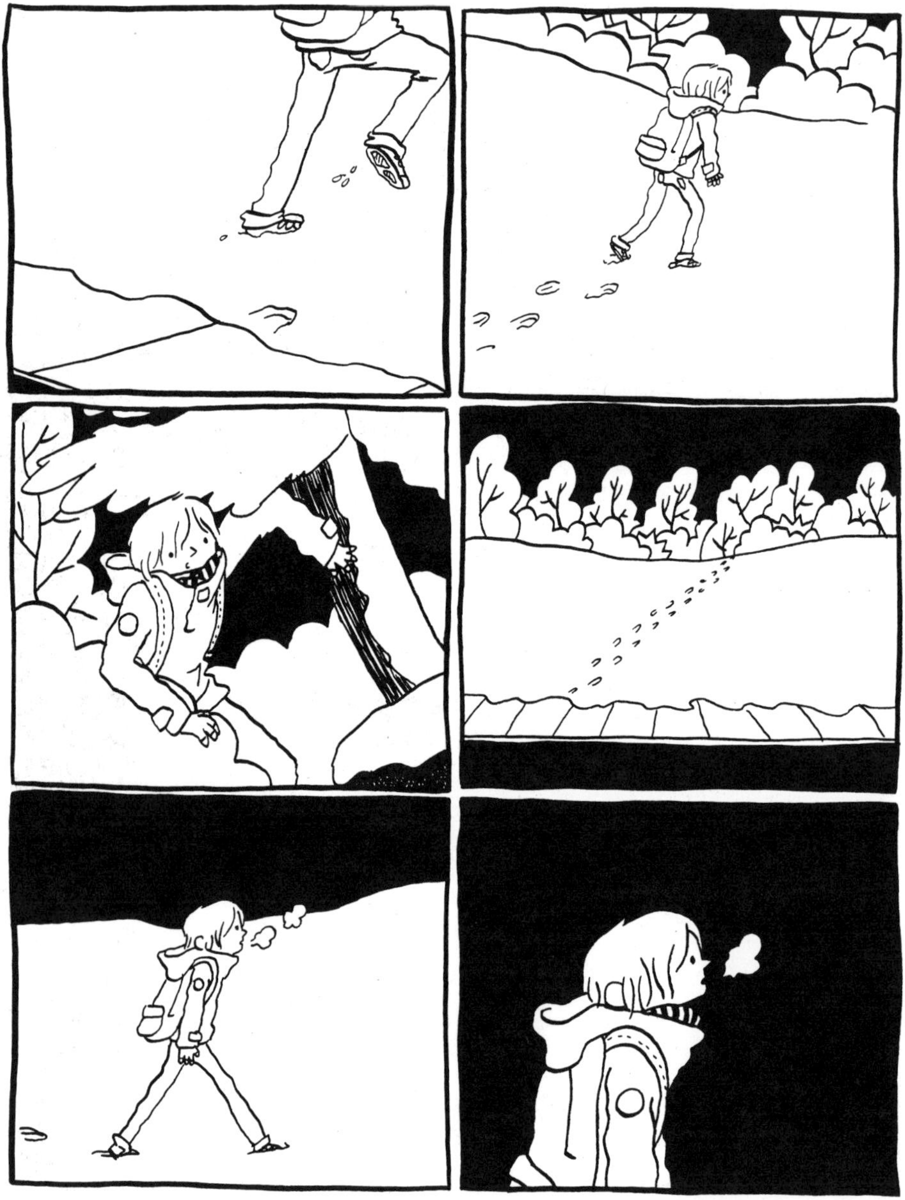

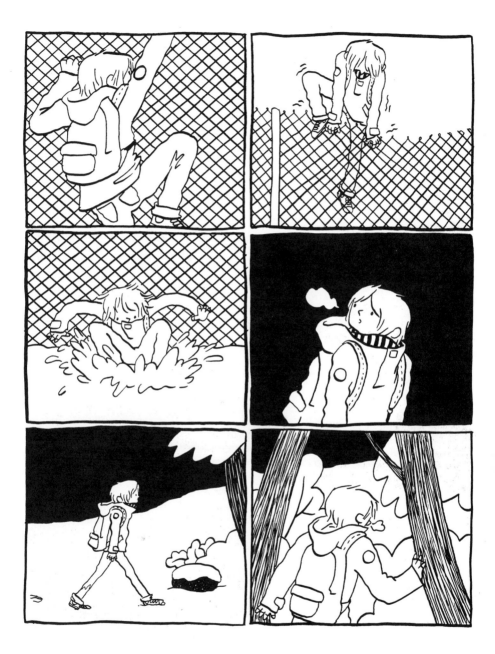

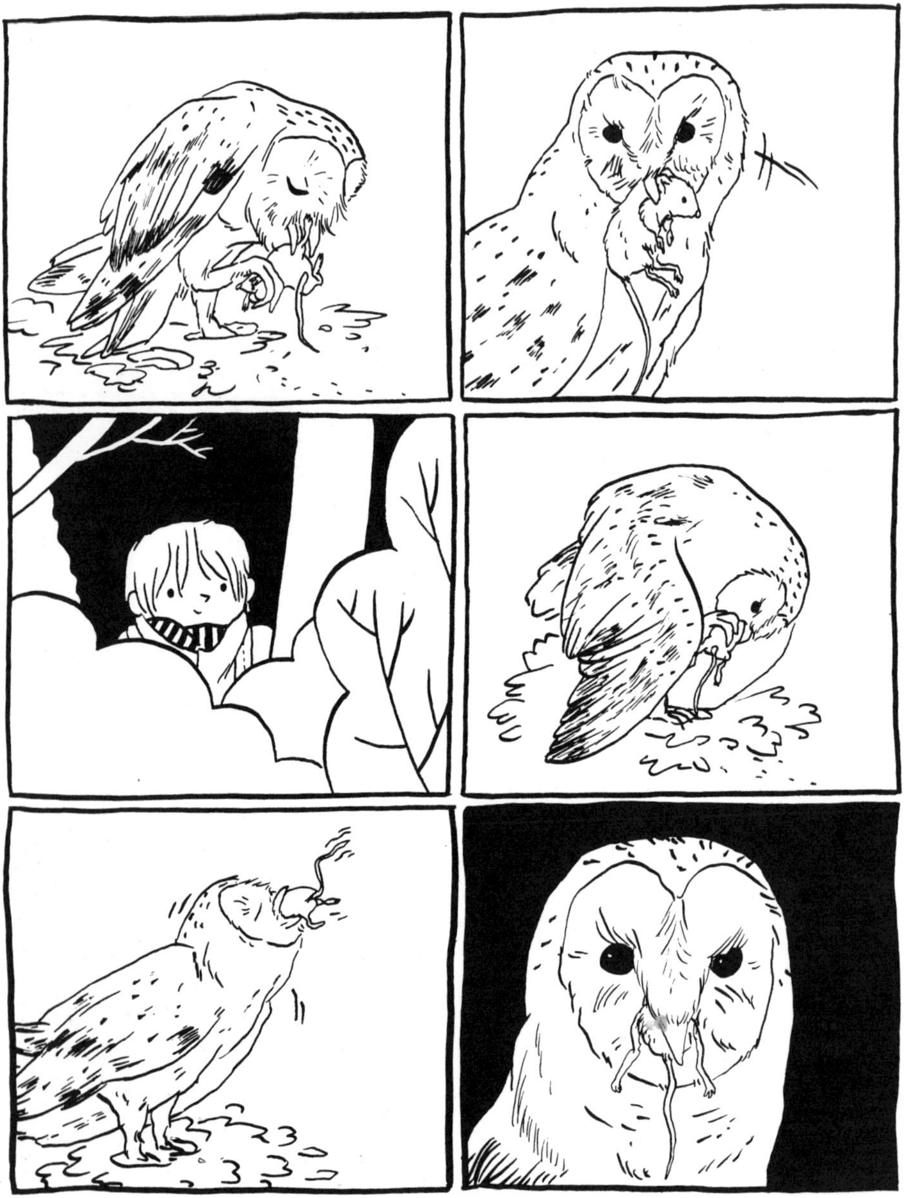

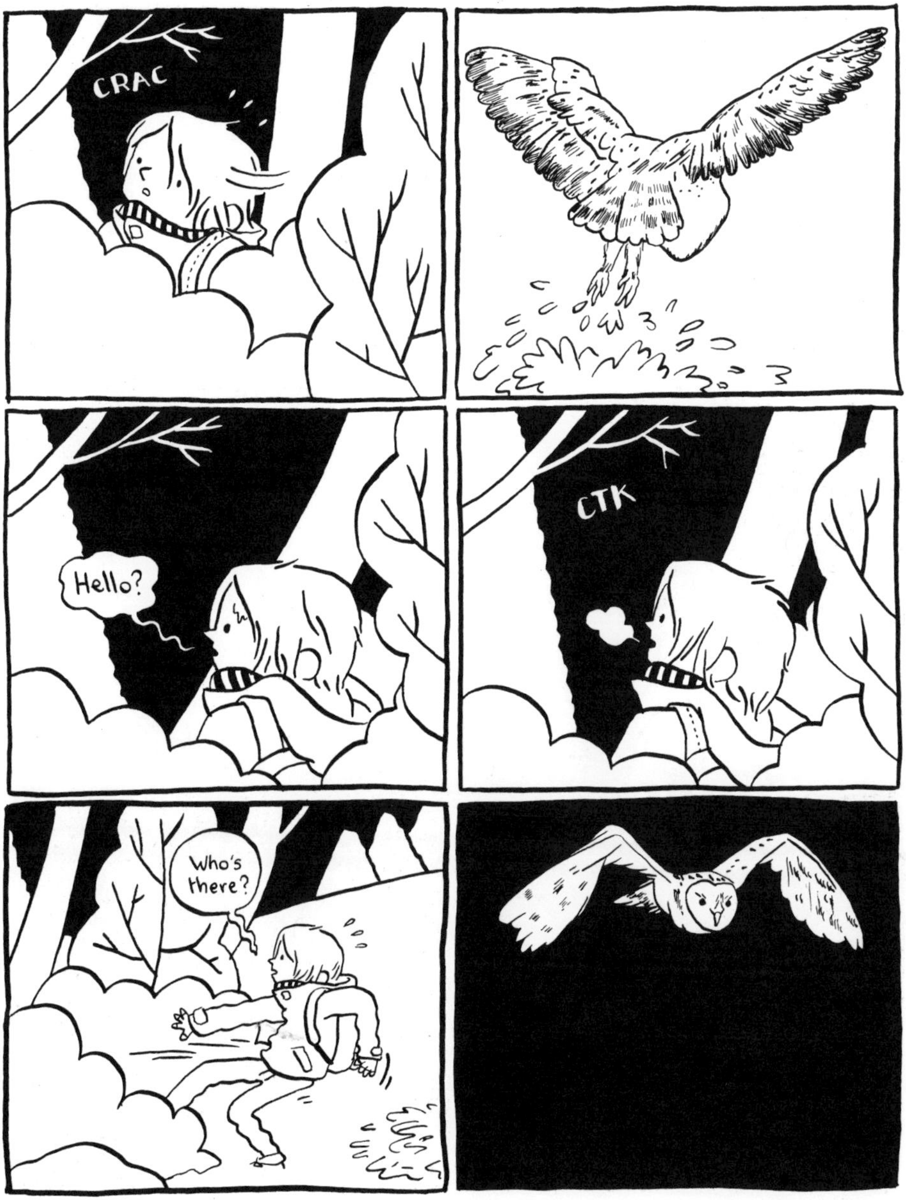
CRAC
Hello?
CTK
Who's there?

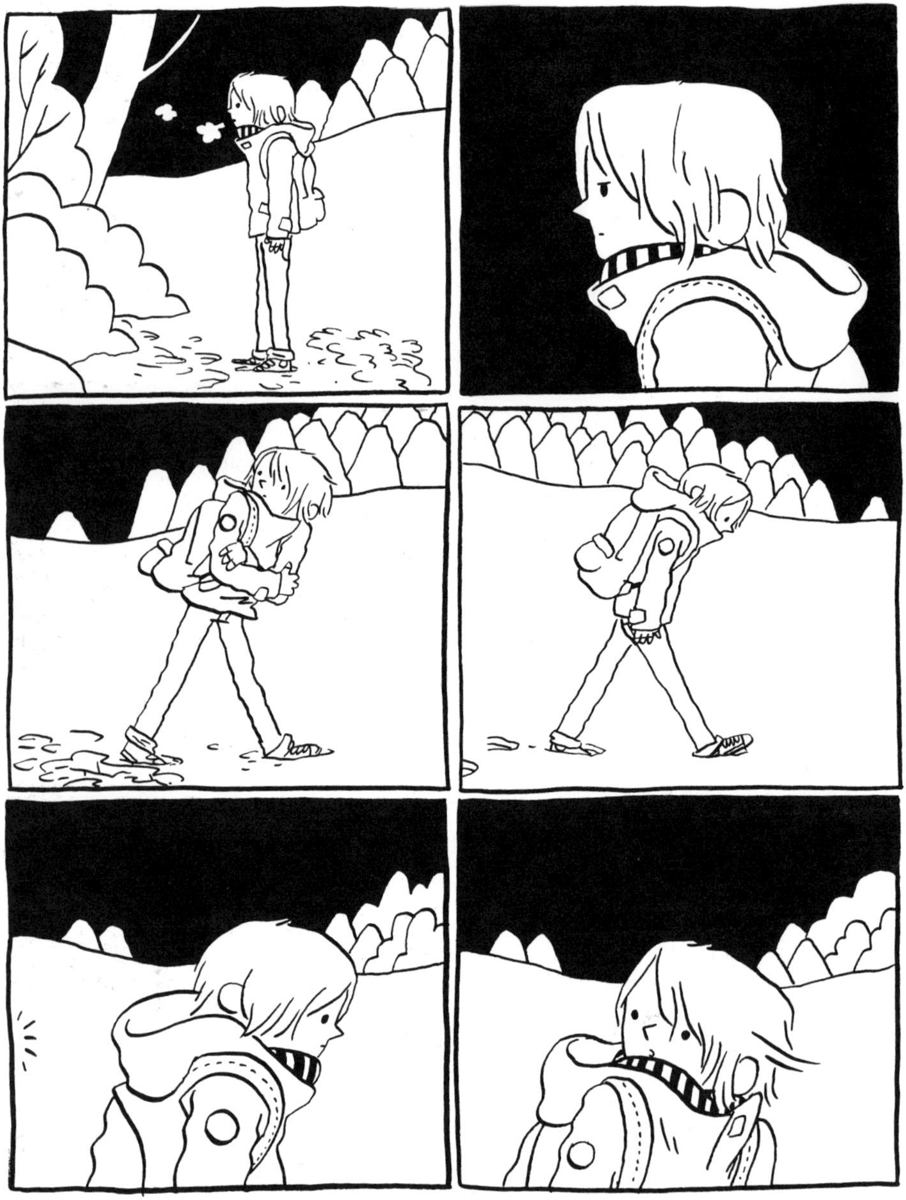

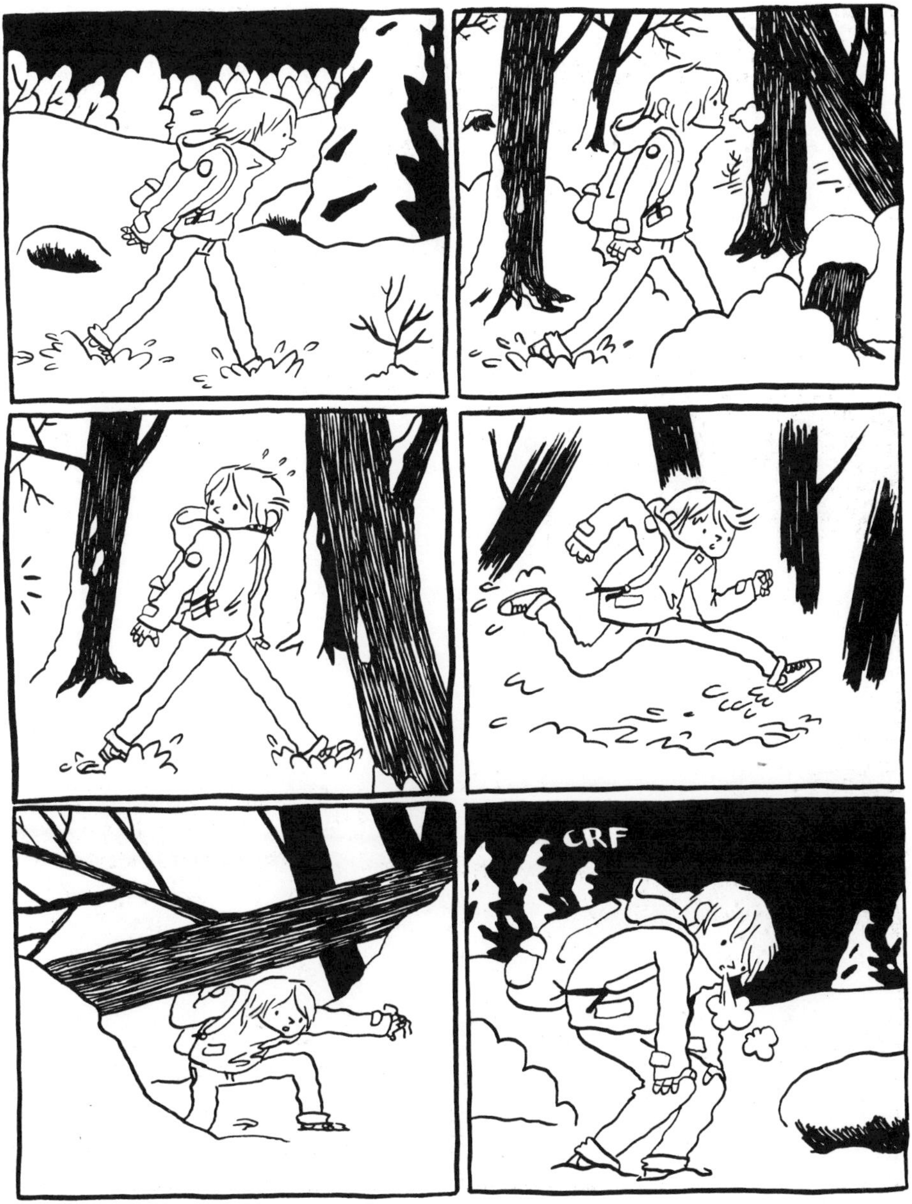
CRF

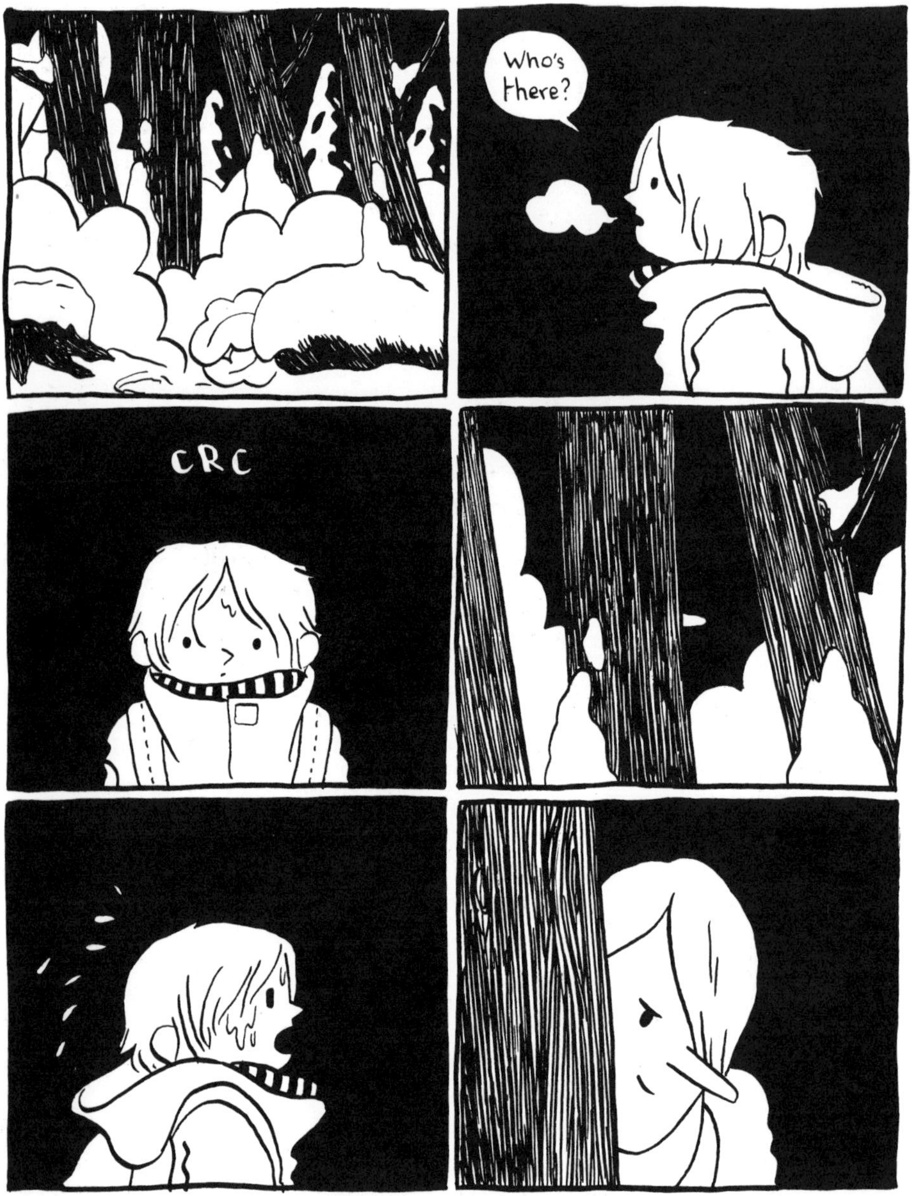
Who's there?
CRC

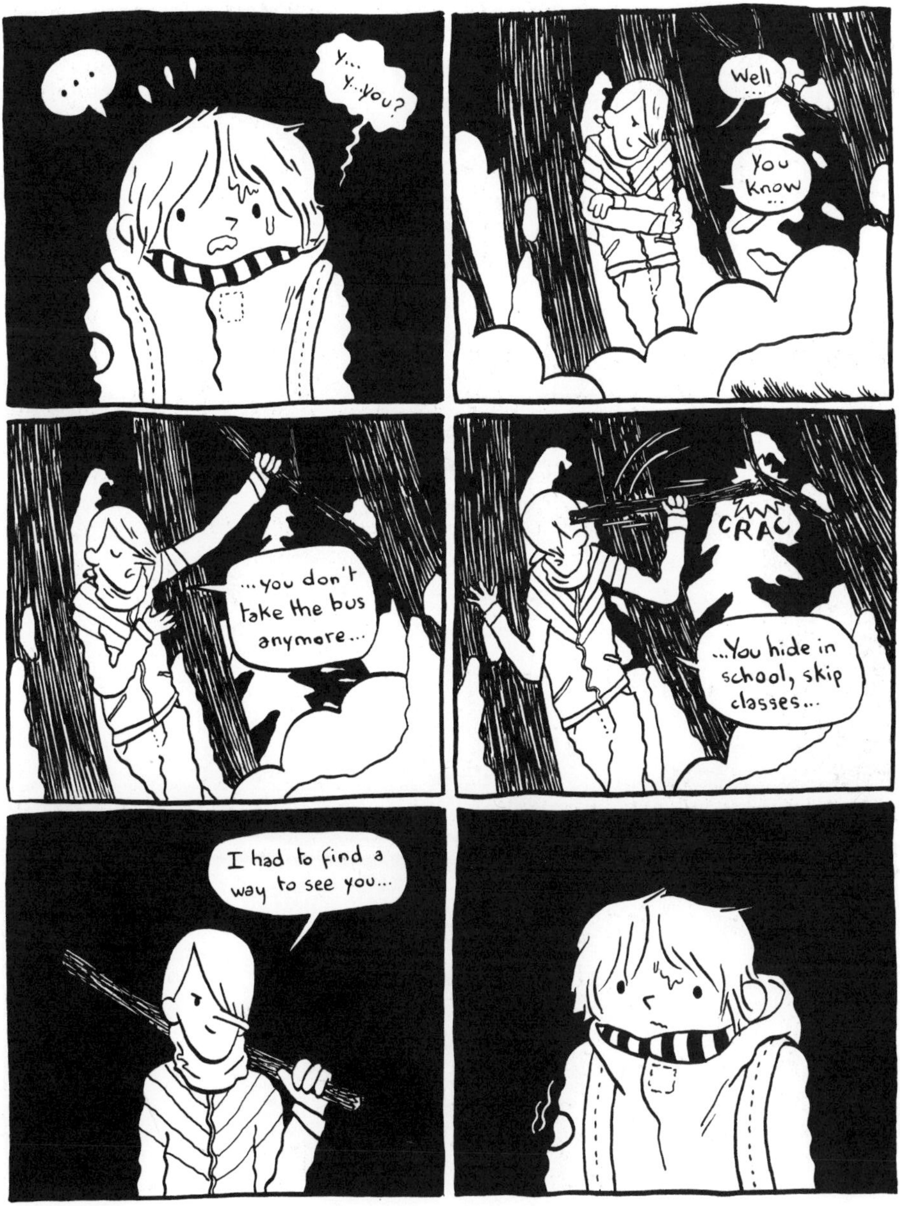
...
Y...
Y...you?
Well
...
You
Know
...
...you don't
take the bus
anymore...
CRAC
...You hide in
school, skip
classes...
I had to find a
way to see you...

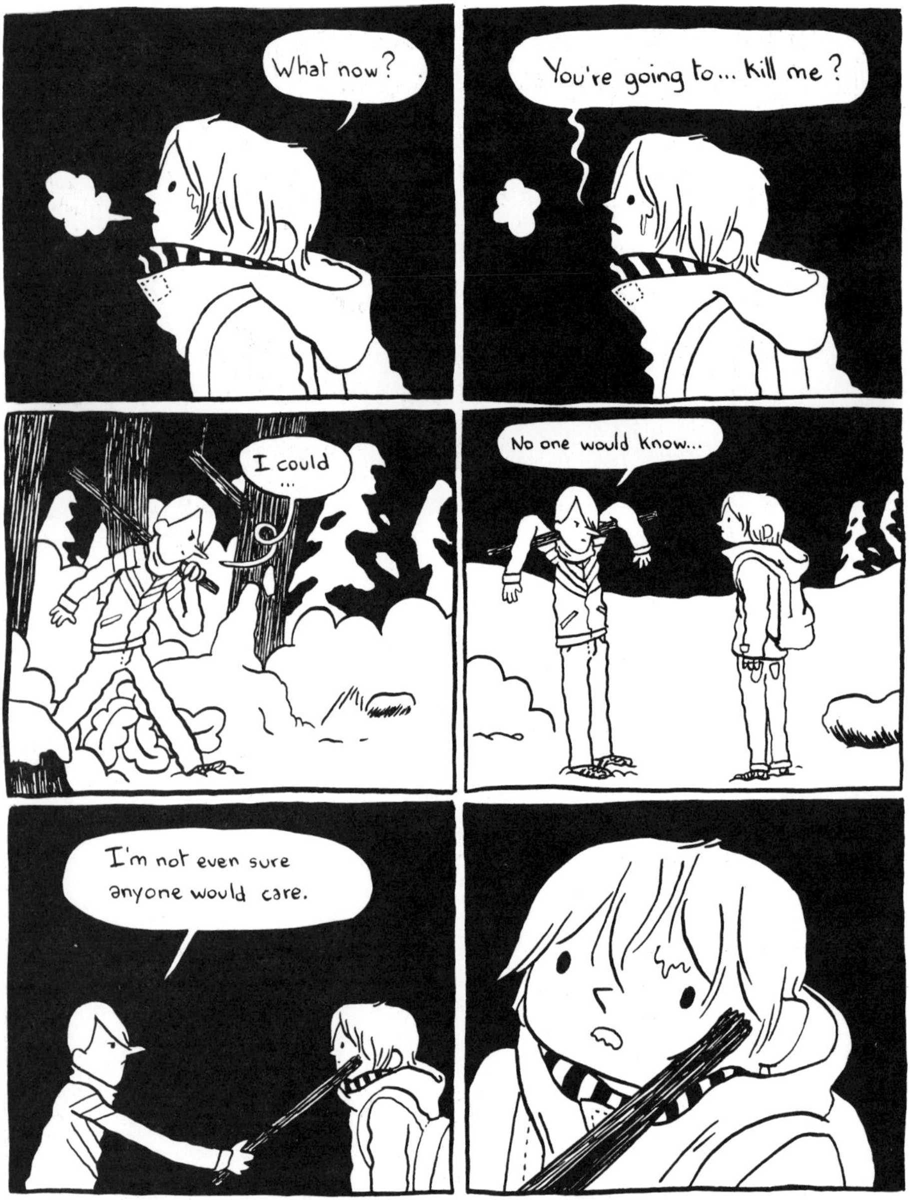
What now?
You're going to... kill me?
I could ...
No one would know...
I'm not even sure anyone would care.

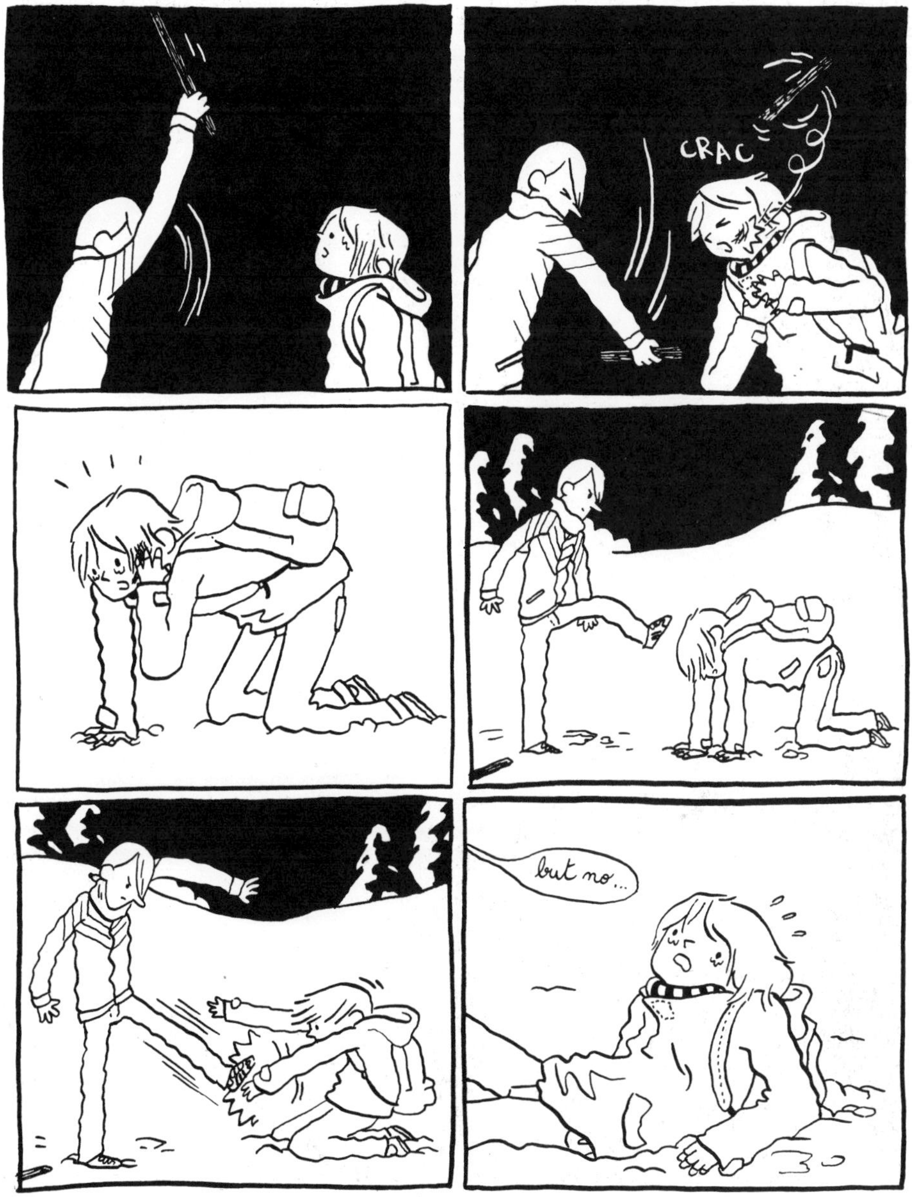
CRAC
but no...

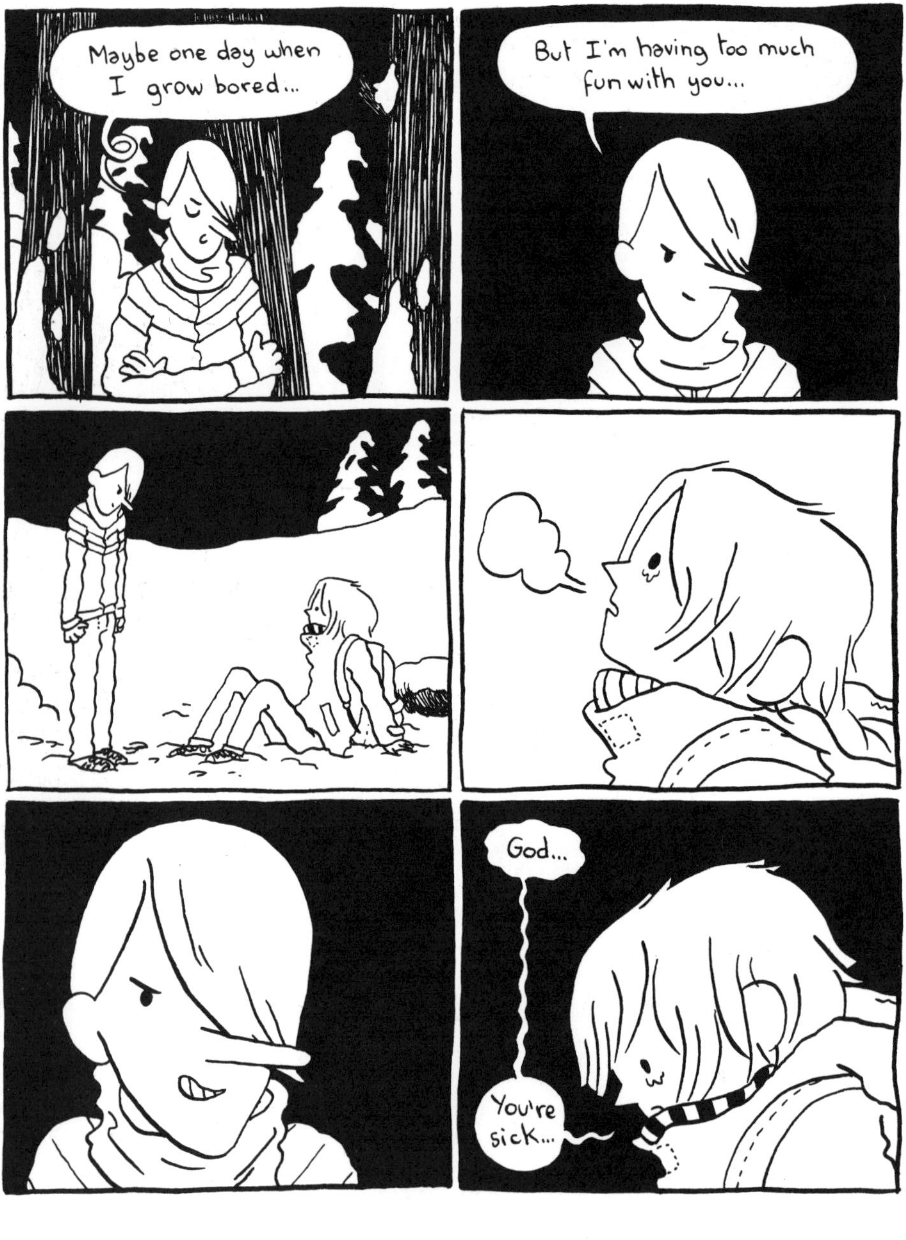
Maybe one day when I grow bored...
But I'm having too much fun with you...
God...
You're sick...

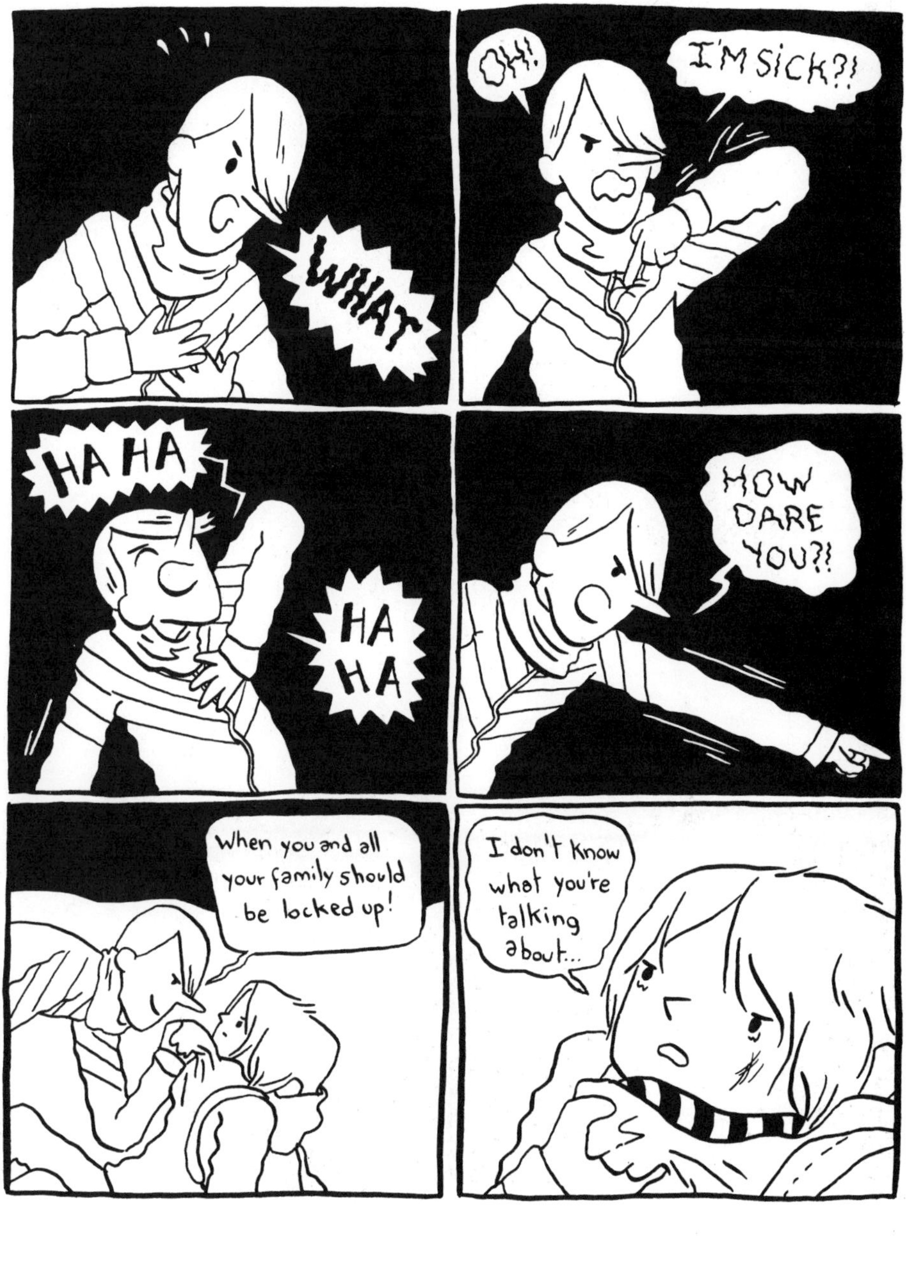
WHAT
OH!
I'M SICK?!
HA HA
HA HA
HOW DARE YOU?!
When you and all your family should be locked up!
I don't know what you're talking about...

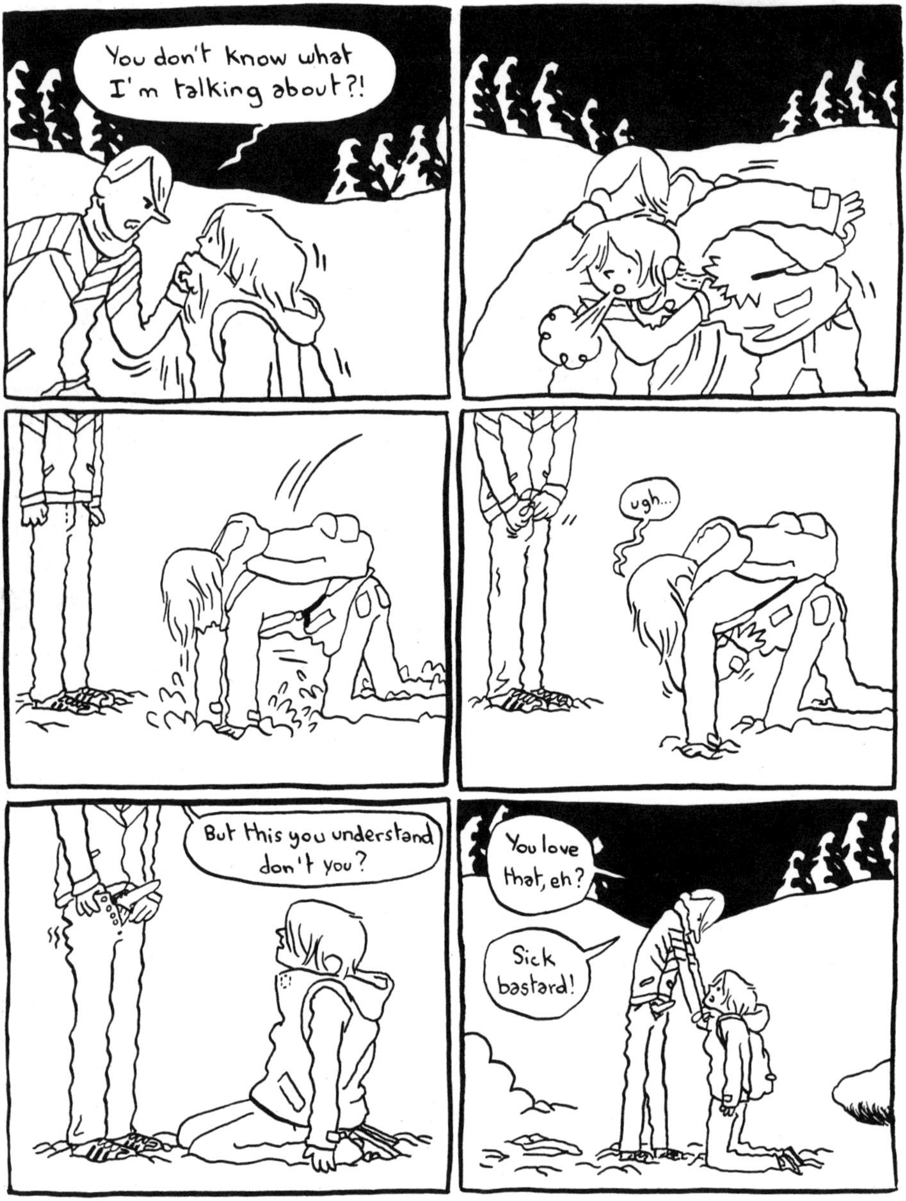
You don't know what I'm talking about?!
ugh...
But this you understand don't you?
You love that, eh?
Sick bastard!

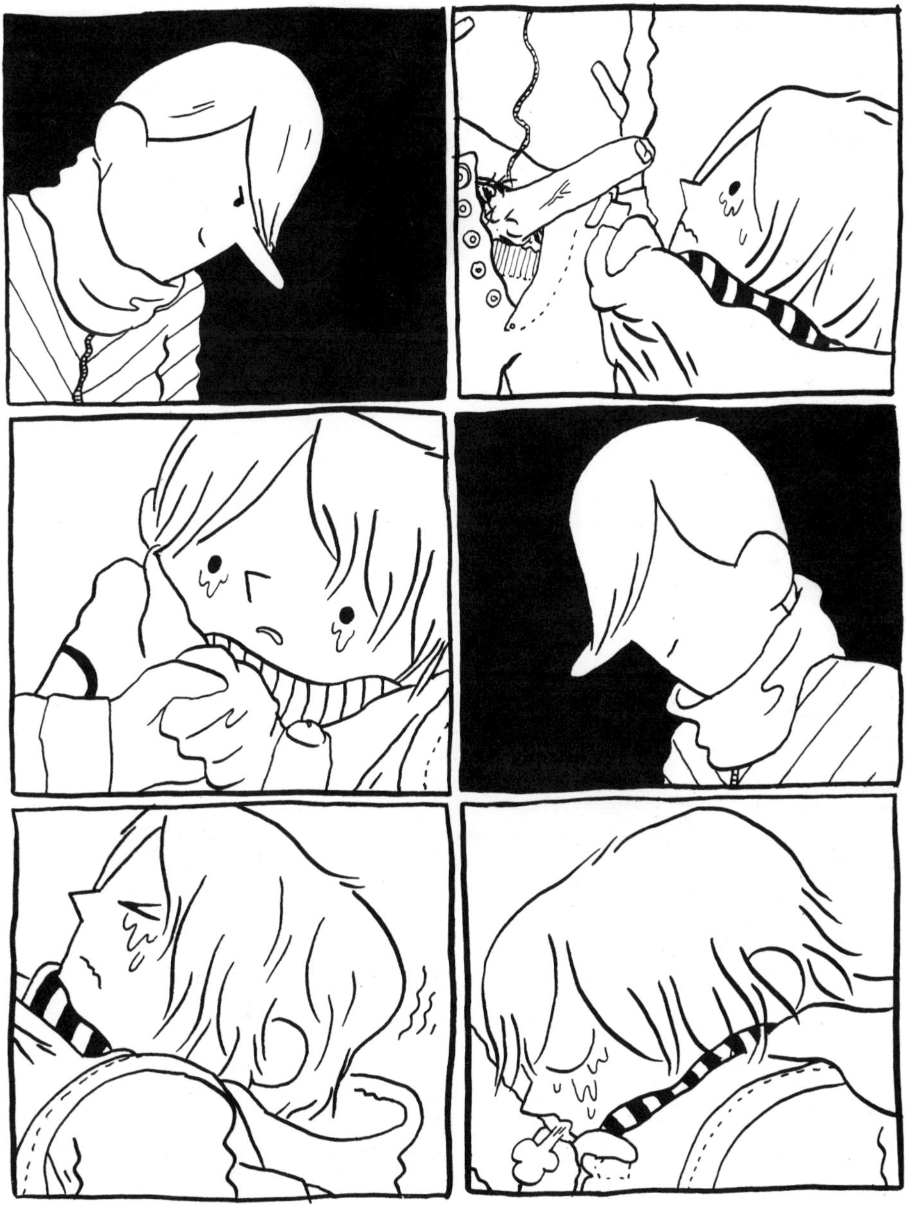

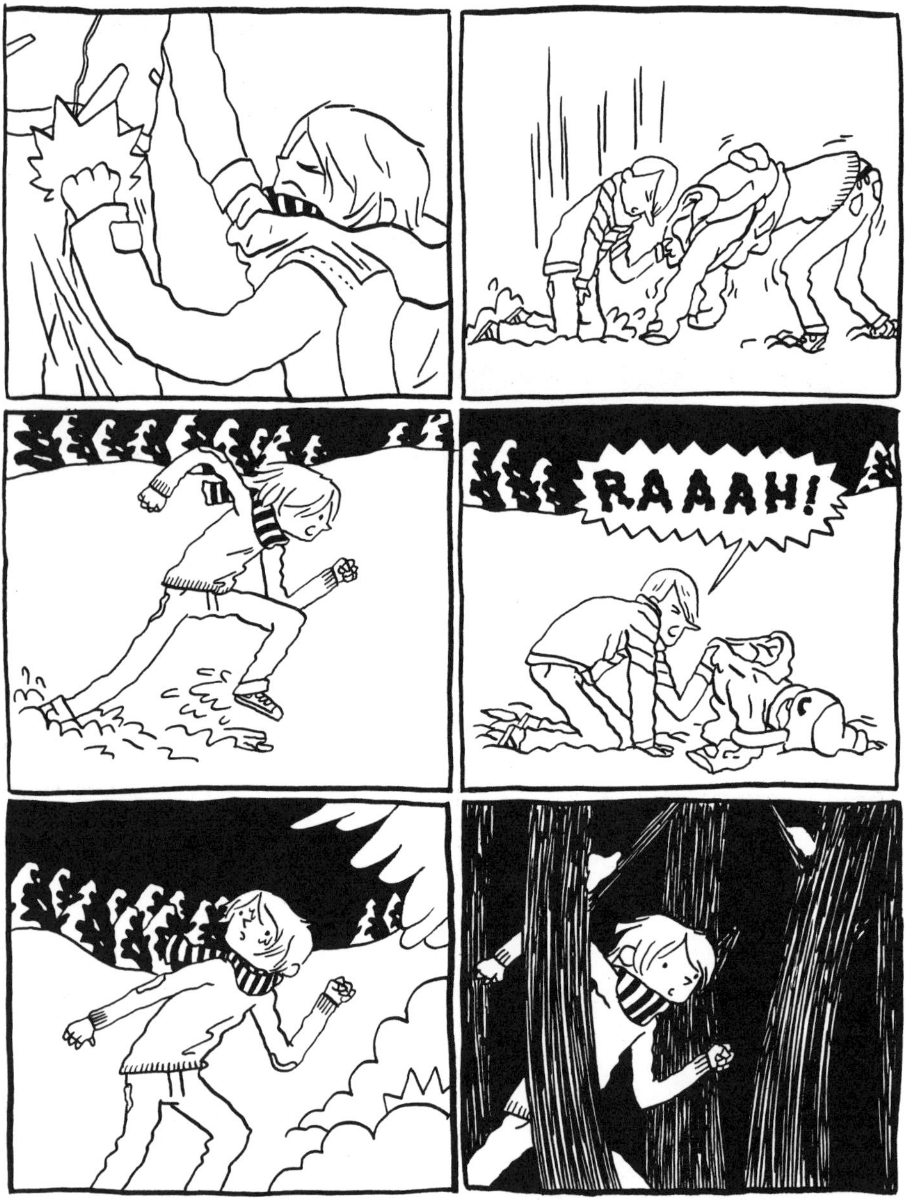
RAAAH!

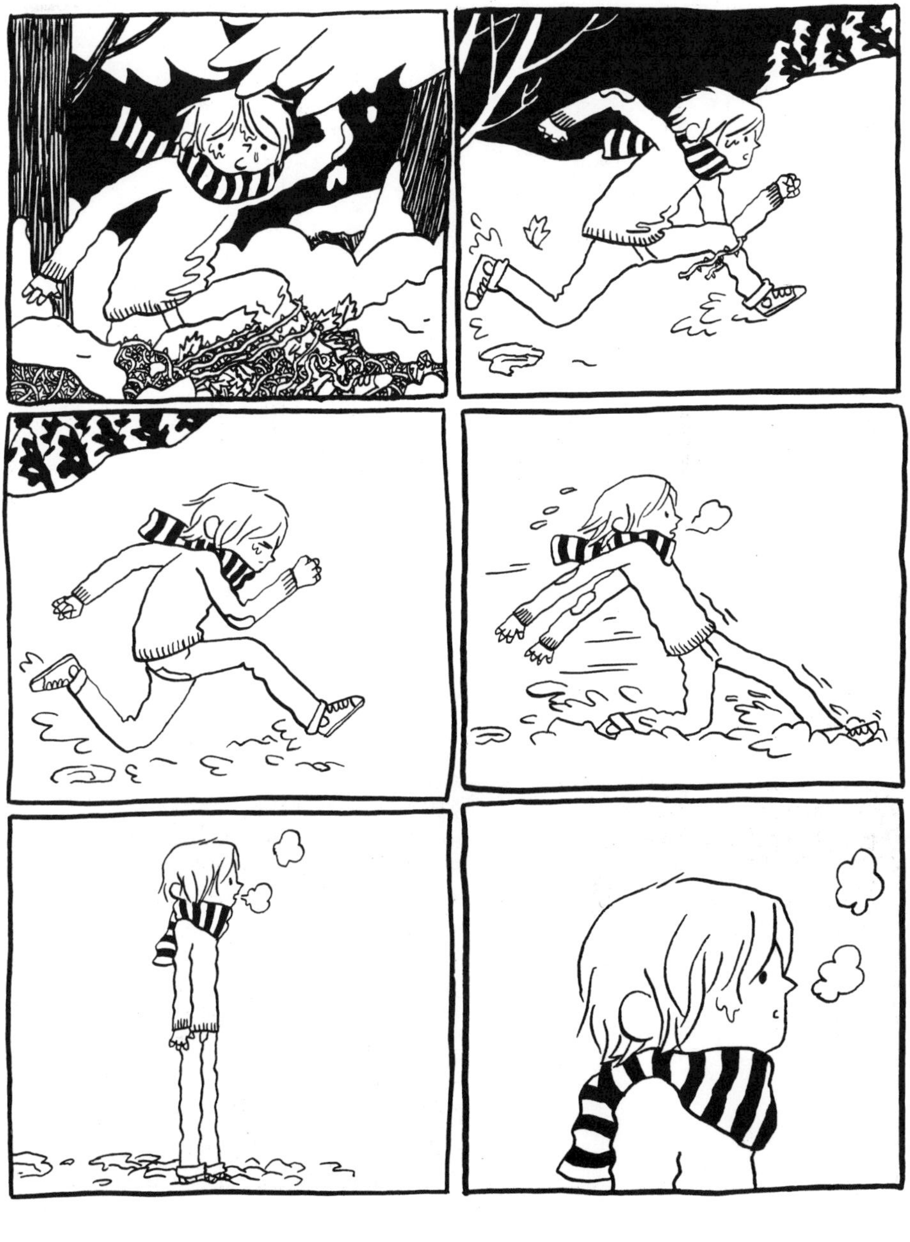

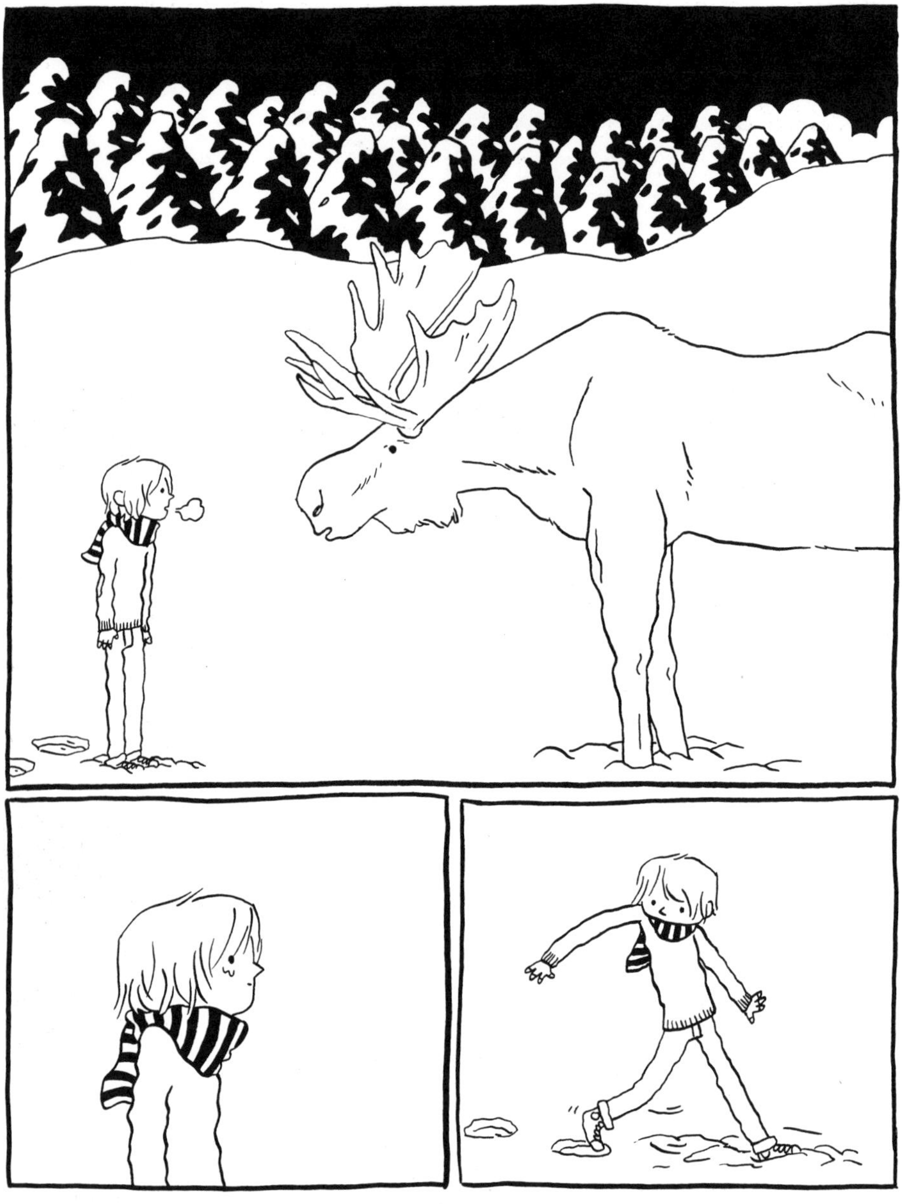

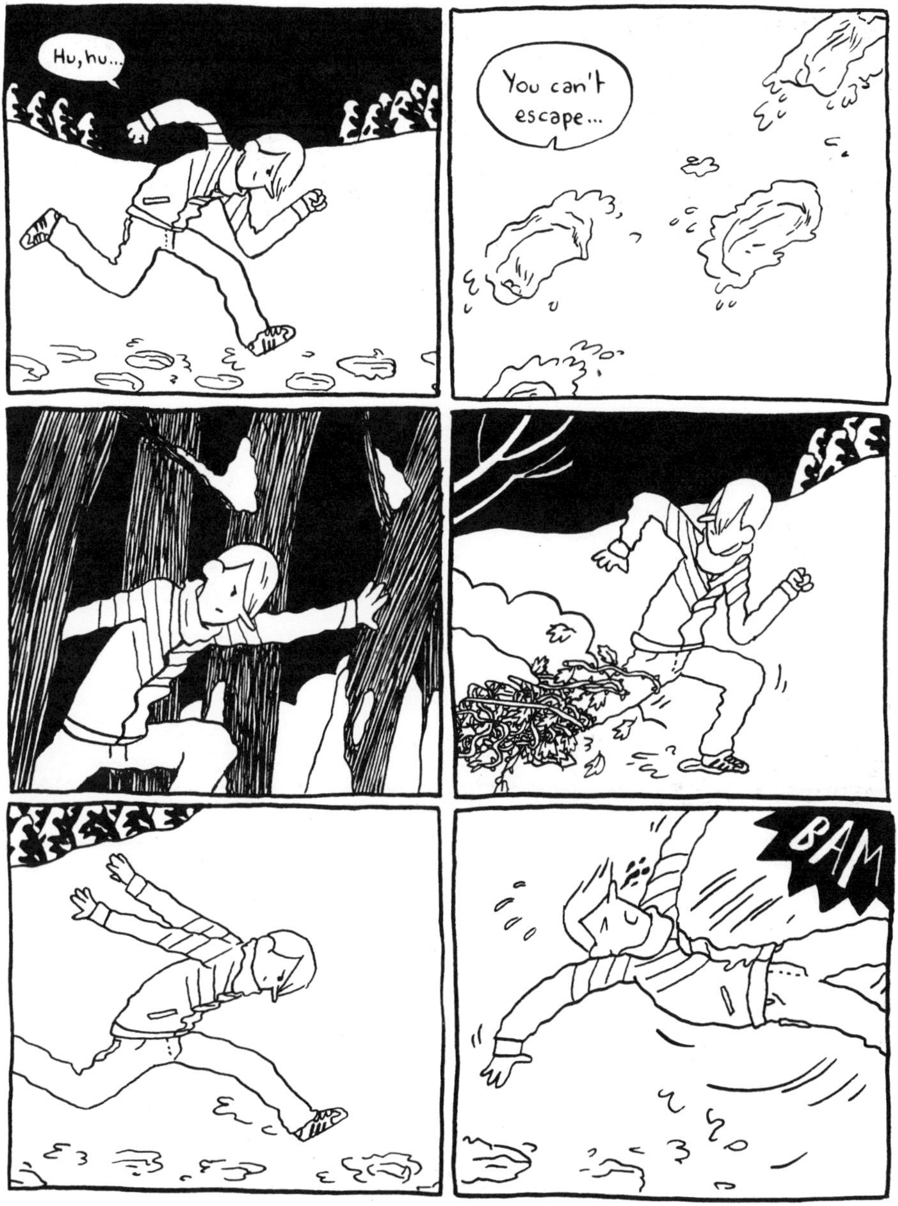
Hu, hu...
You can't escape...
BAM

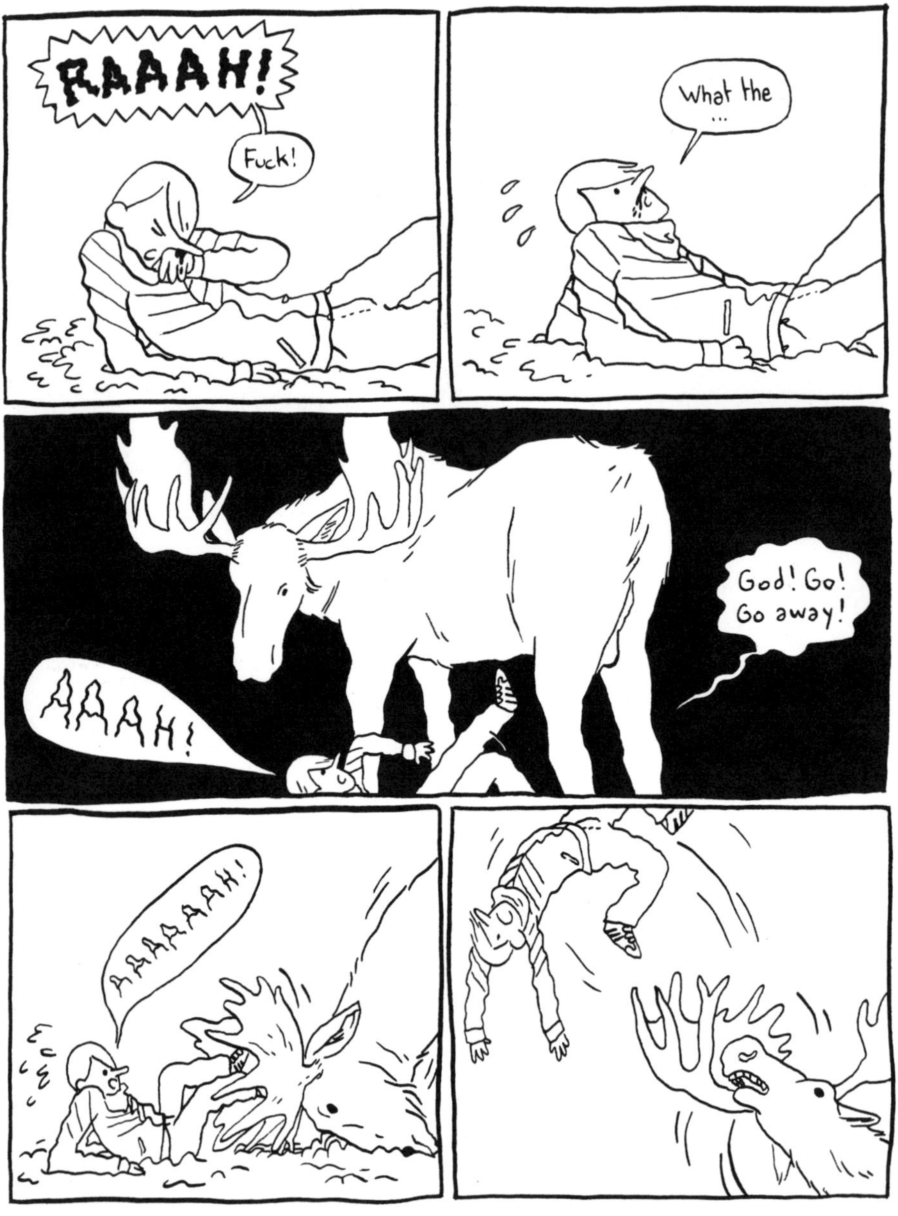
RAAAH!
Fuck!
What the ...
God! Go! Go away!
AAAH!
AAAAAAAH!

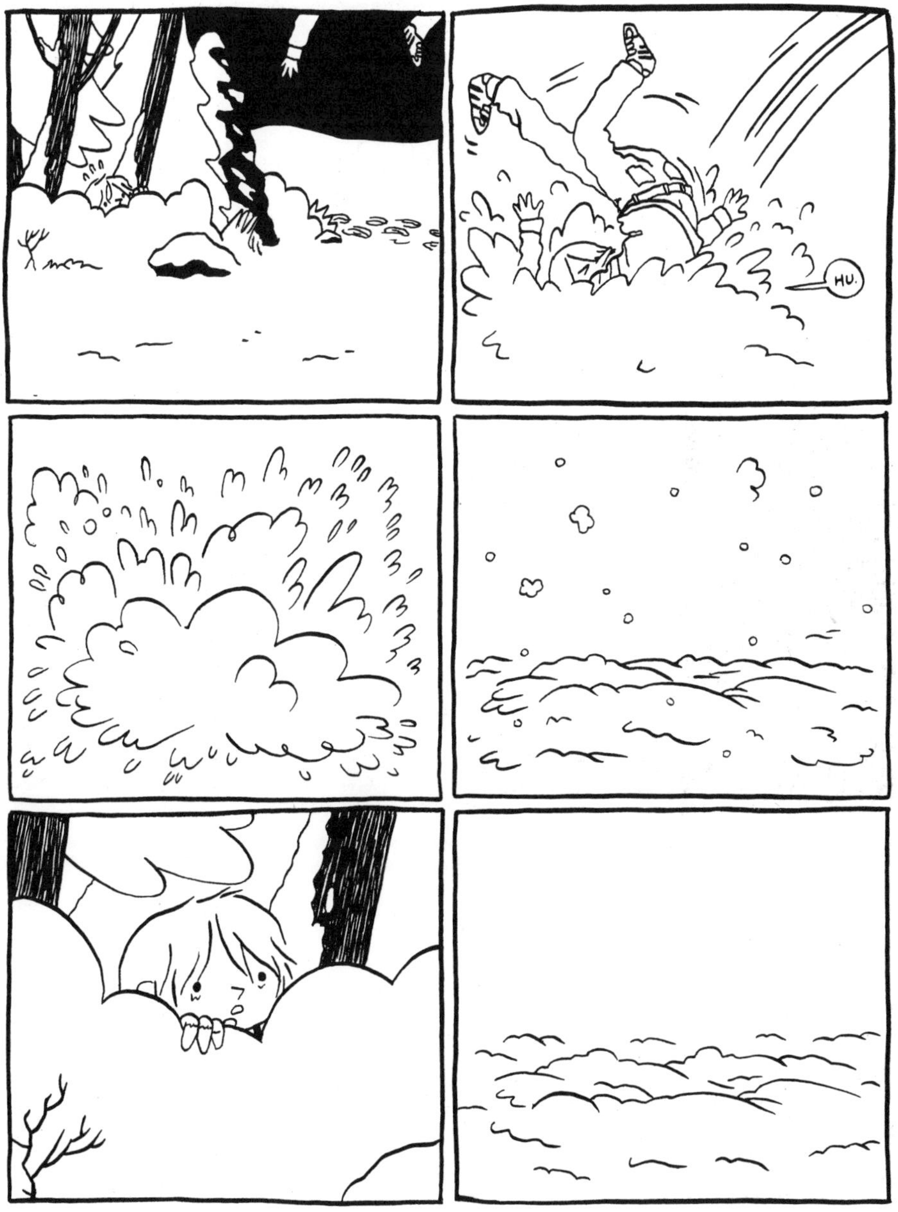
HU.

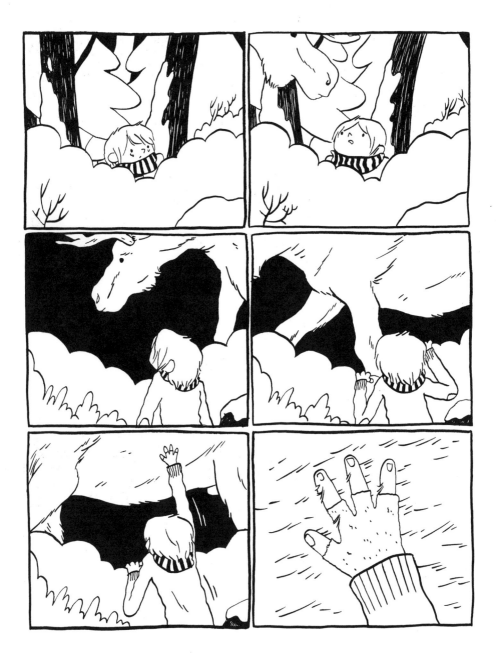

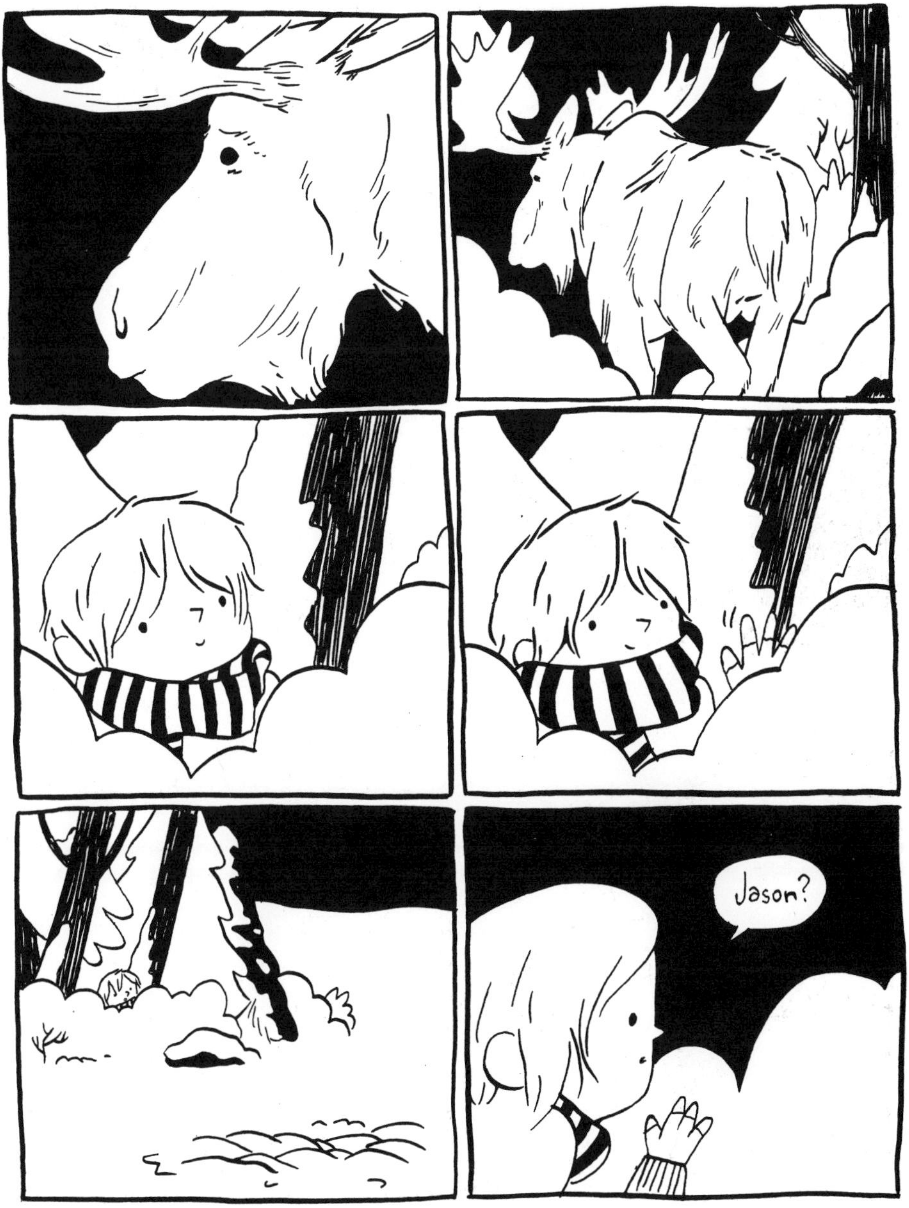
Jason?

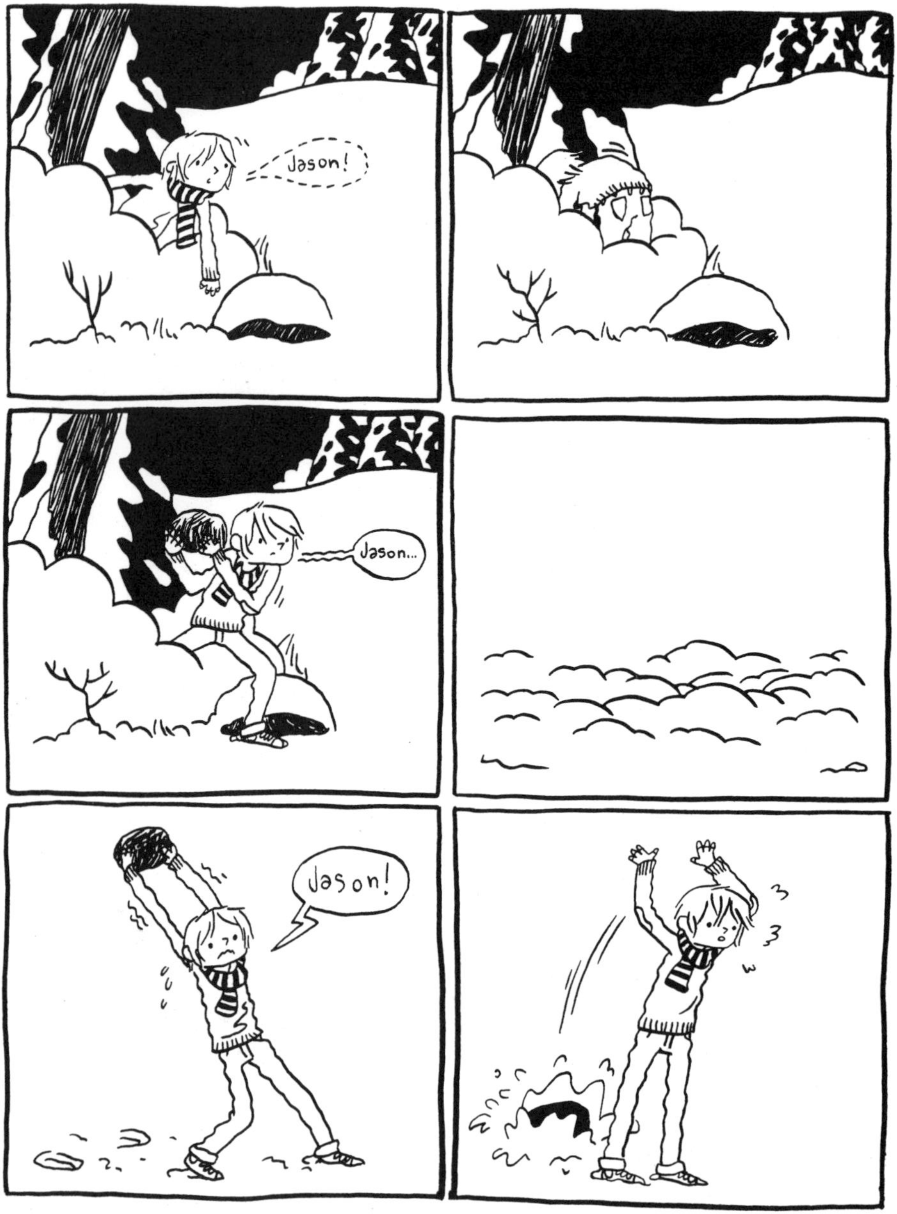
Jason!
Jason...
Jason!

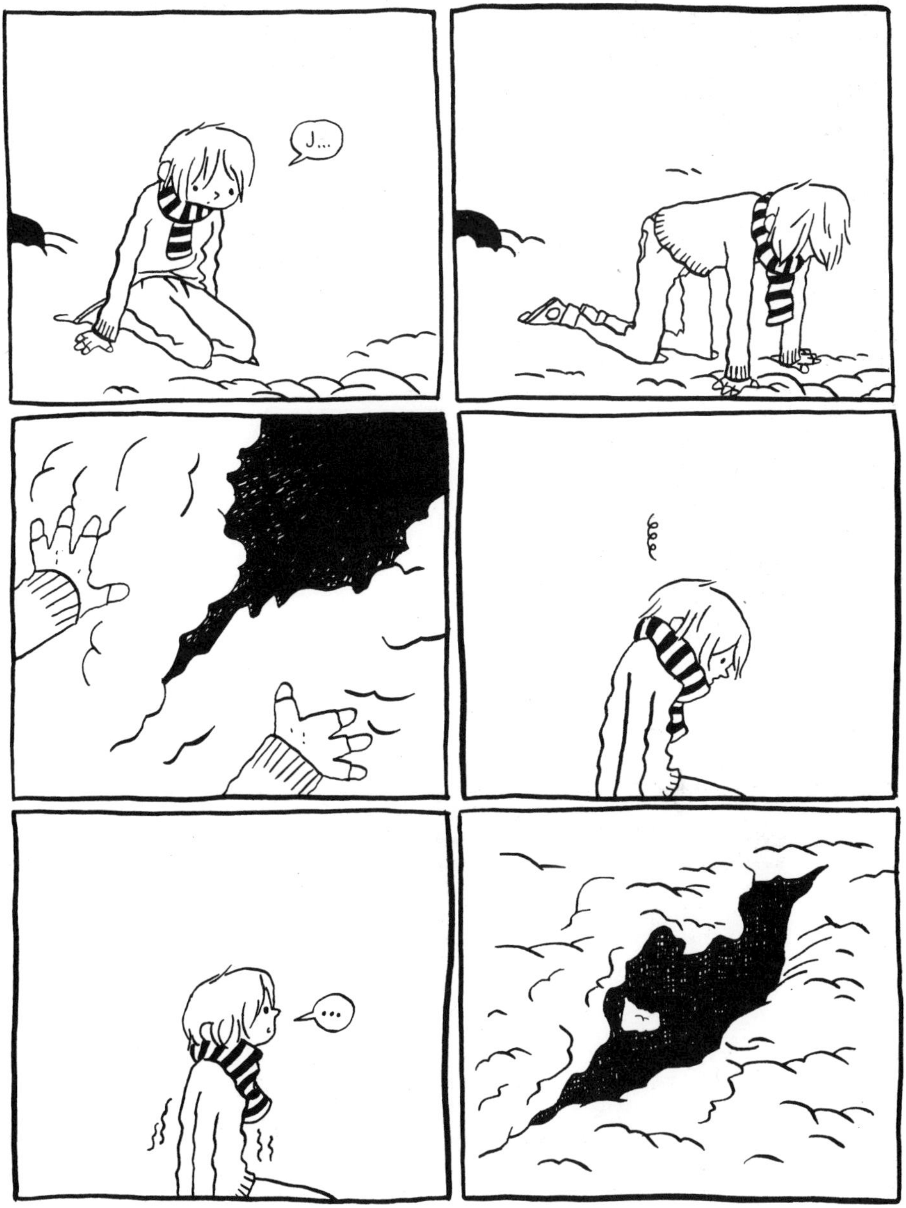
J...
...

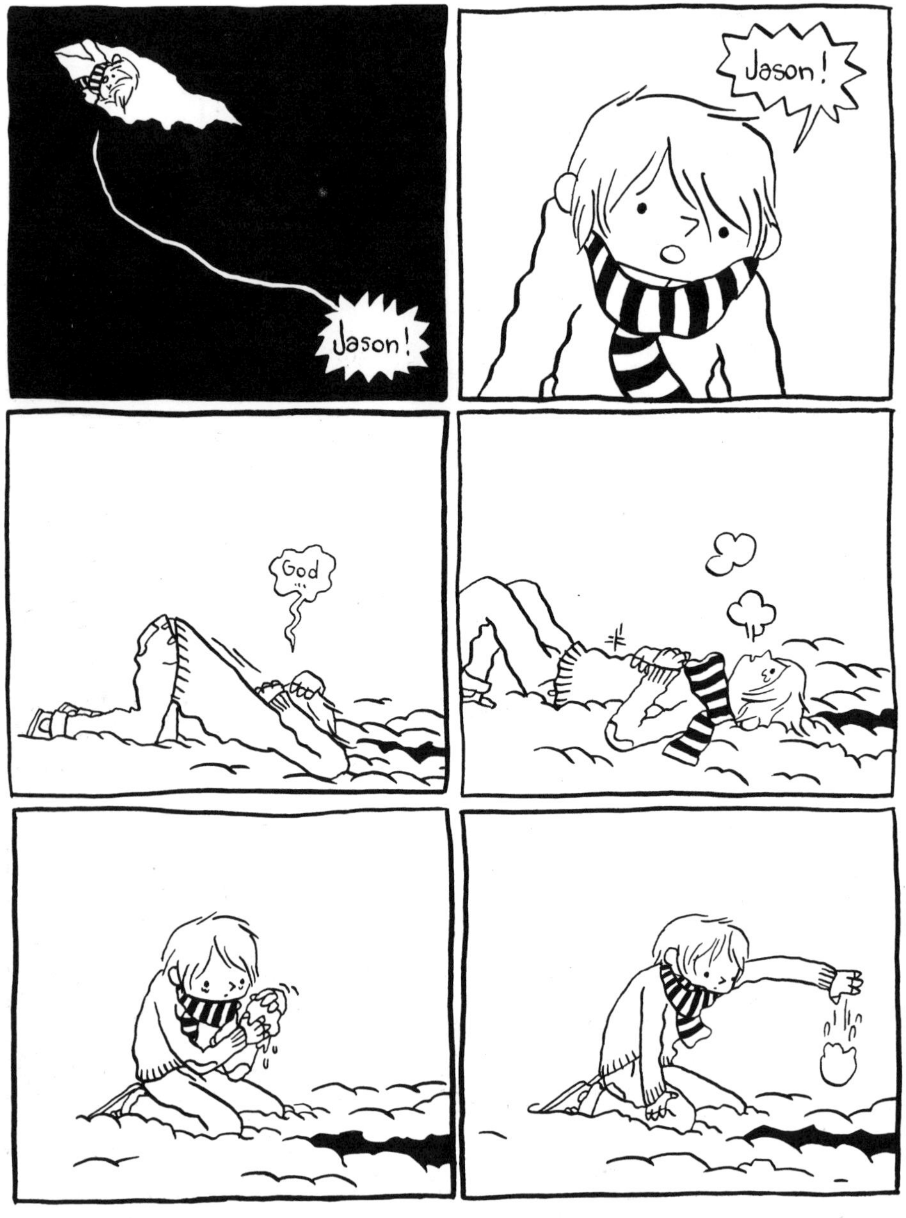

Jason!
Jason!
God

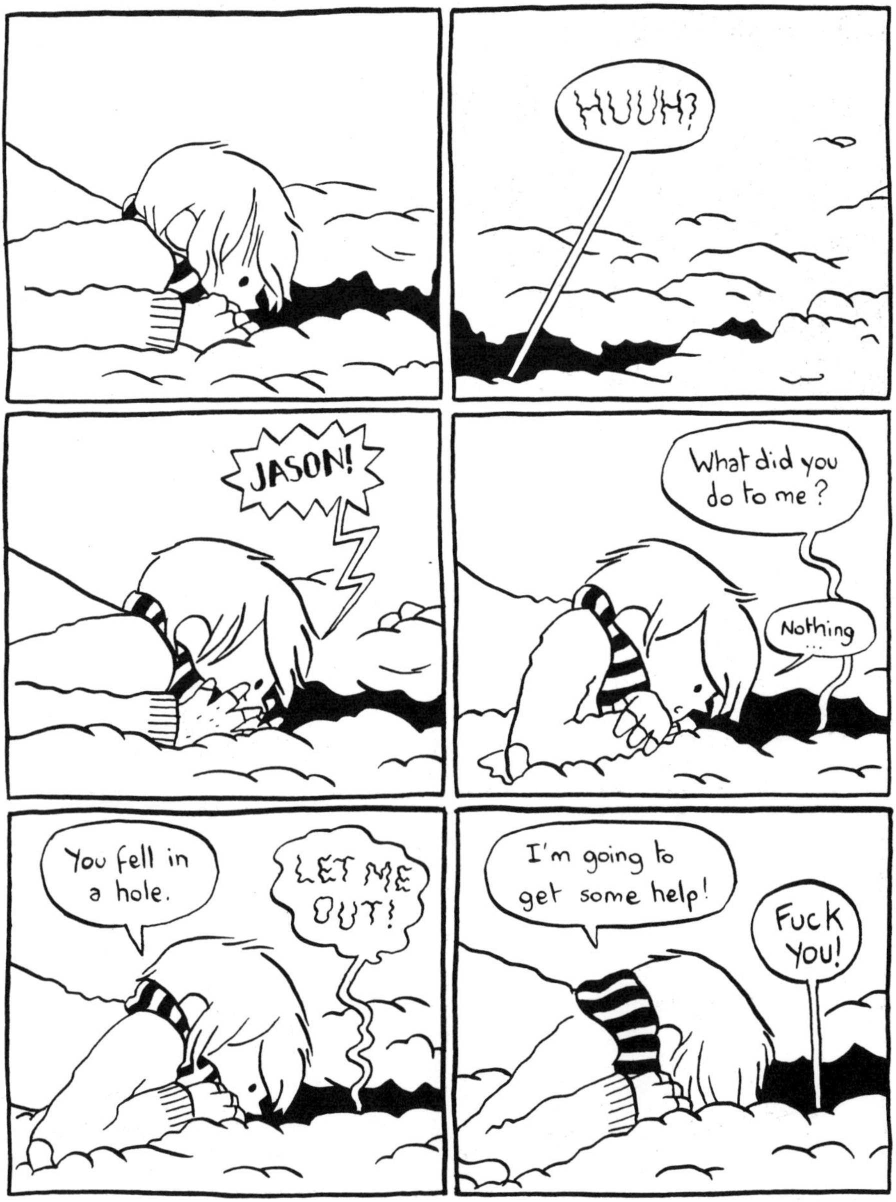
HUUH?
JASON!
What did you do to me?
Nothing...
You fell in a hole.
LET ME OUT!
I'm going to get some help!
Fuck you!

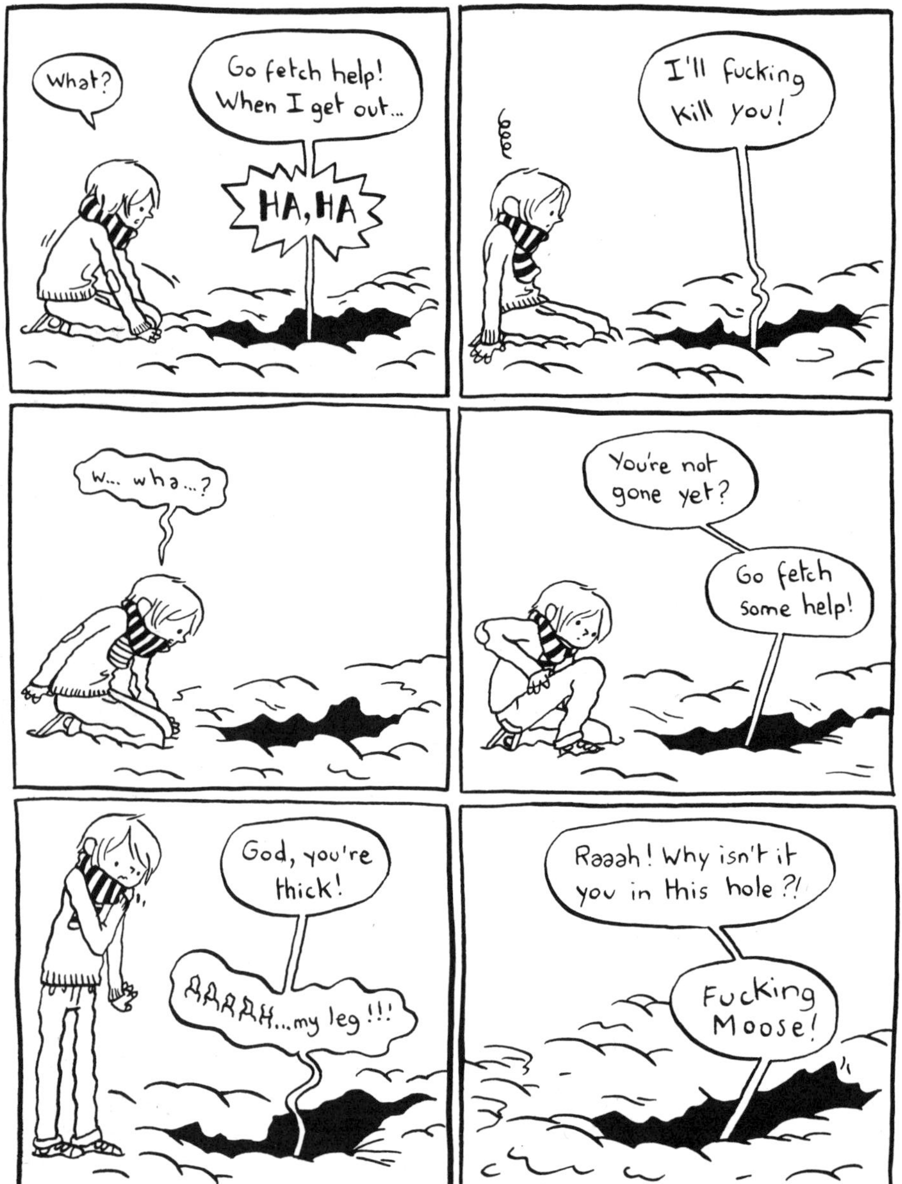
What?
Go fetch help! When I get out...
HA, HA
I'll fucking kill you!
w... wha...?
You're not gone yet?
Go fetch some help!
God, you're thick!
AAAAH... my leg!!!
Raaah! Why isn't it you in this hole?!
Fucking Moose!

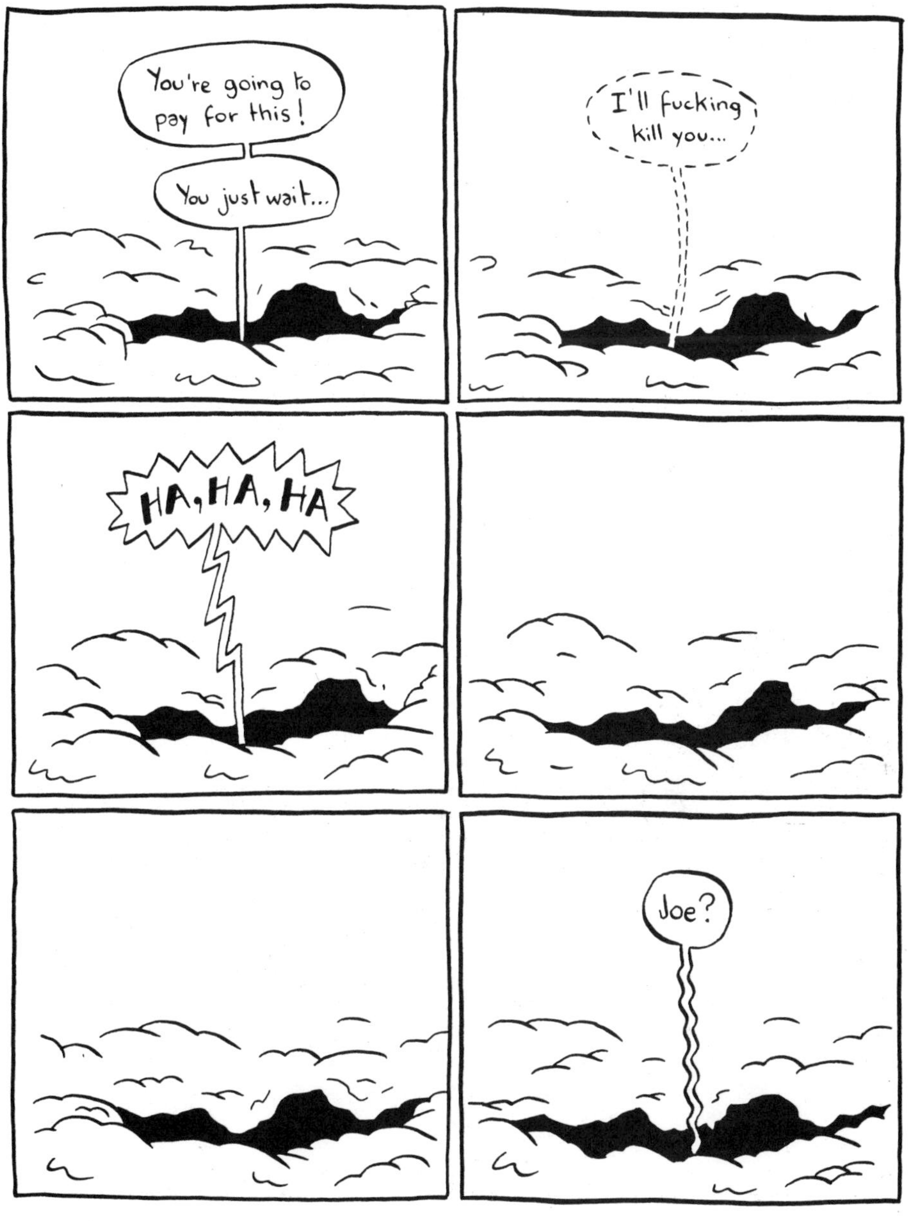
You're going to pay for this!
You just wait...
I'll fucking kill you...
HA, HA, HA
Joe?

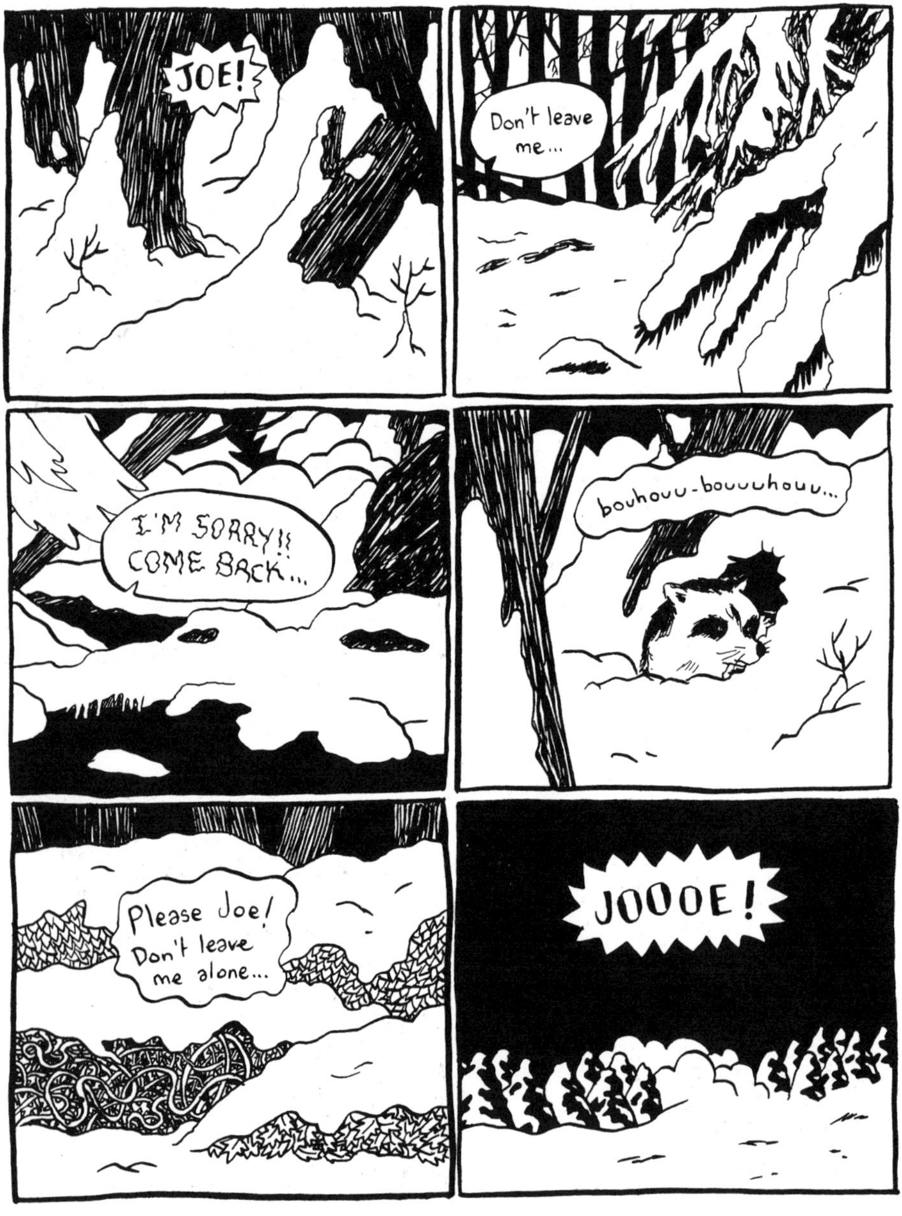
JOE!
Don't leave me...
I'M SORRY!! COME BACK...
bouhouu-bouuuhouu...
Please Joe! Don't leave me alone...
JOOOE!

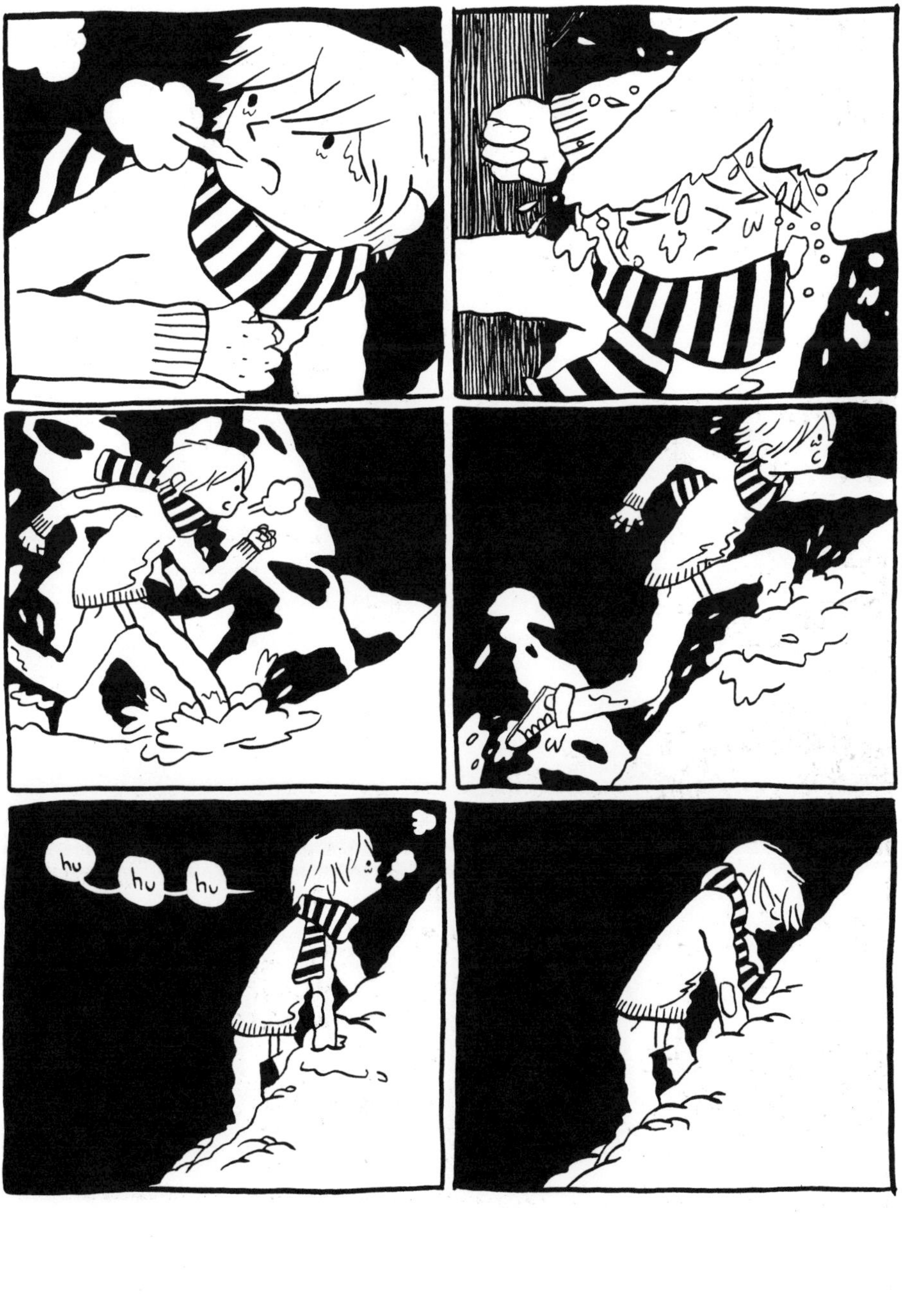
hu
hu
hu

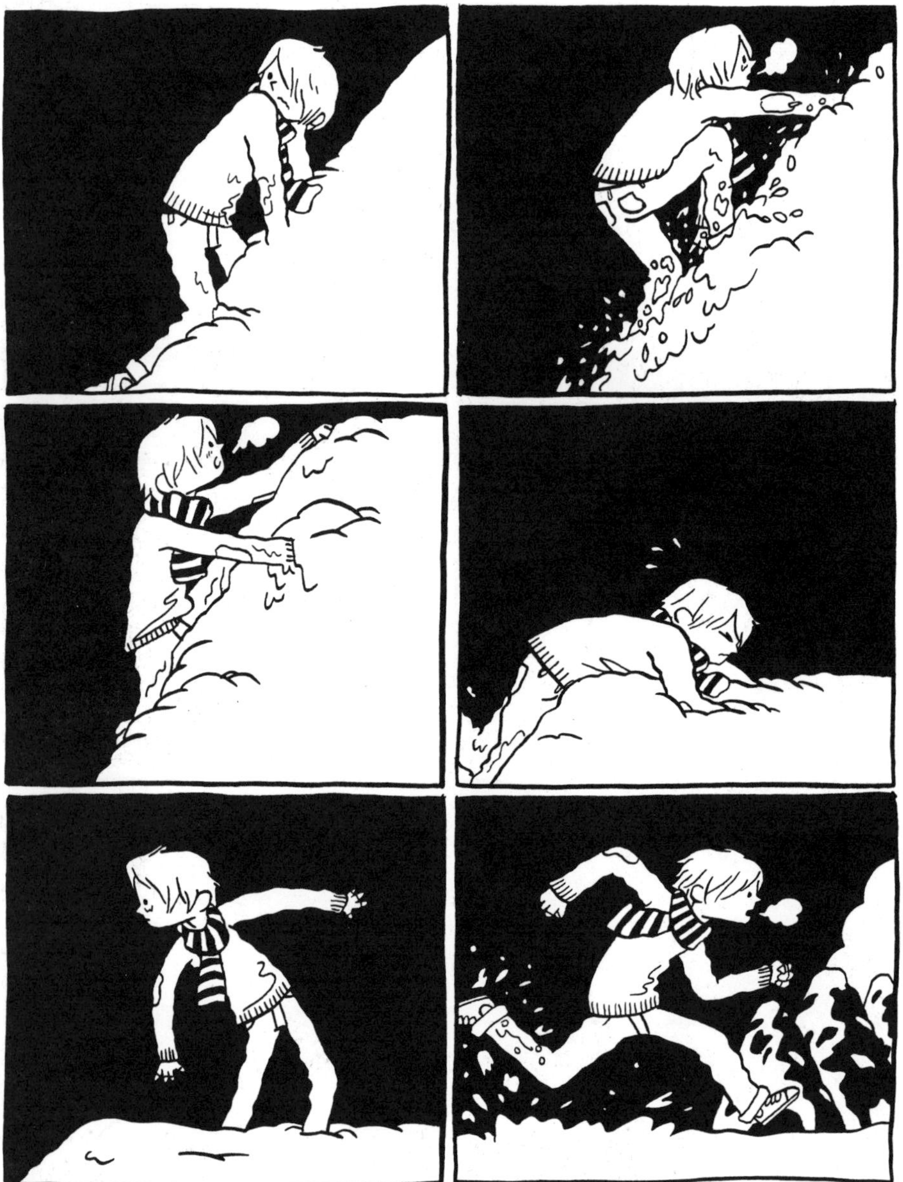

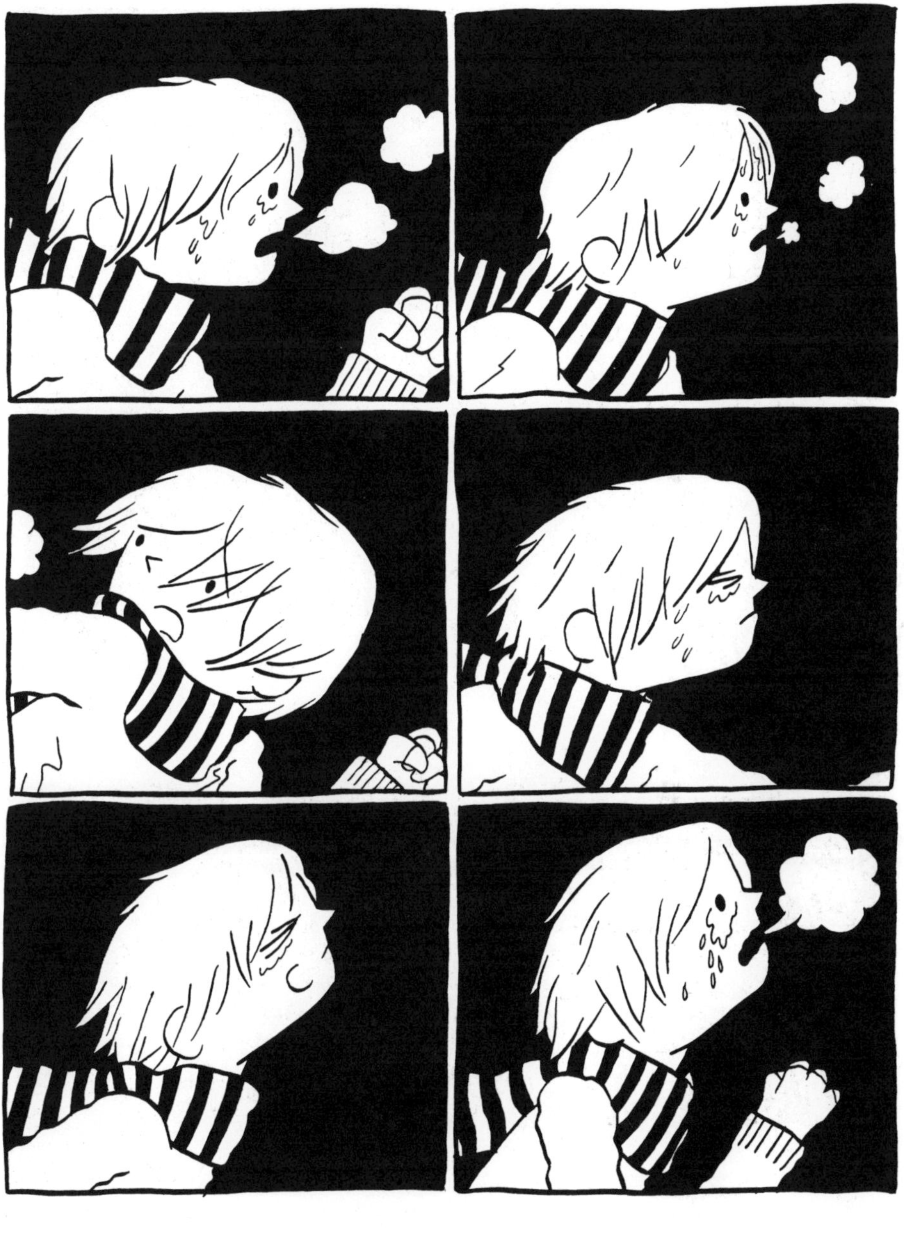

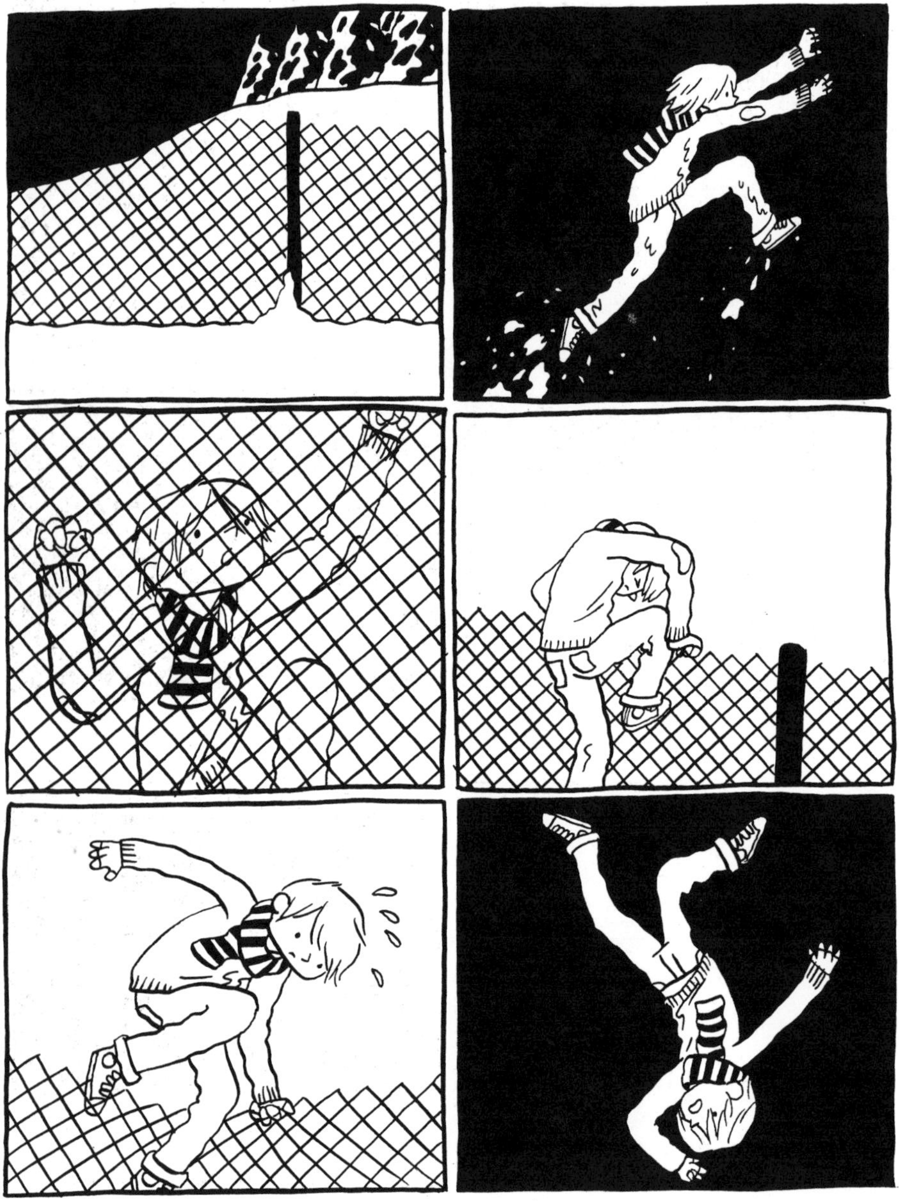

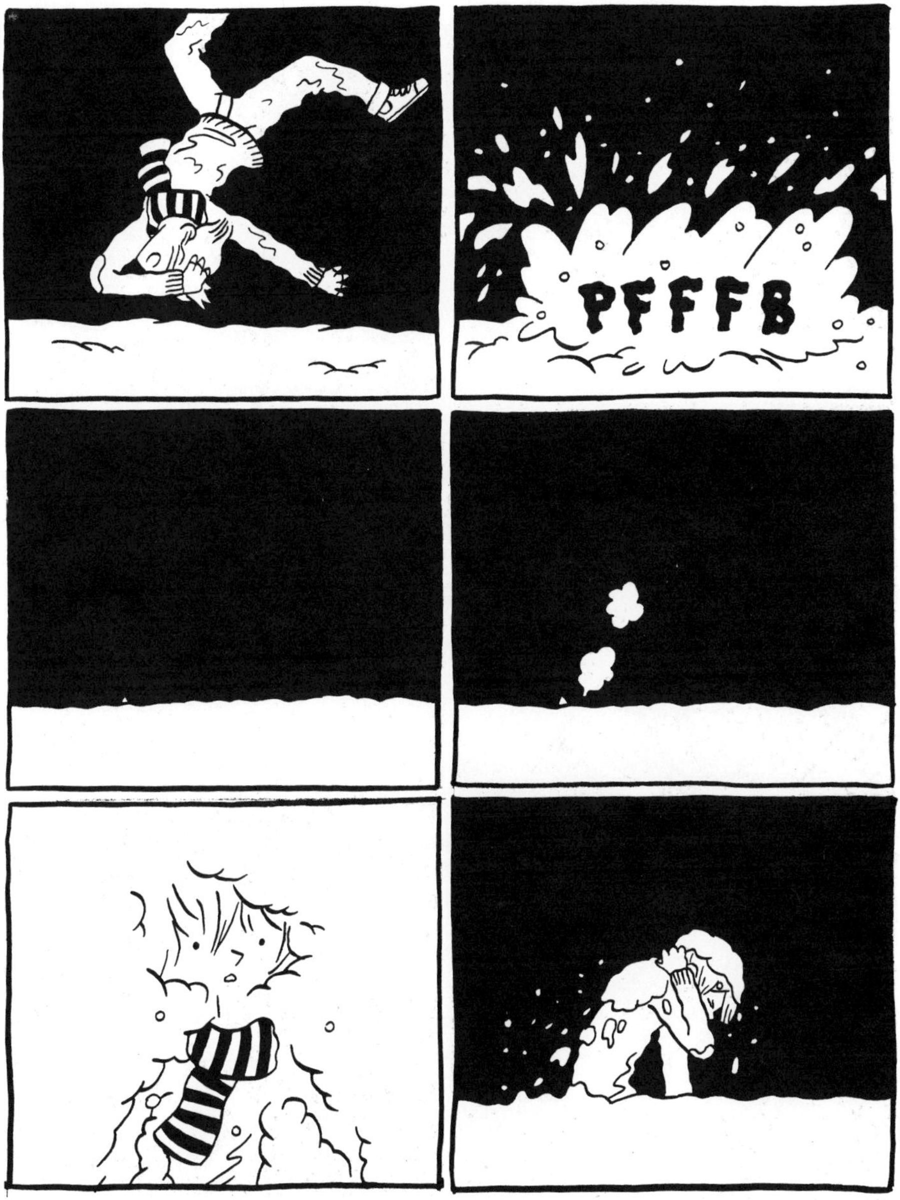
PFFFB

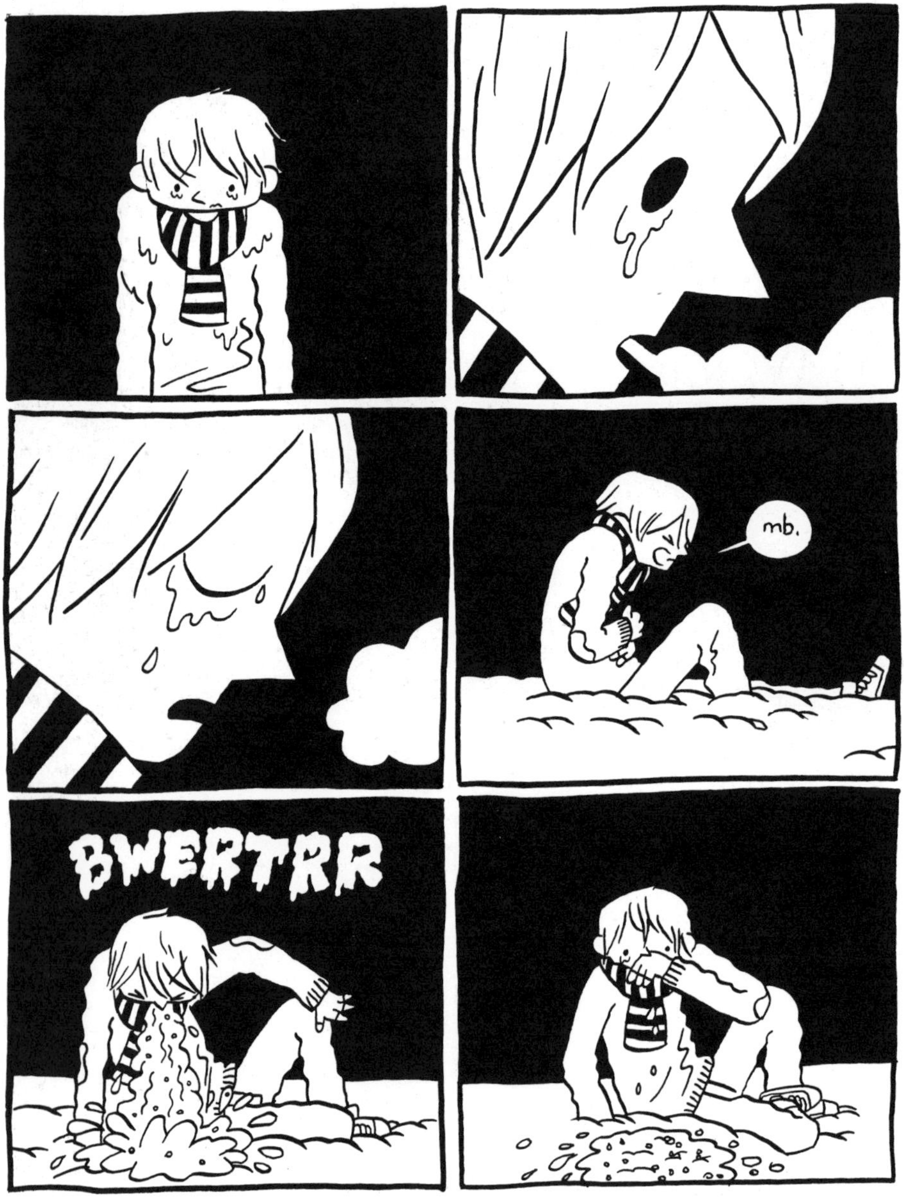
mb.
BWERTRR

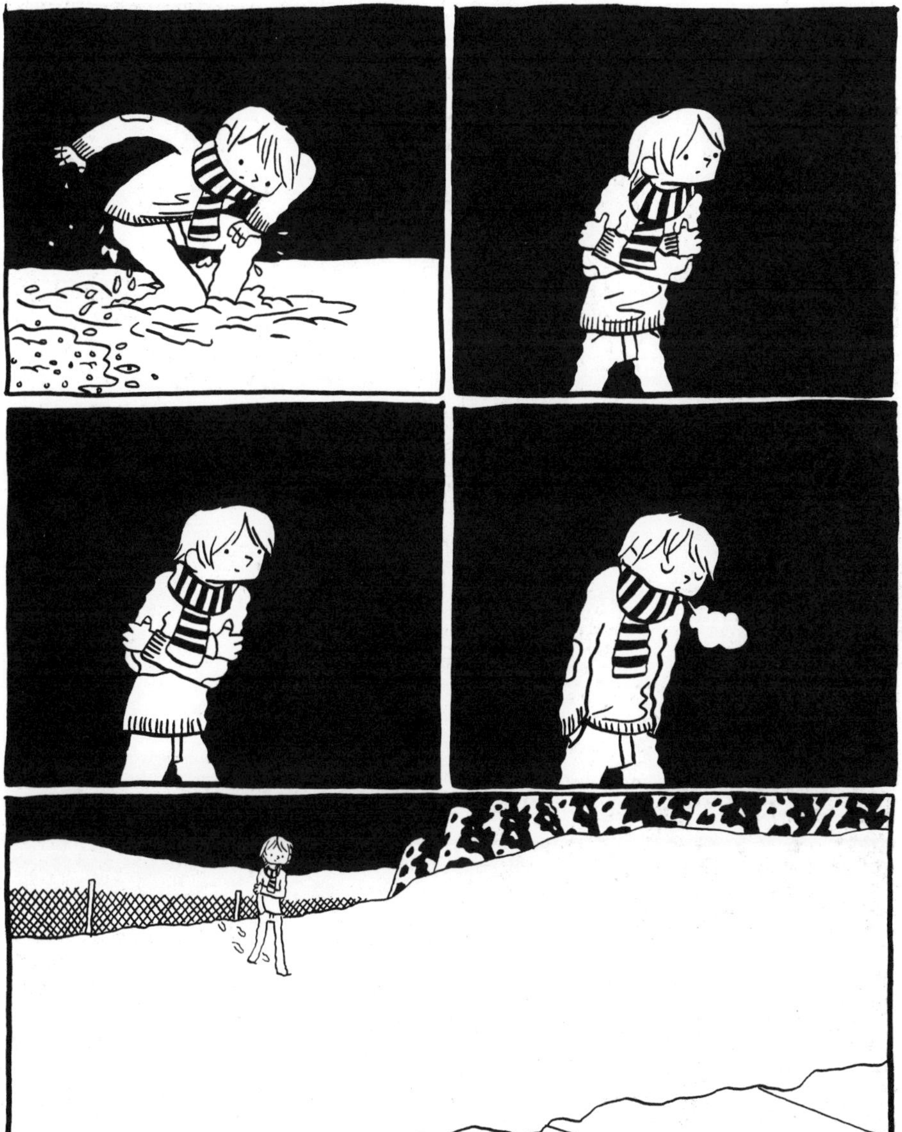

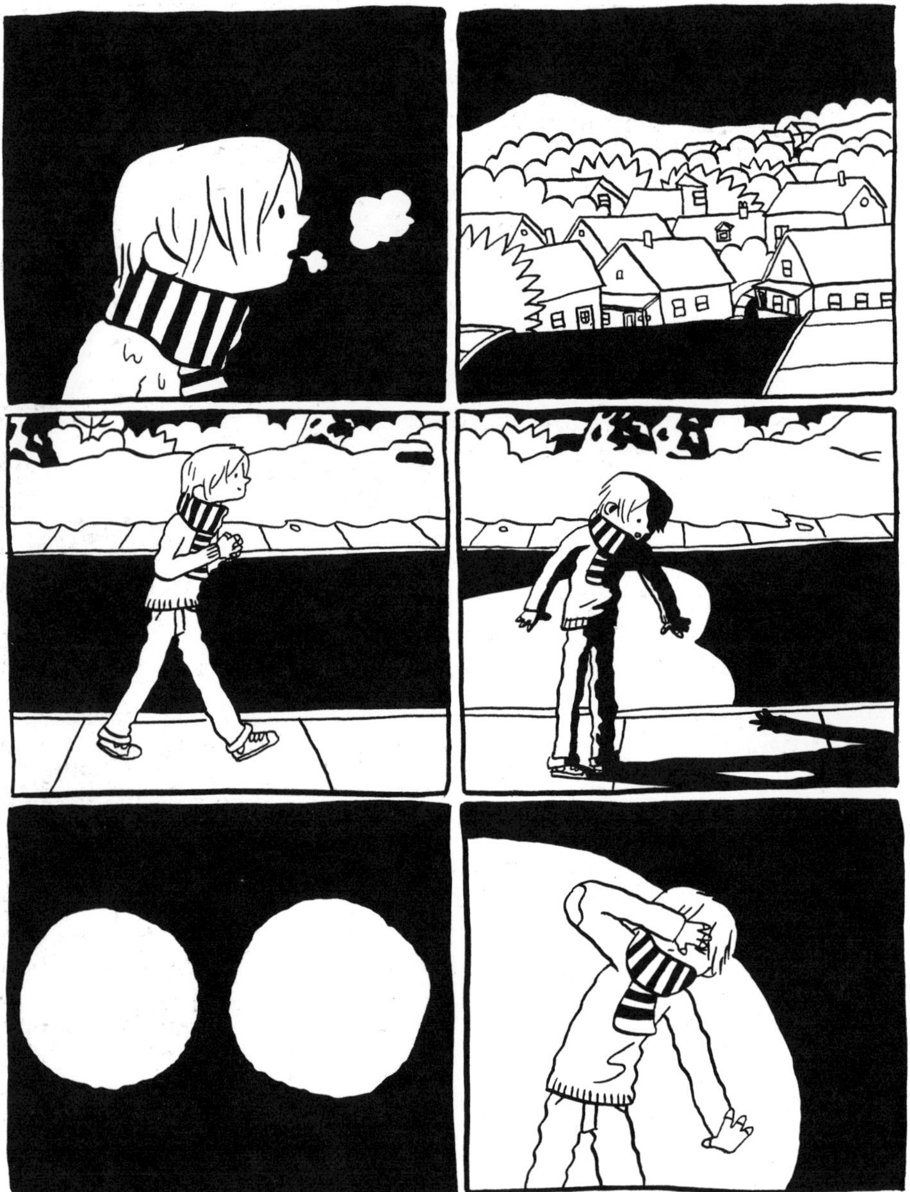

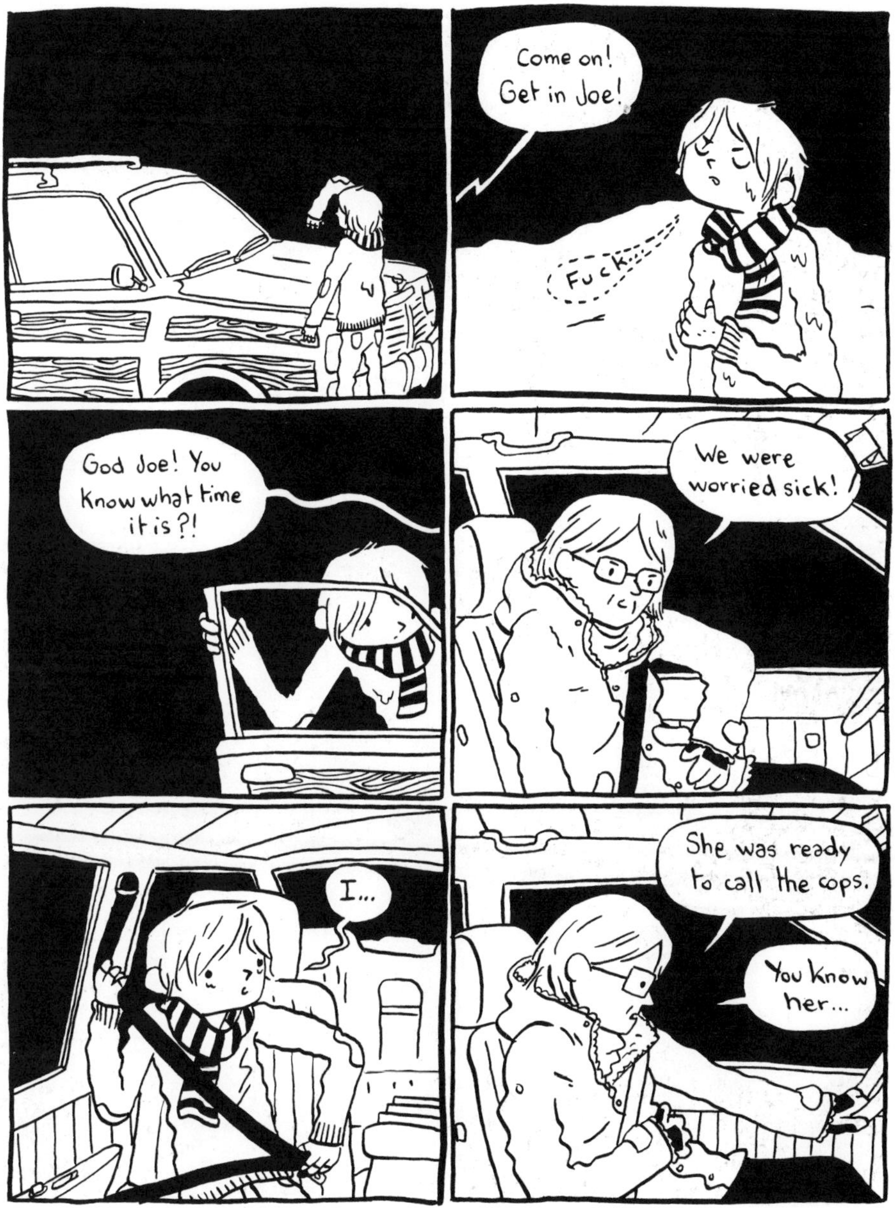

Come on! Get in Joe!
Fuck.
God Joe! You Know what time it is?!
We were worried sick!
I...
She was ready to call the cops.
You know her...

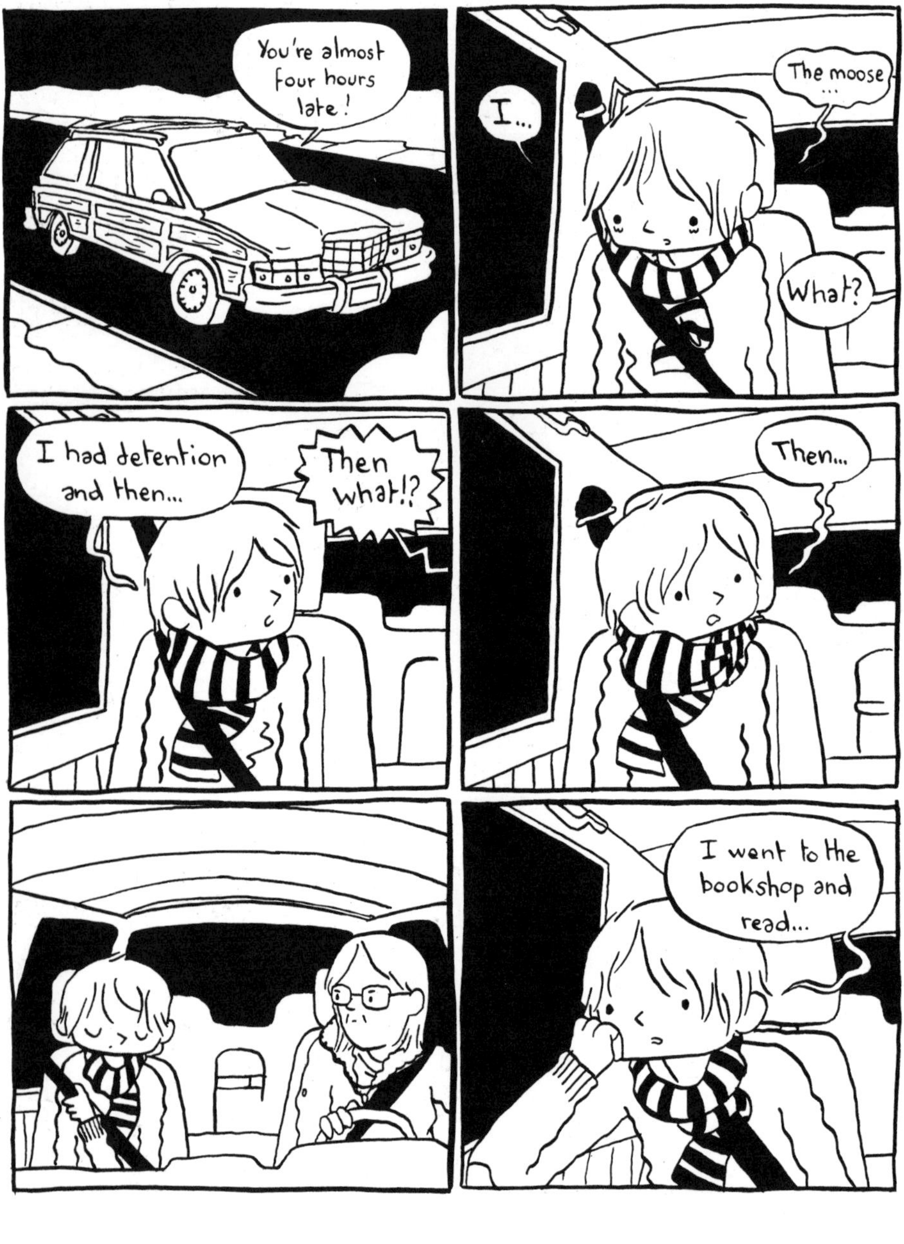
You're almost four hours late!
I...
The moose ...
What?
I had detention and then...
Then what!?
Then...
I went to the bookshop and read...

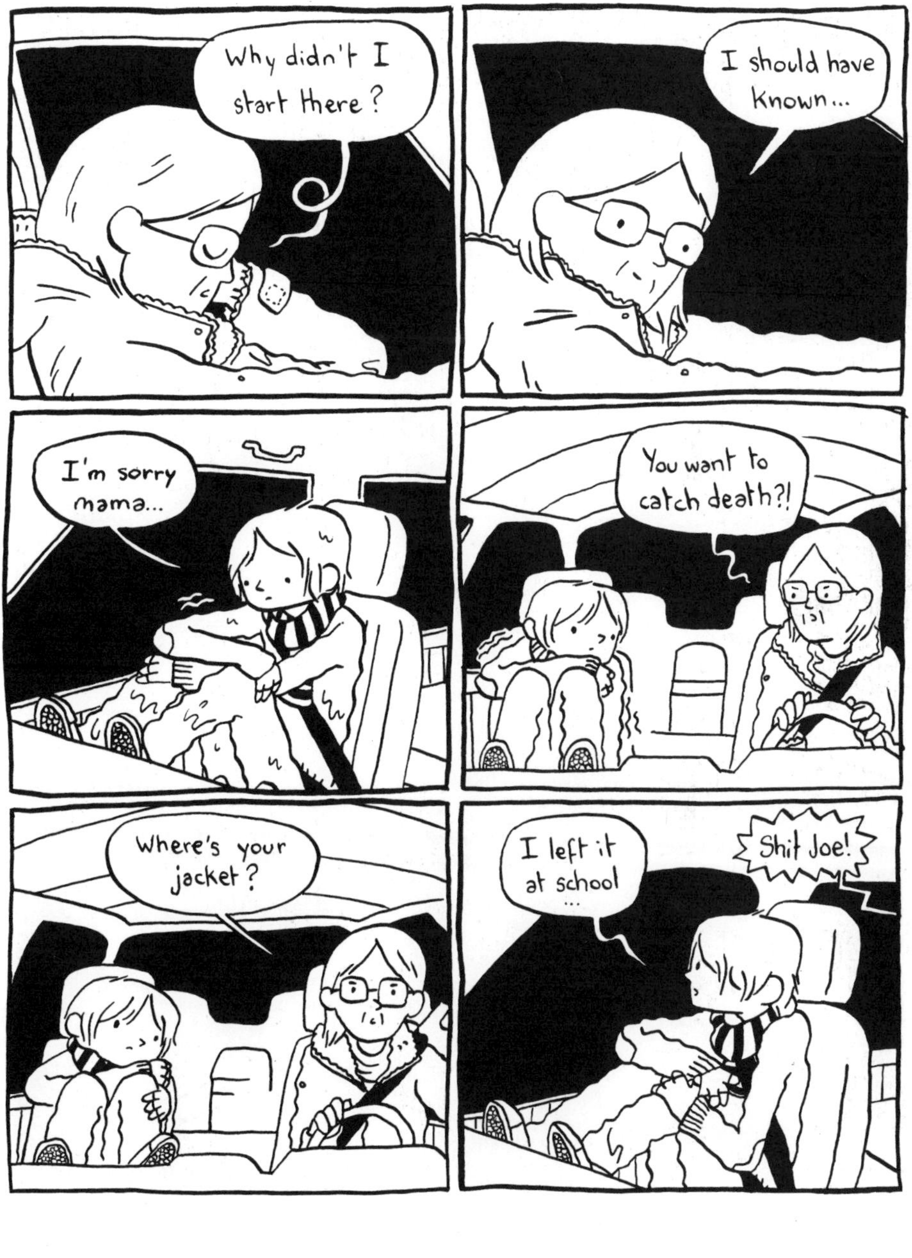
Why didn't I start there?
I should have known...
I'm sorry mama...
You want to catch death?!
Where's your jacket?
I left it at school ...
Shit Joe!

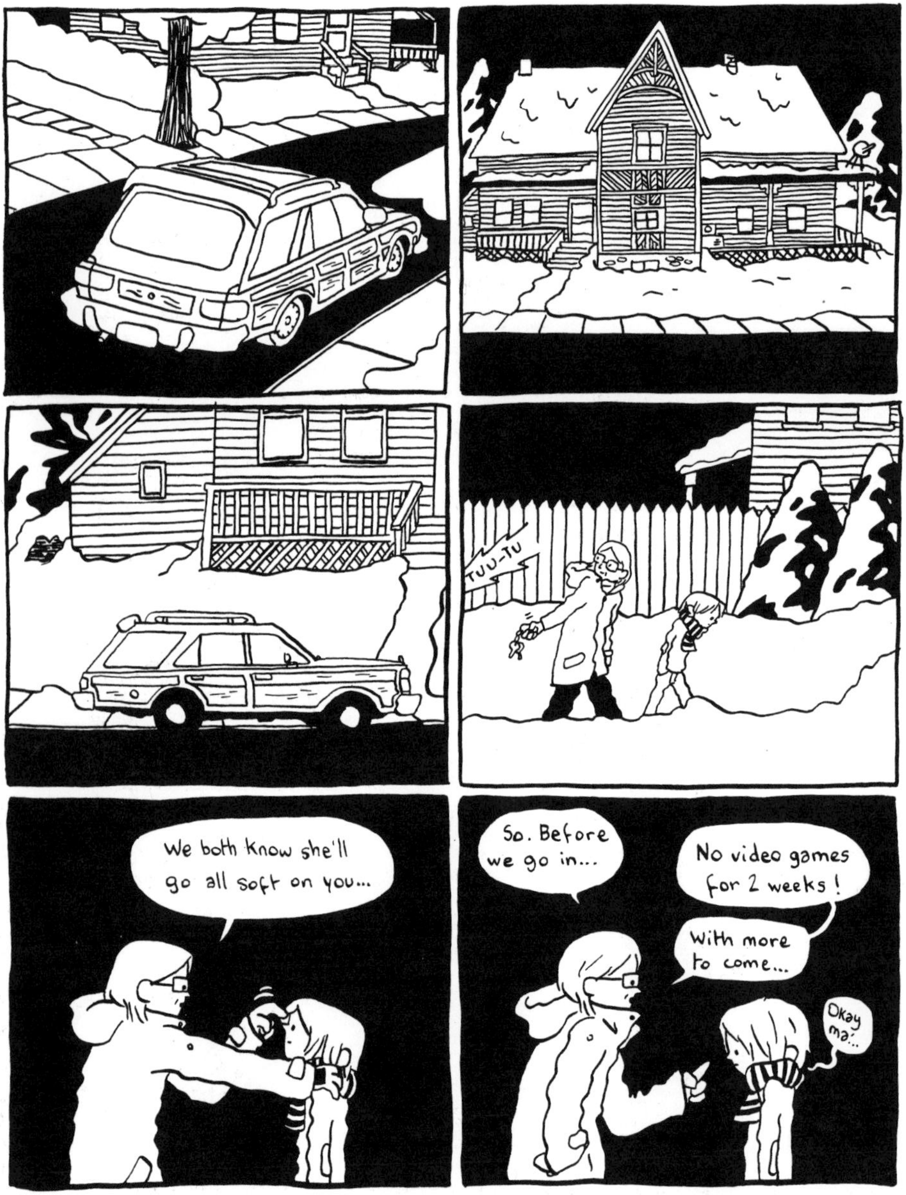
TUU-TU
We both know she'll go all soft on you...
So. Before we go in...
No video games for 2 weeks!
With more to come...
Okay ma'...

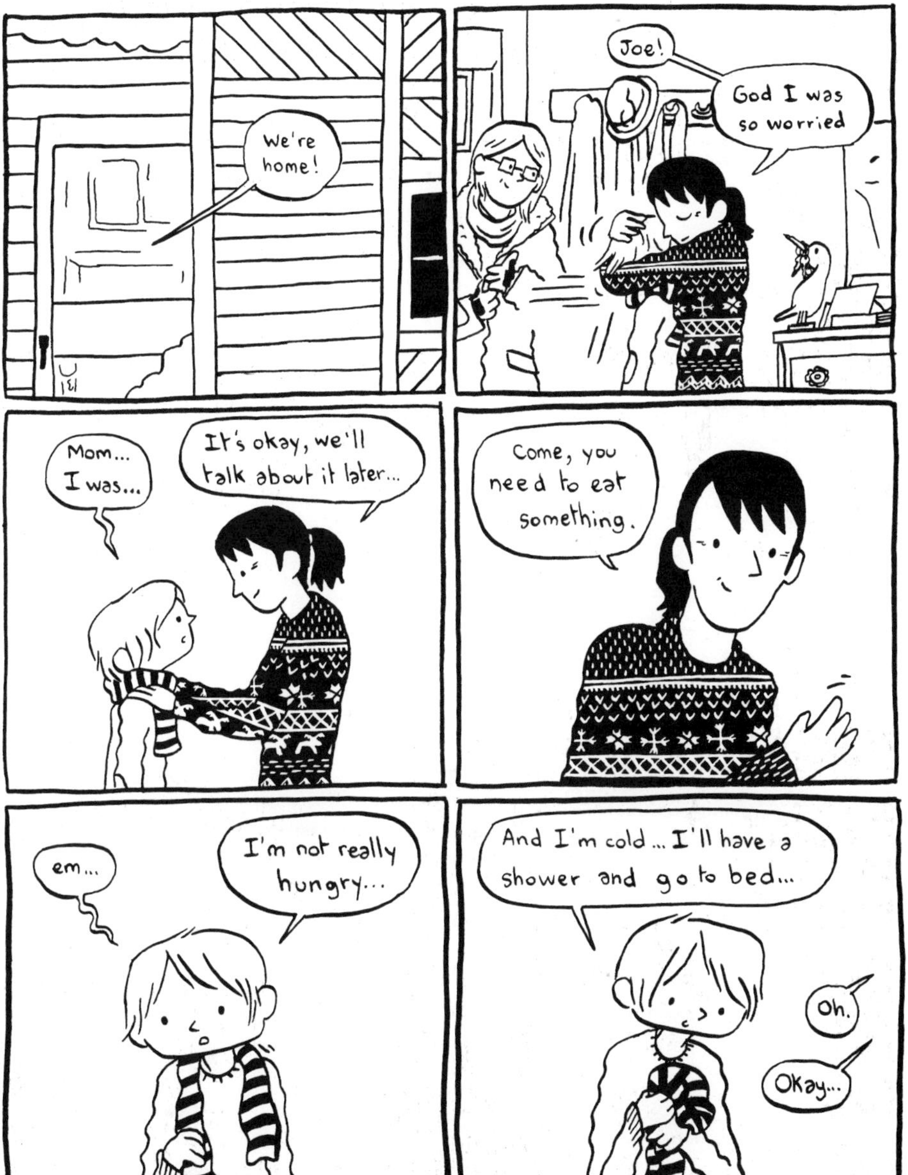
We're home!
Joe!
God I was so worried
Mom... I was...
It's okay, we'll talk about it later...
Come, you need to eat something.
em...
I'm not really hungry...
And I'm cold... I'll have a shower and go to bed...
Oh.
Okay...

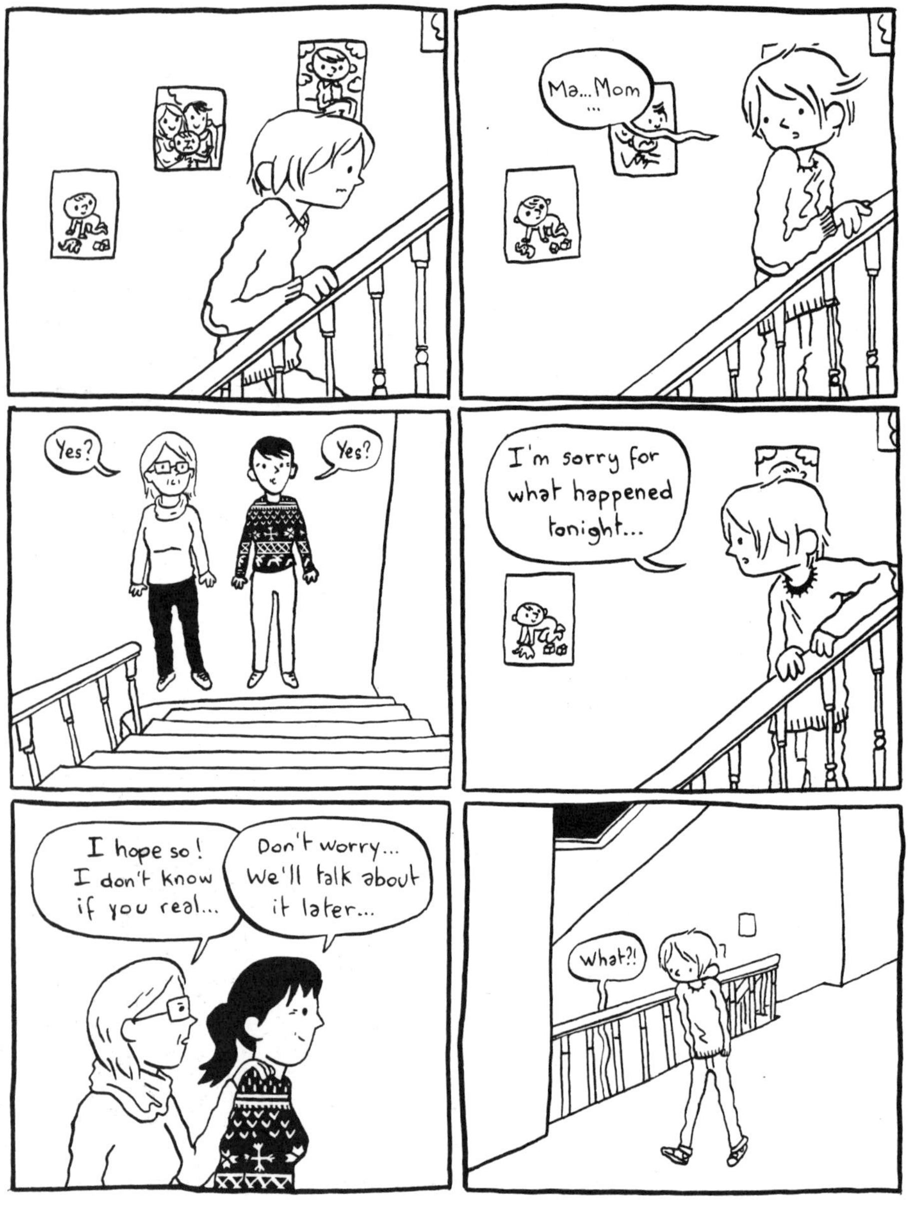
Ma...Mom
...
Yes?
Yes?
I'm sorry for what happened tonight...
I hope so! I don't know if you real...
Don't worry... We'll talk about it later...
What?!

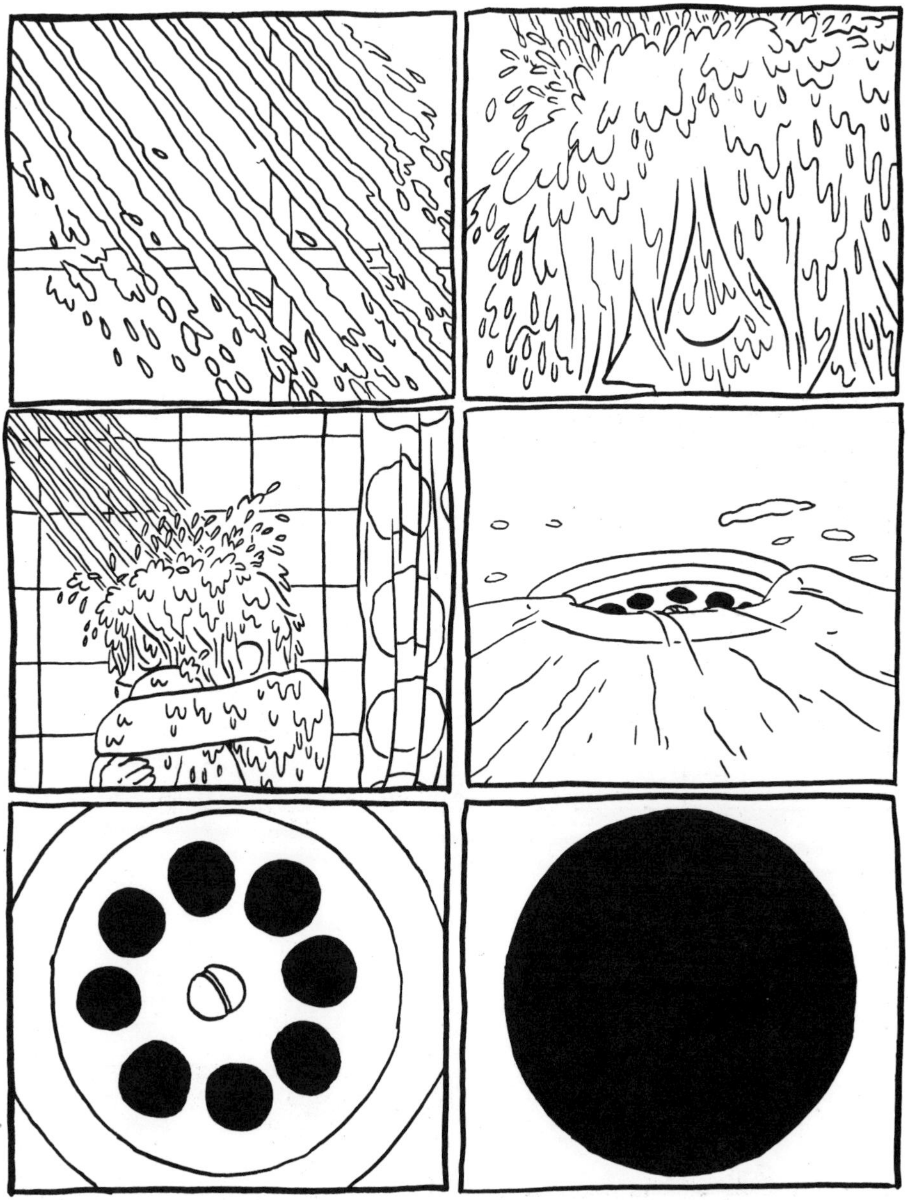

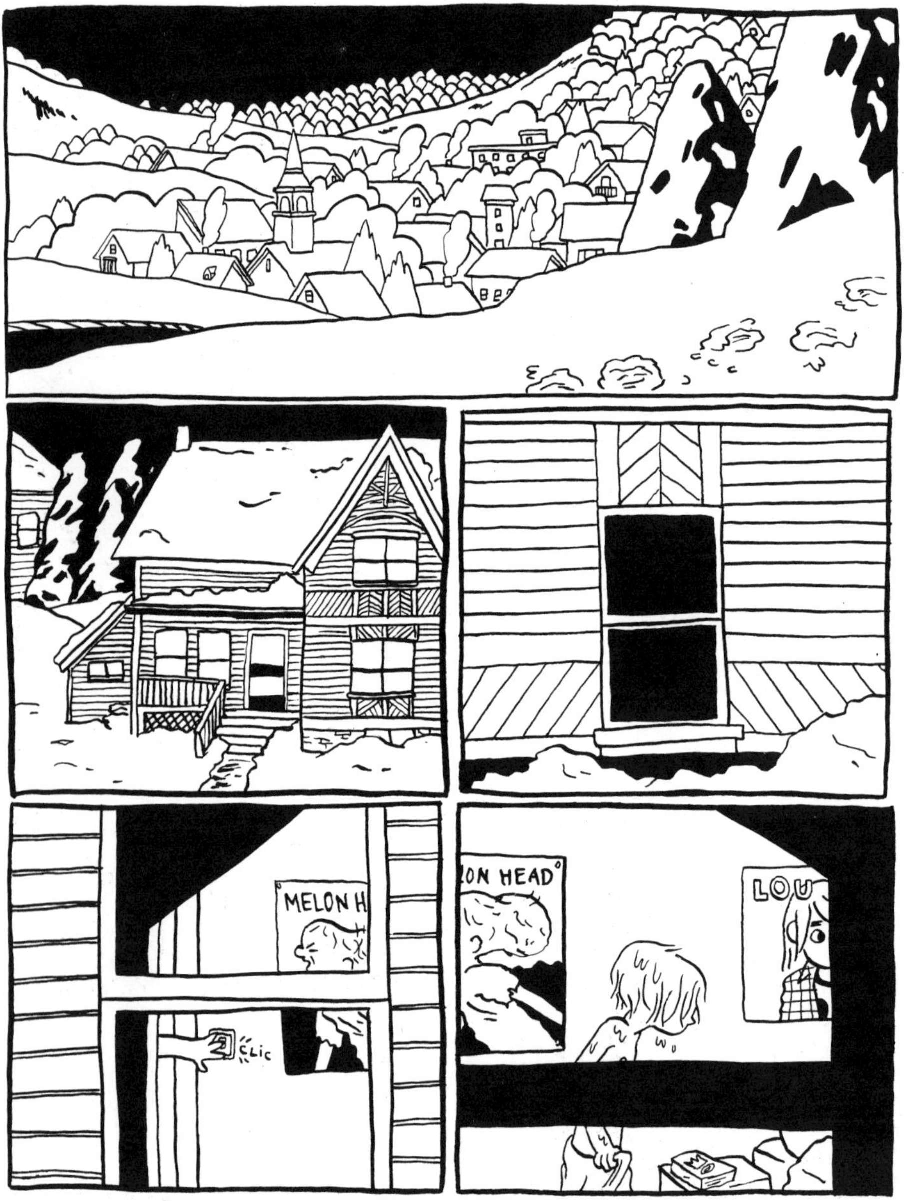
MELON H
CLIC
ON HEAD
LOU

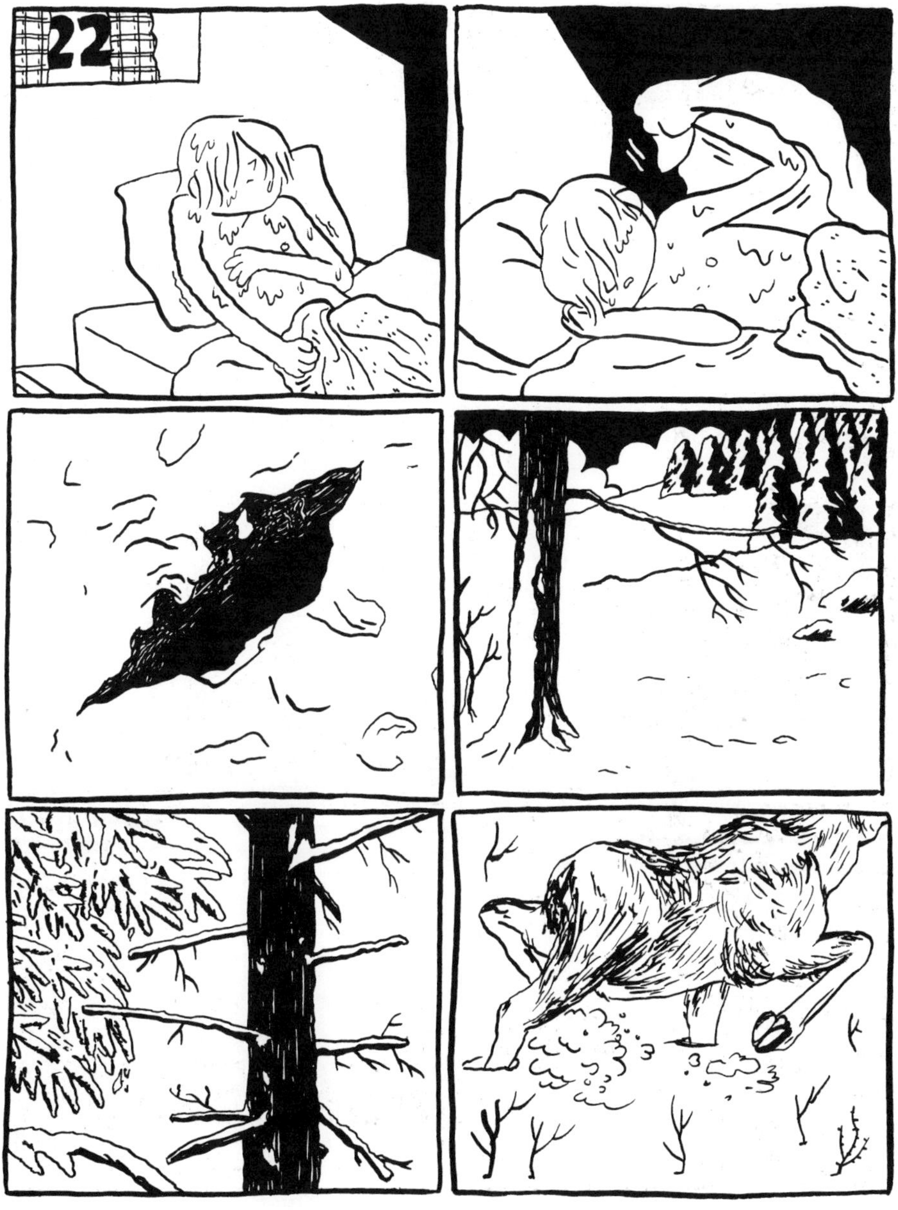
22

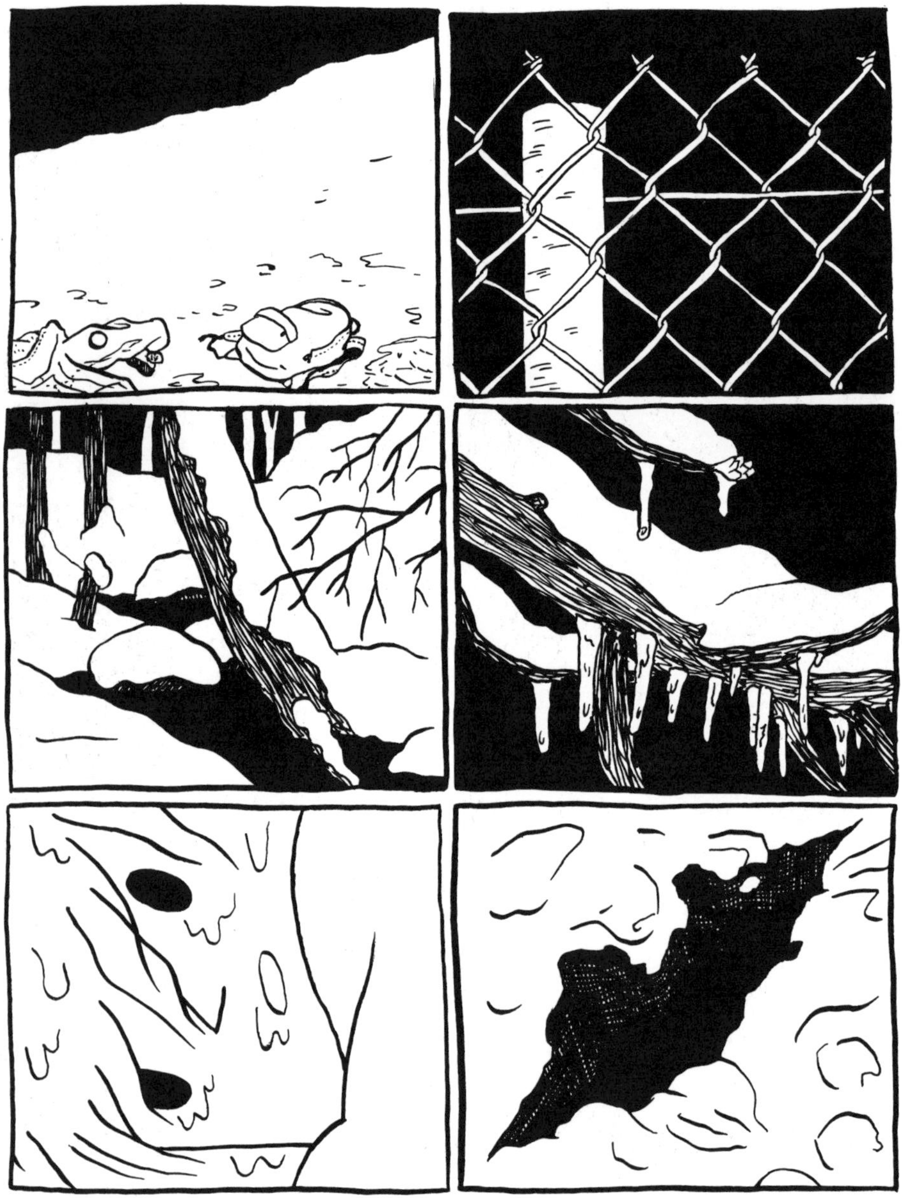

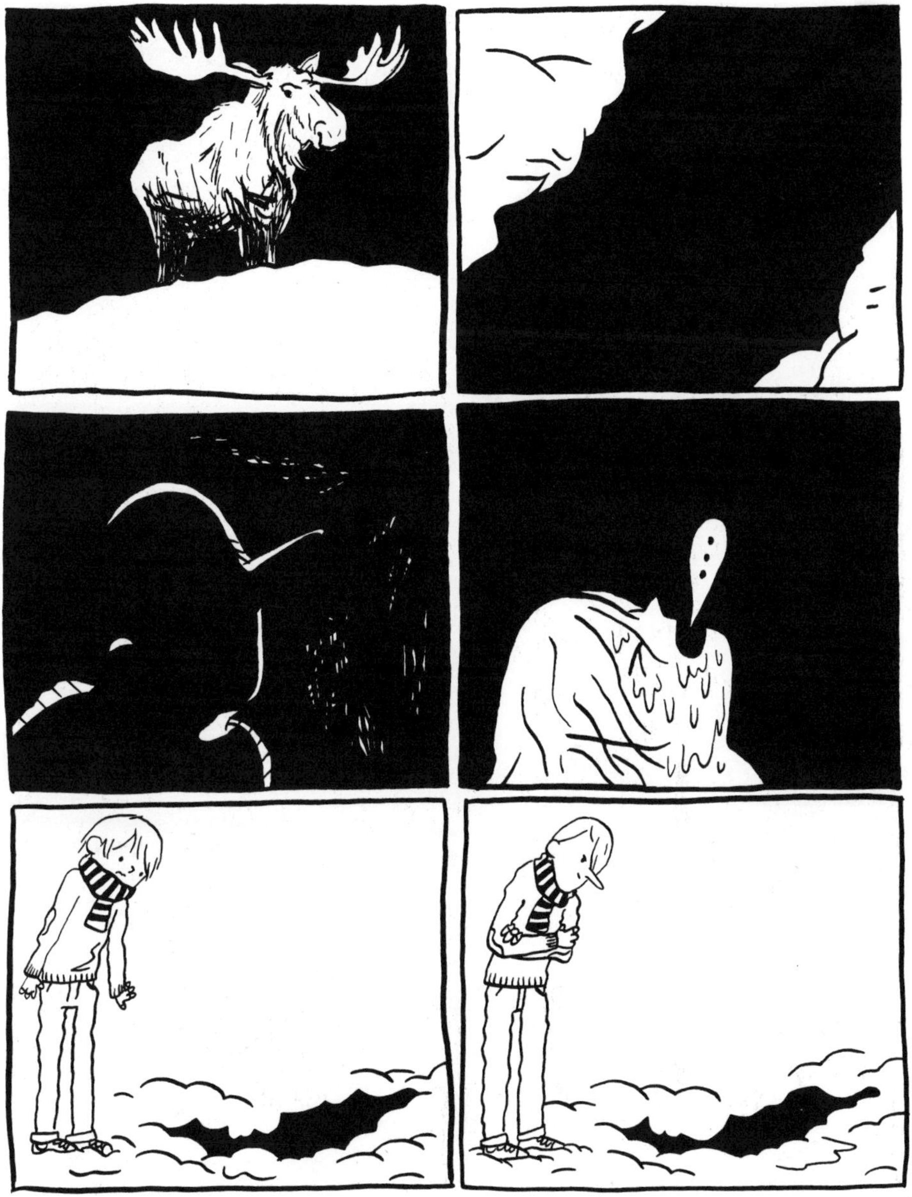

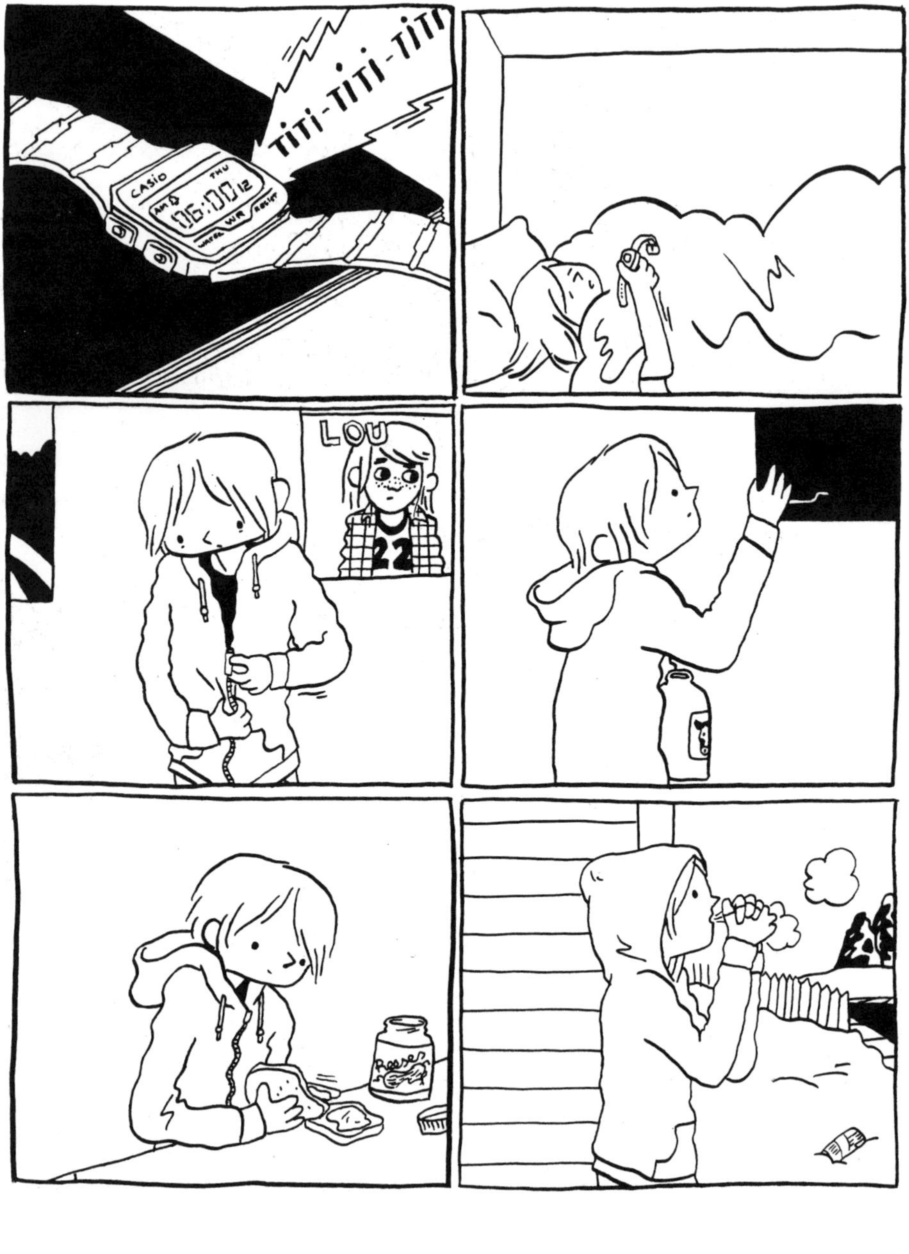
TITI-TITI-TITI
CASIO
THU
06:00 12
LOU
22
Reeses

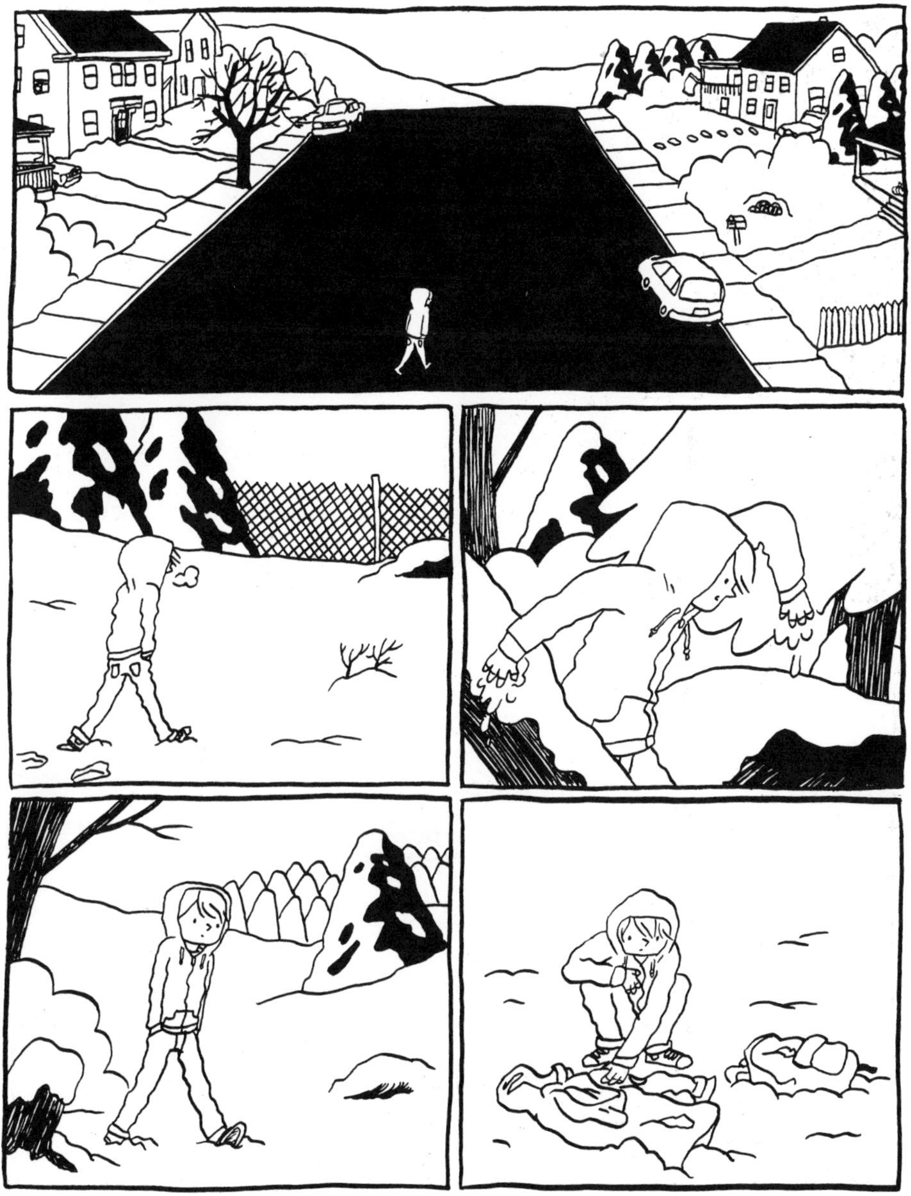

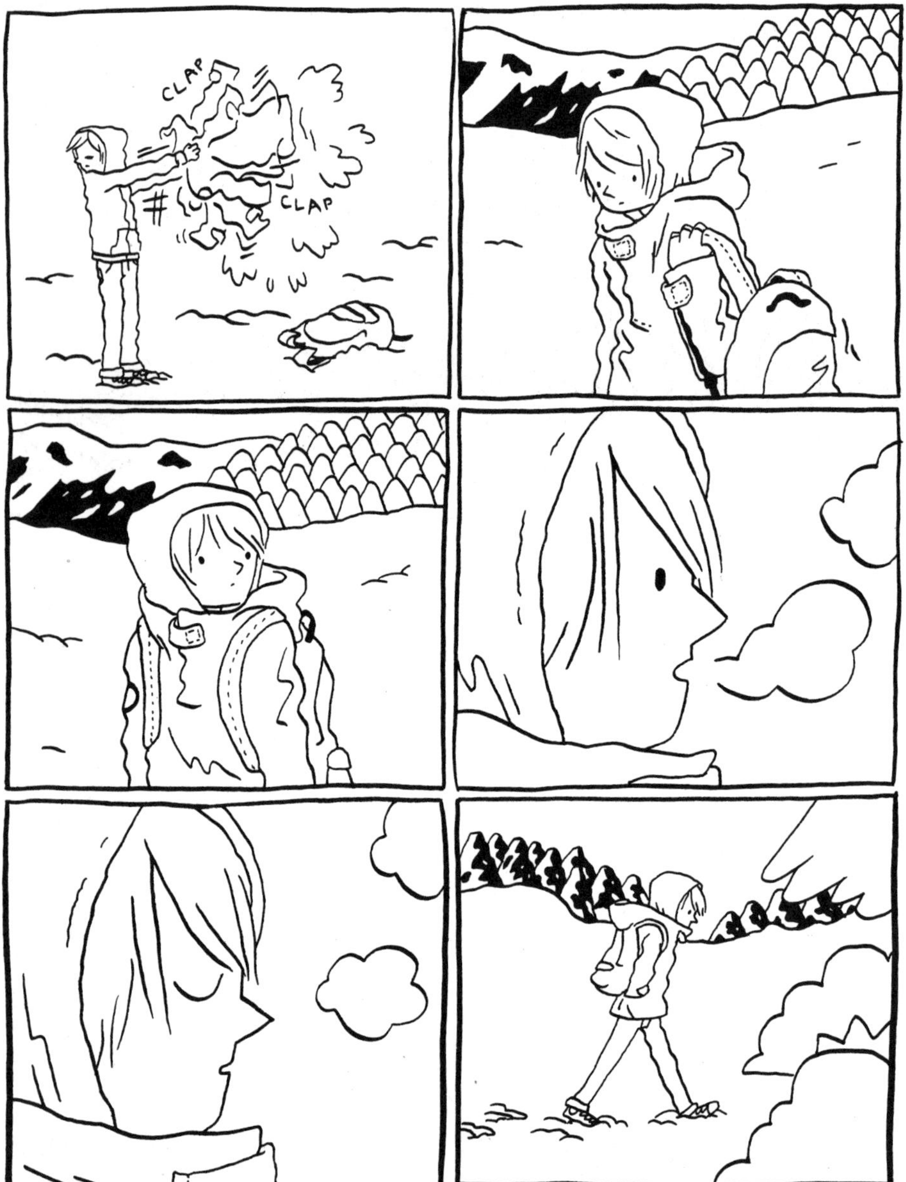
CLAP
CLAP

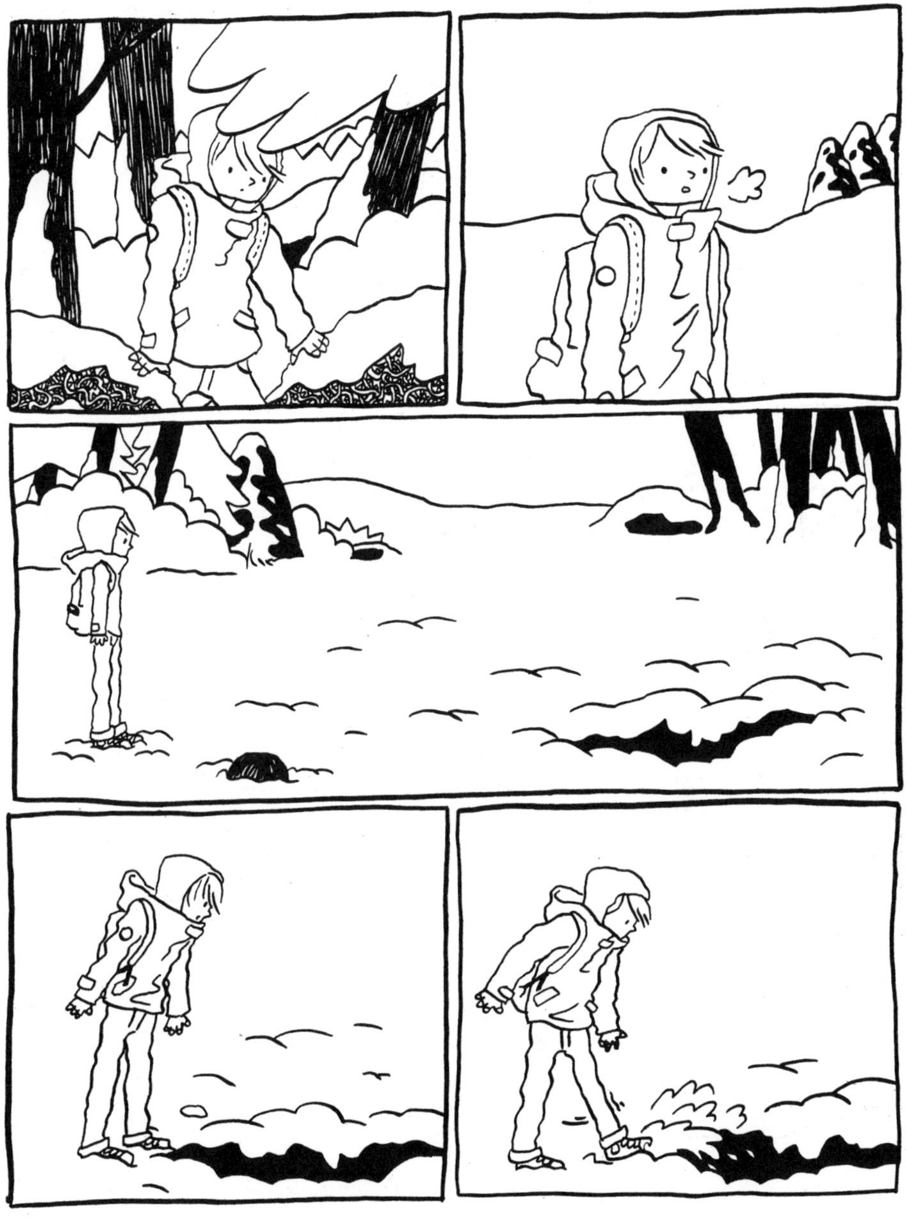

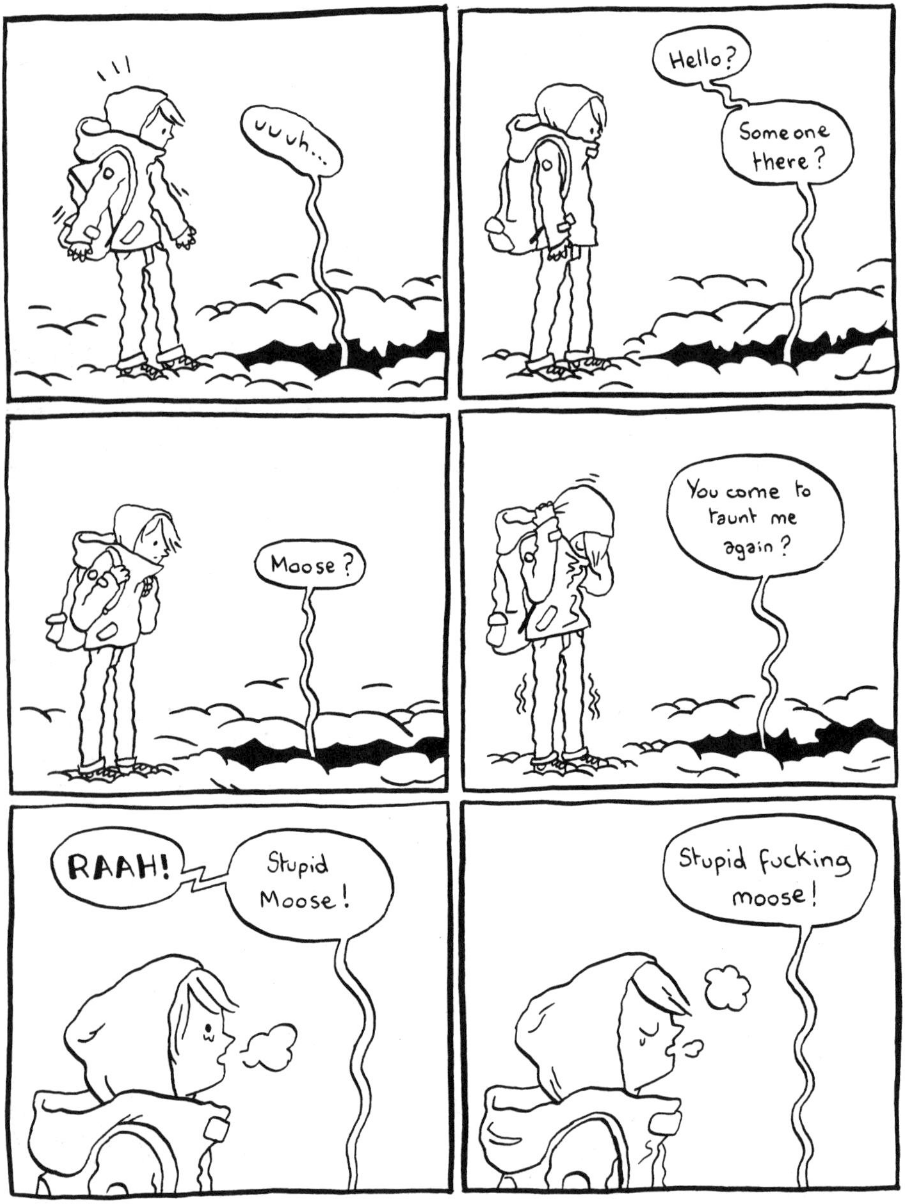
uuuh...
Hello?
Someone there?
Moose?
You come to taunt me again?
RAAH!
Stupid Moose!
Stupid fucking moose!

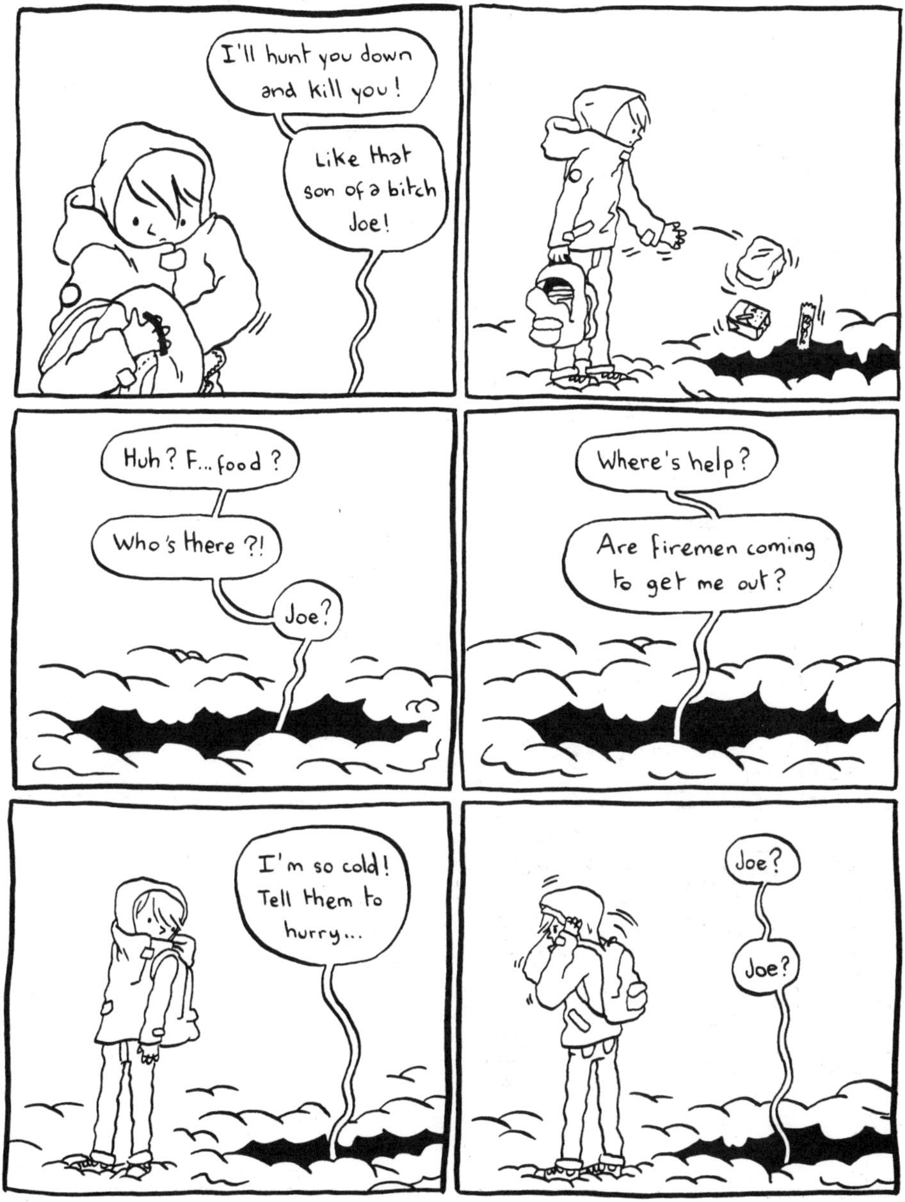
I'll hunt you down and kill you!
Like that son of a bitch Joe!
Huh? F... food?
Who's there?!
Joe?
Where's help?
Are firemen coming to get me out?
I'm so cold! Tell them to hurry...
Joe?
Joe?

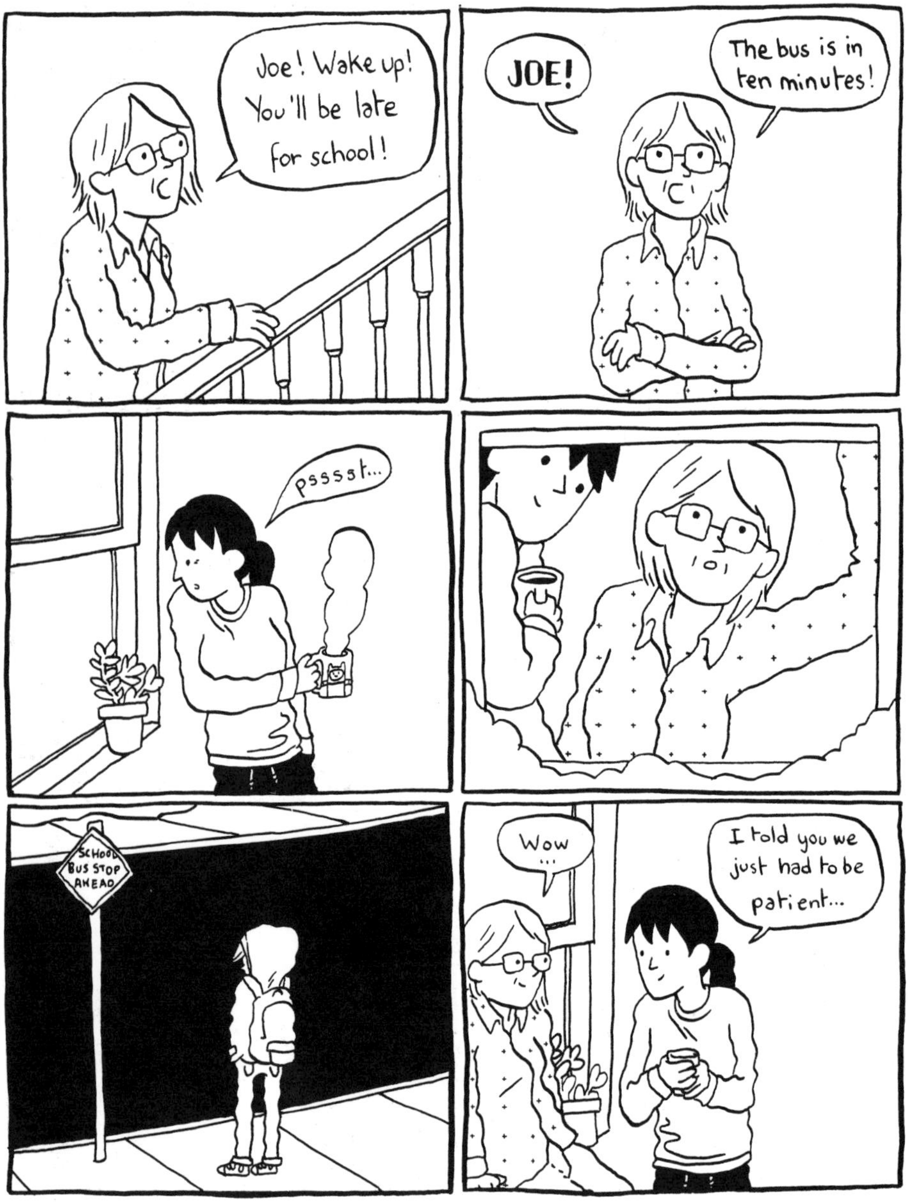
Joe! Wake up! You'll be late for school!
JOE!
The bus is in ten minutes!
psssst...
SCHOOL BUS STOP AHEAD
Wow...
I told you we just had to be patient...

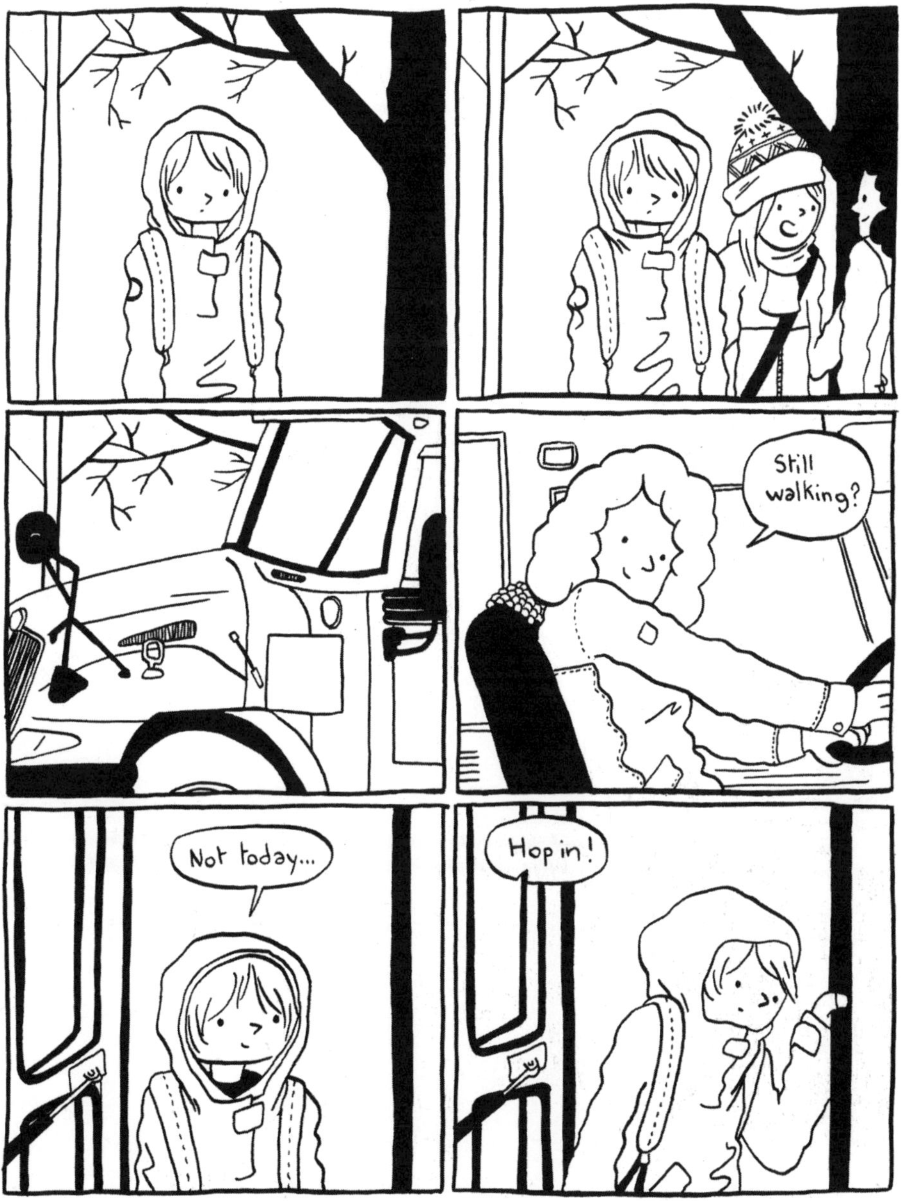
Still walking?
Not today...
Hop in!

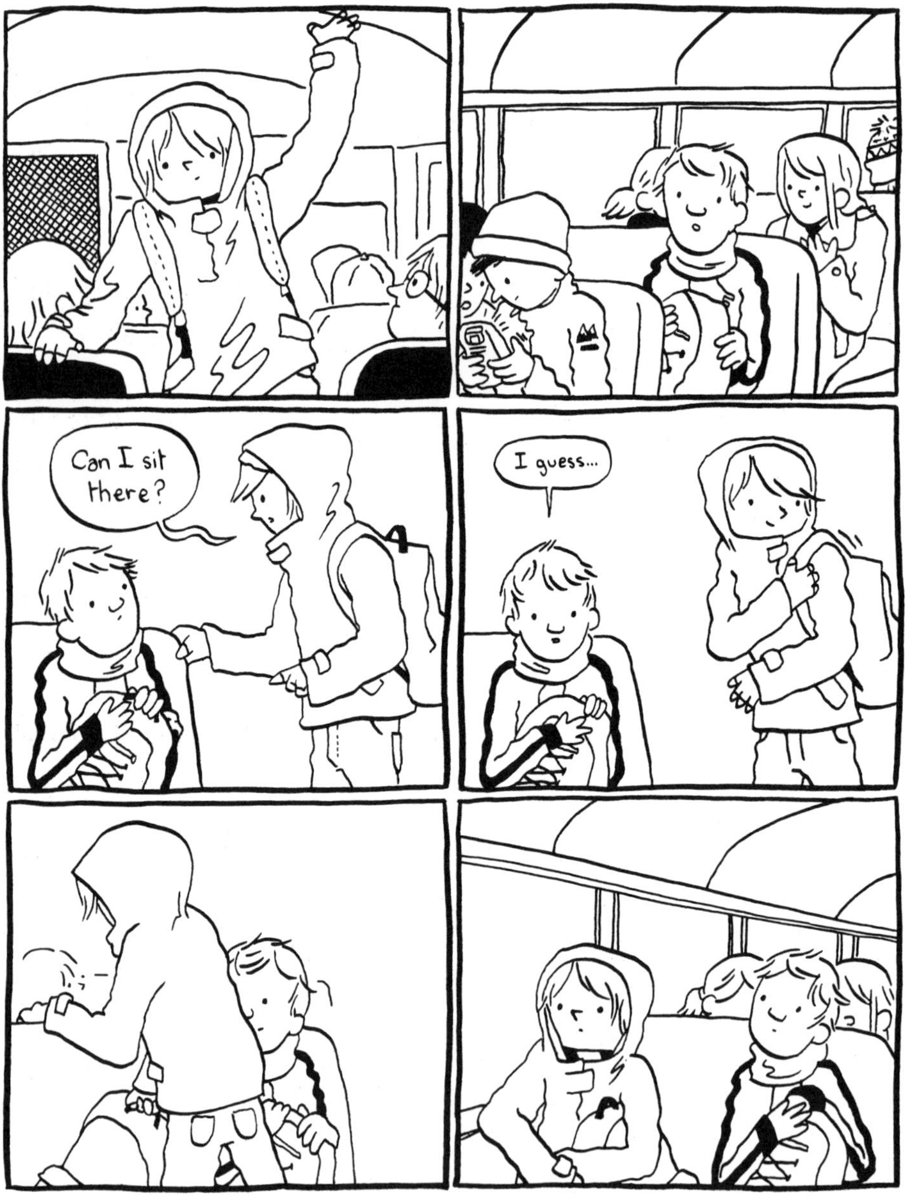
Can I sit there?
I guess...

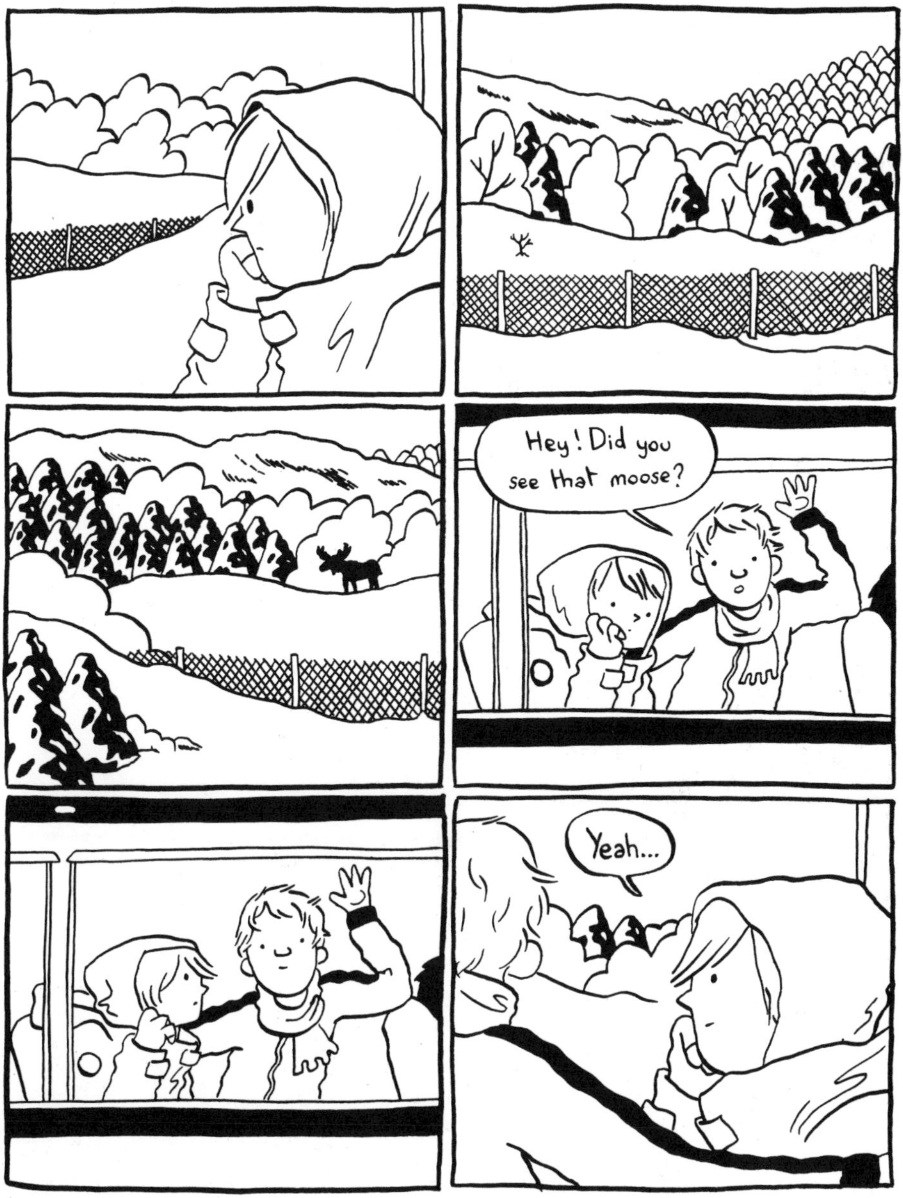
Hey! Did you see that moose?
Yeah...

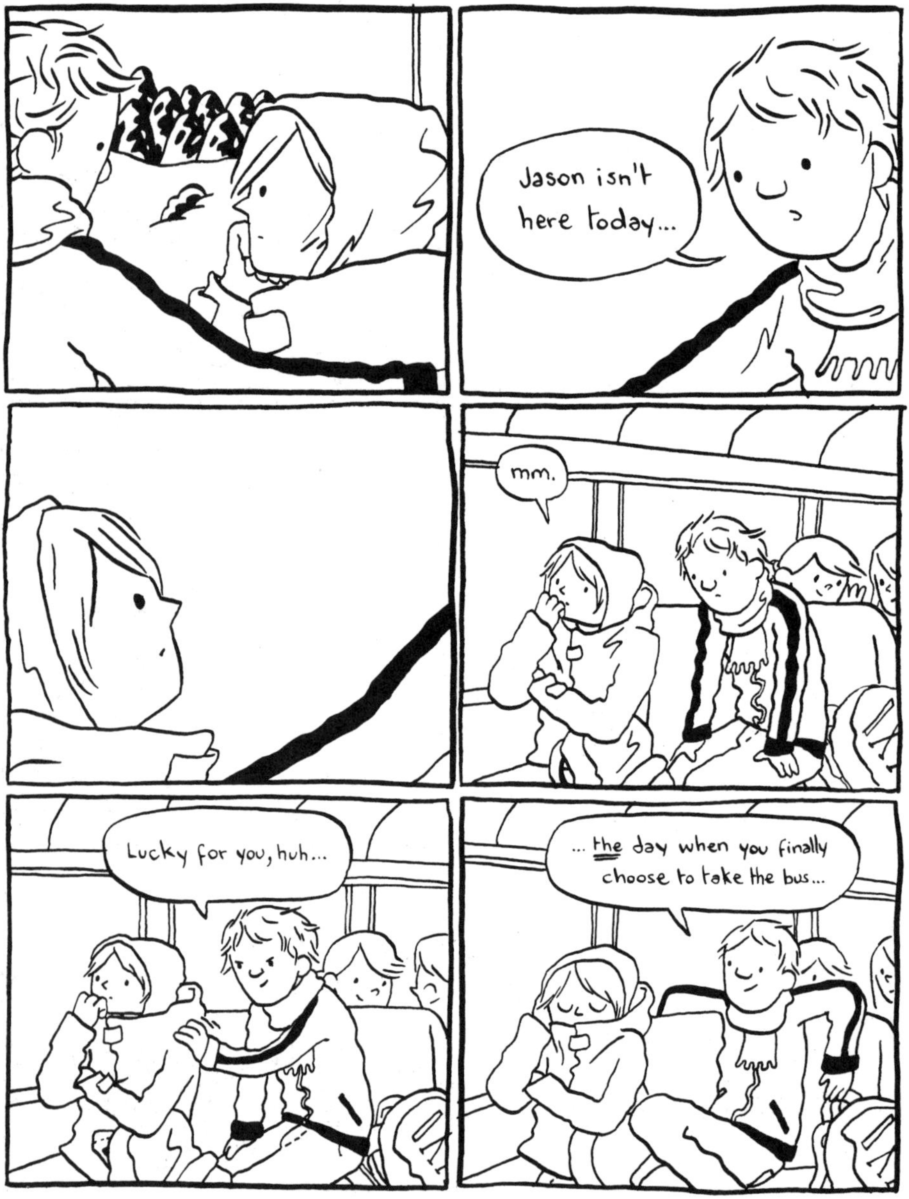
Jason isn't here today...
mm.
Lucky for you, huh...
... the day when you finally choose to take the bus...

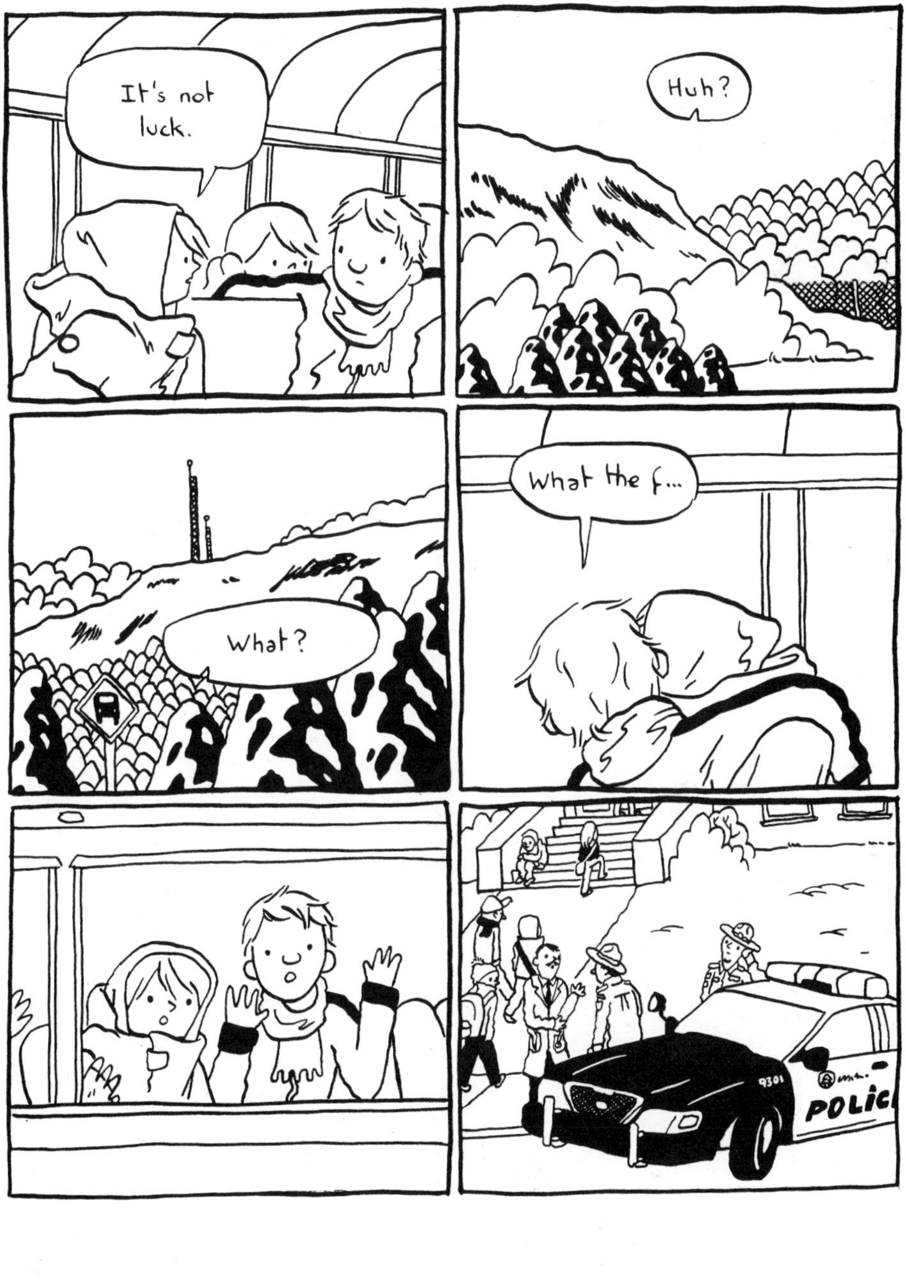
It's not luck.
Huh?
What?
What the f...
POLIC

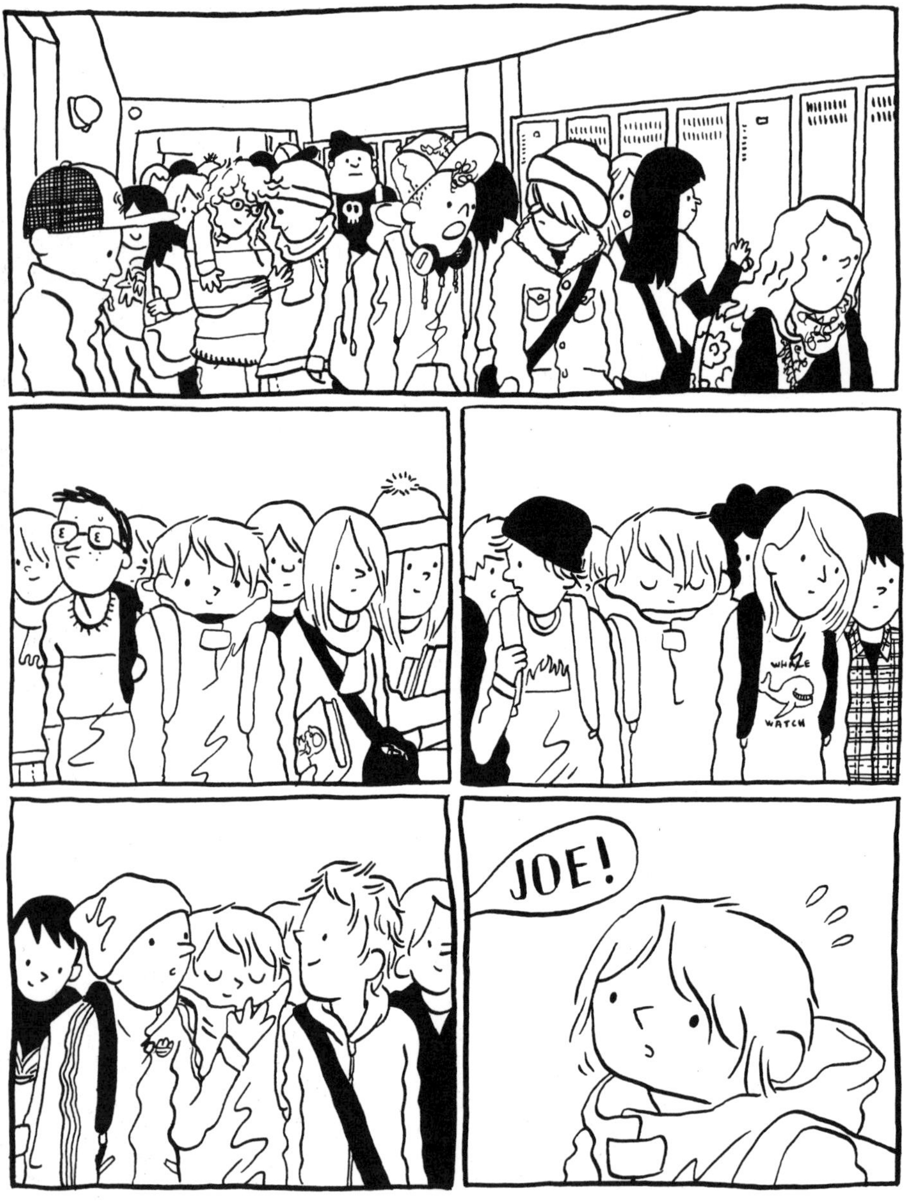
WHALE
WATCH
JOE!

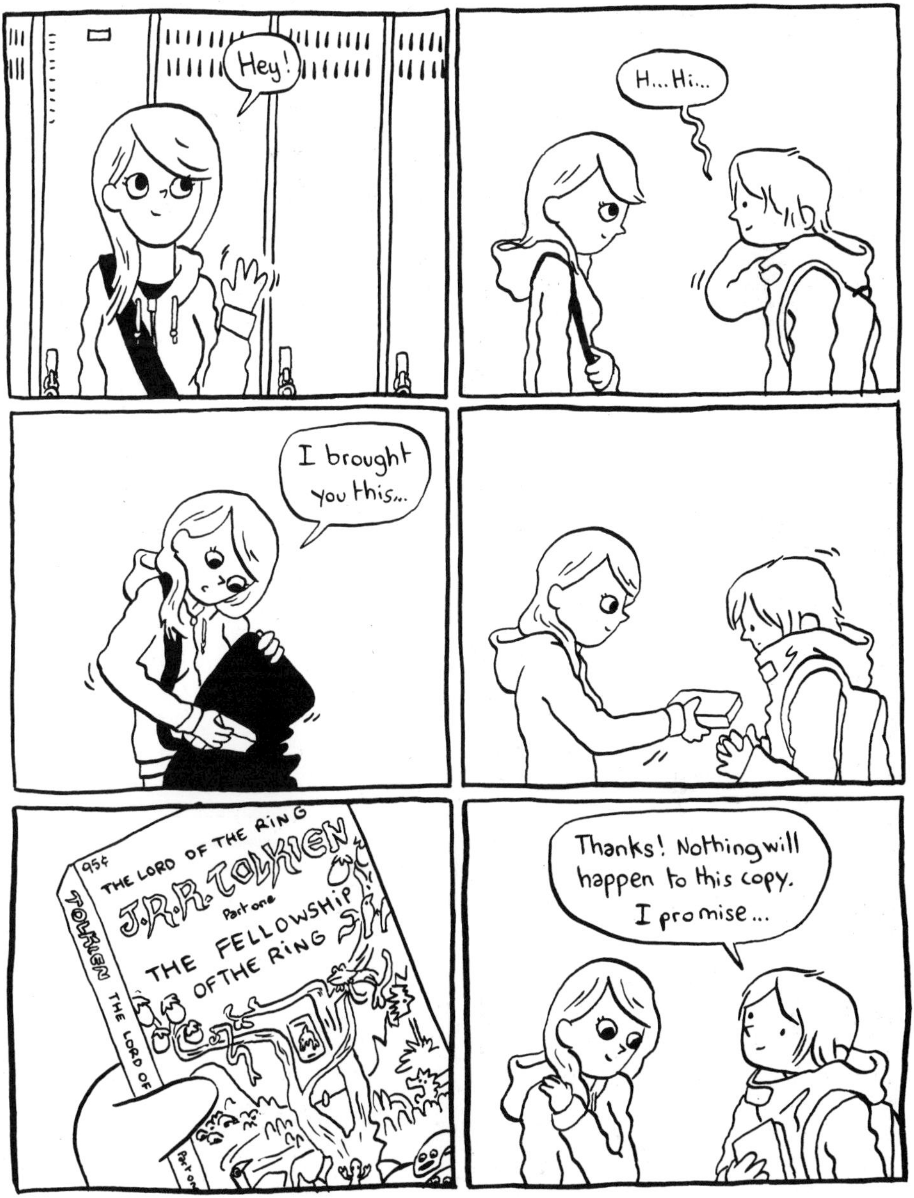
Hey!
H... Hi...
I brought you this...
THE LORD OF THE RING
95¢
J.R.R. TOLKIEN
Part one
THE FELLOWSHIP OF THE RING
TOLKIEN THE LORD OF
Thanks! Nothing will happen to this copy. I promise...

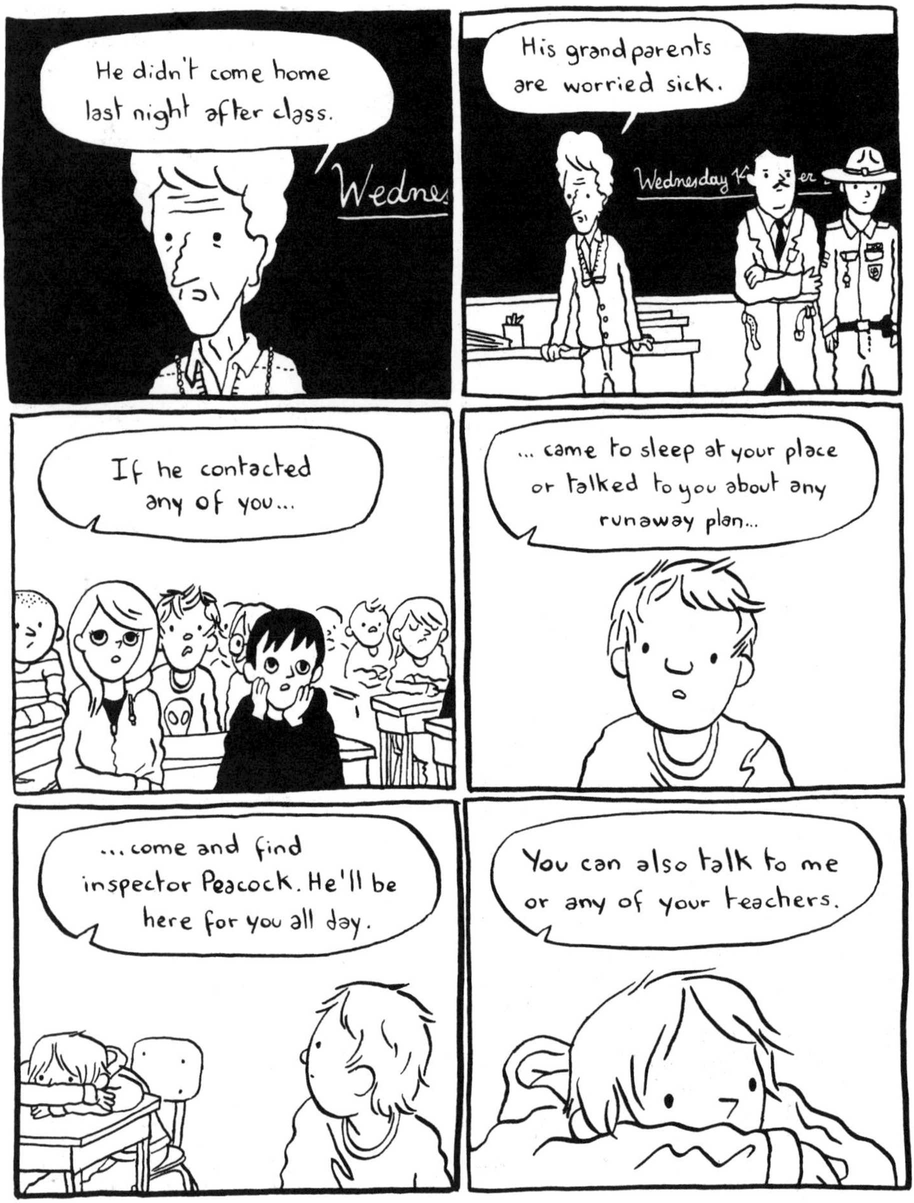
He didn't come home last night after class.
Wednes
His grandparents are worried sick.
If he contacted any of you...
... came to sleep at your place or talked to you about any runaway plan...
...come and find inspector Peacock. He'll be here for you all day.
You can also talk to me or any of your teachers.

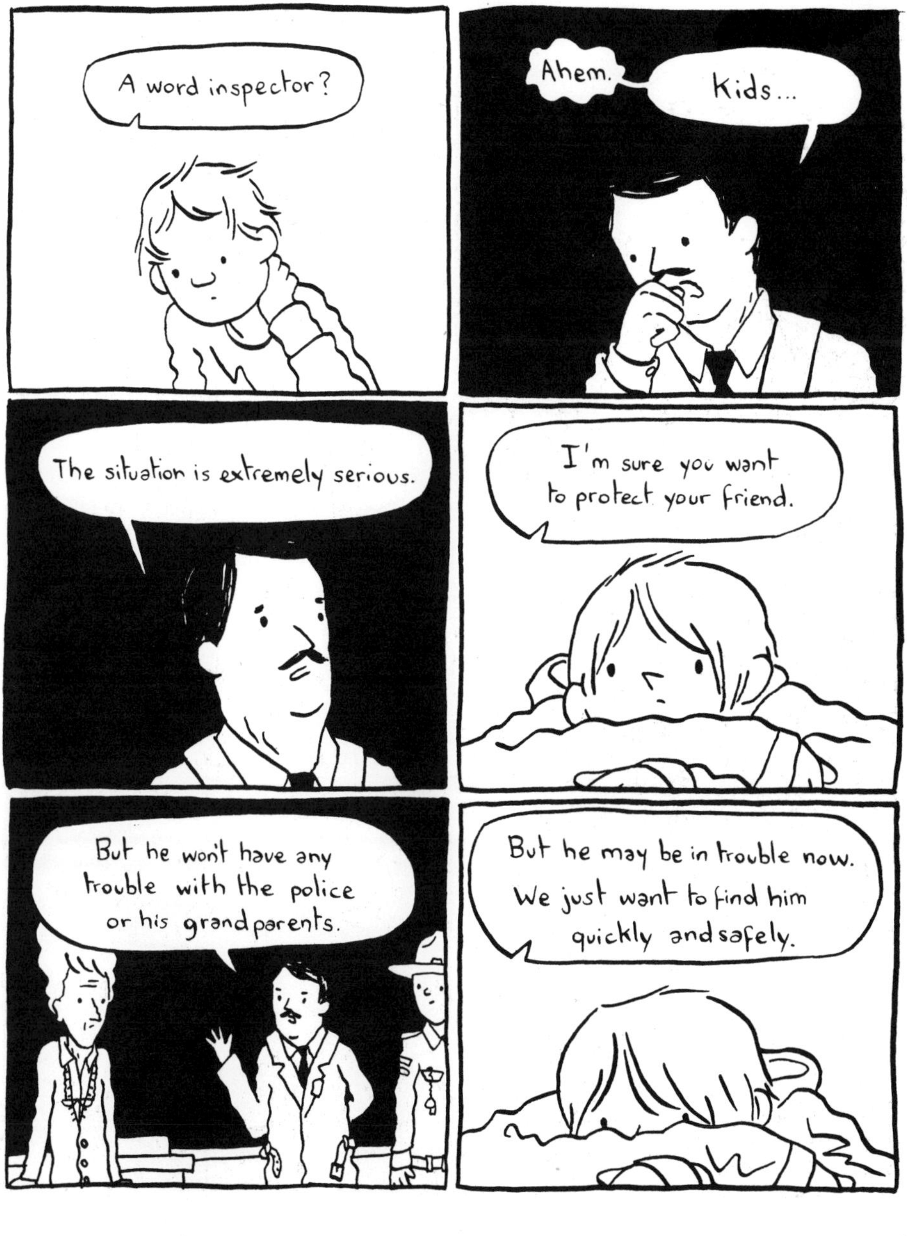
A word inspector?
Ahem.
Kids...
The situation is extremely serious.
I'm sure you want to protect your friend.
But he won't have any trouble with the police or his grandparents.
But he may be in trouble now. We just want to find him quickly and safely.

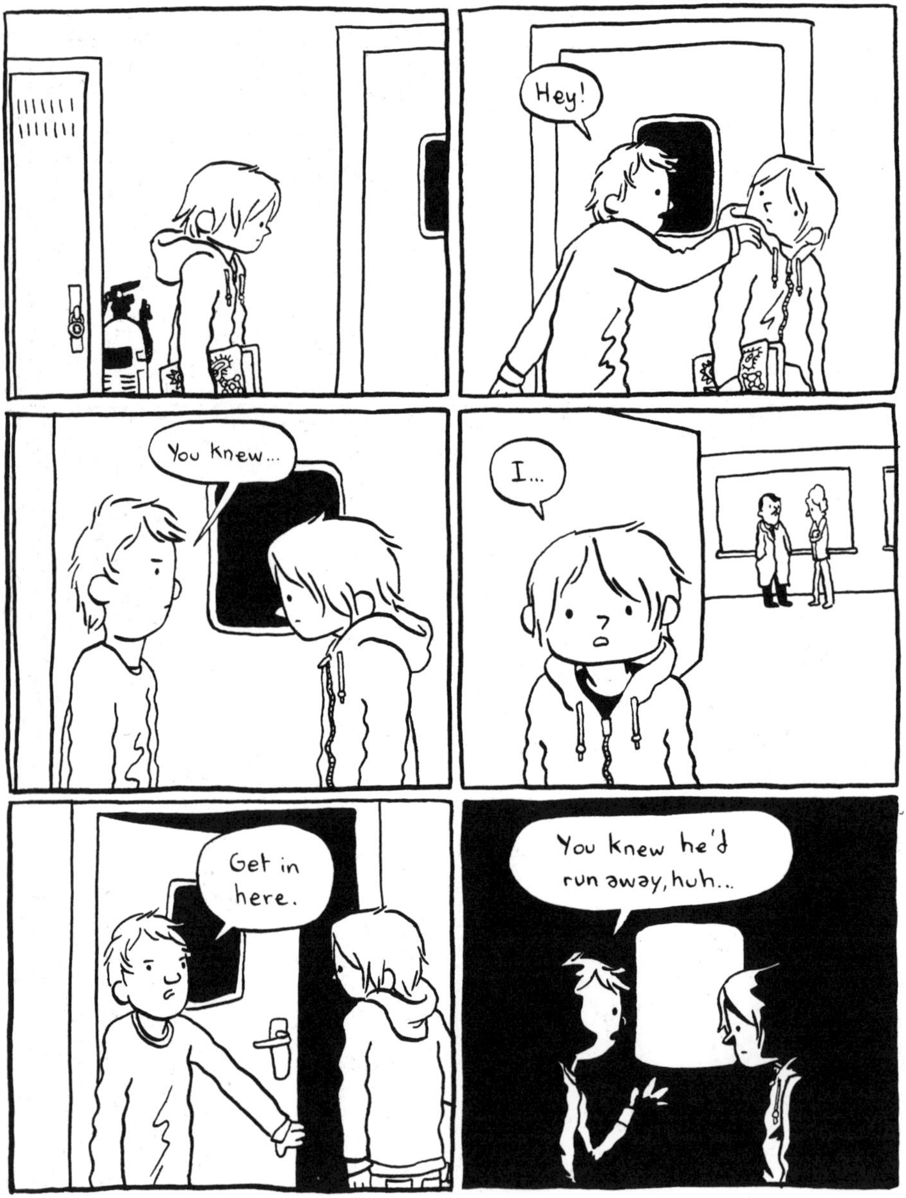
Hey!
You knew...
I...
Get in here.
You knew he'd run away, huh...

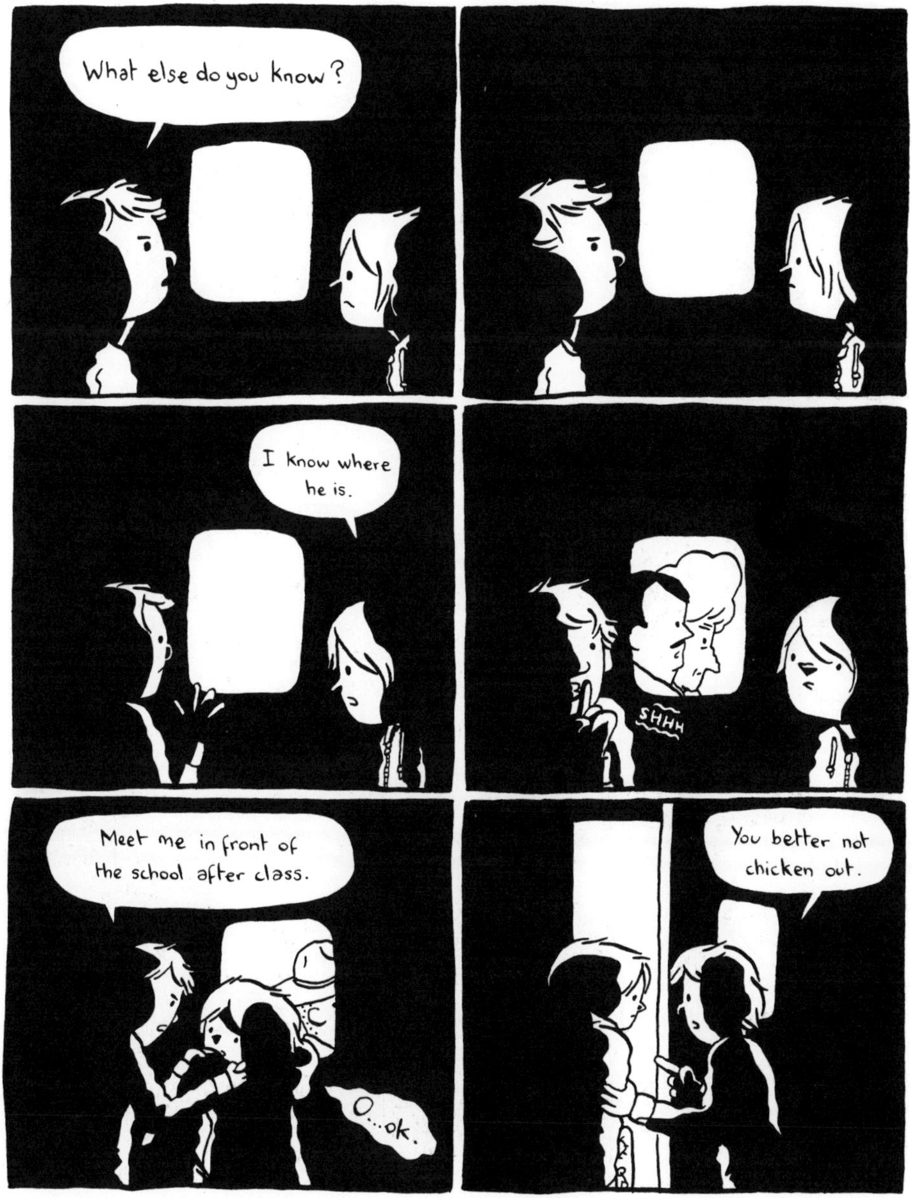
What else do you know?
I know where he is.
SHHH
Meet me in front of the school after class.
O...ok.
You better not chicken out.

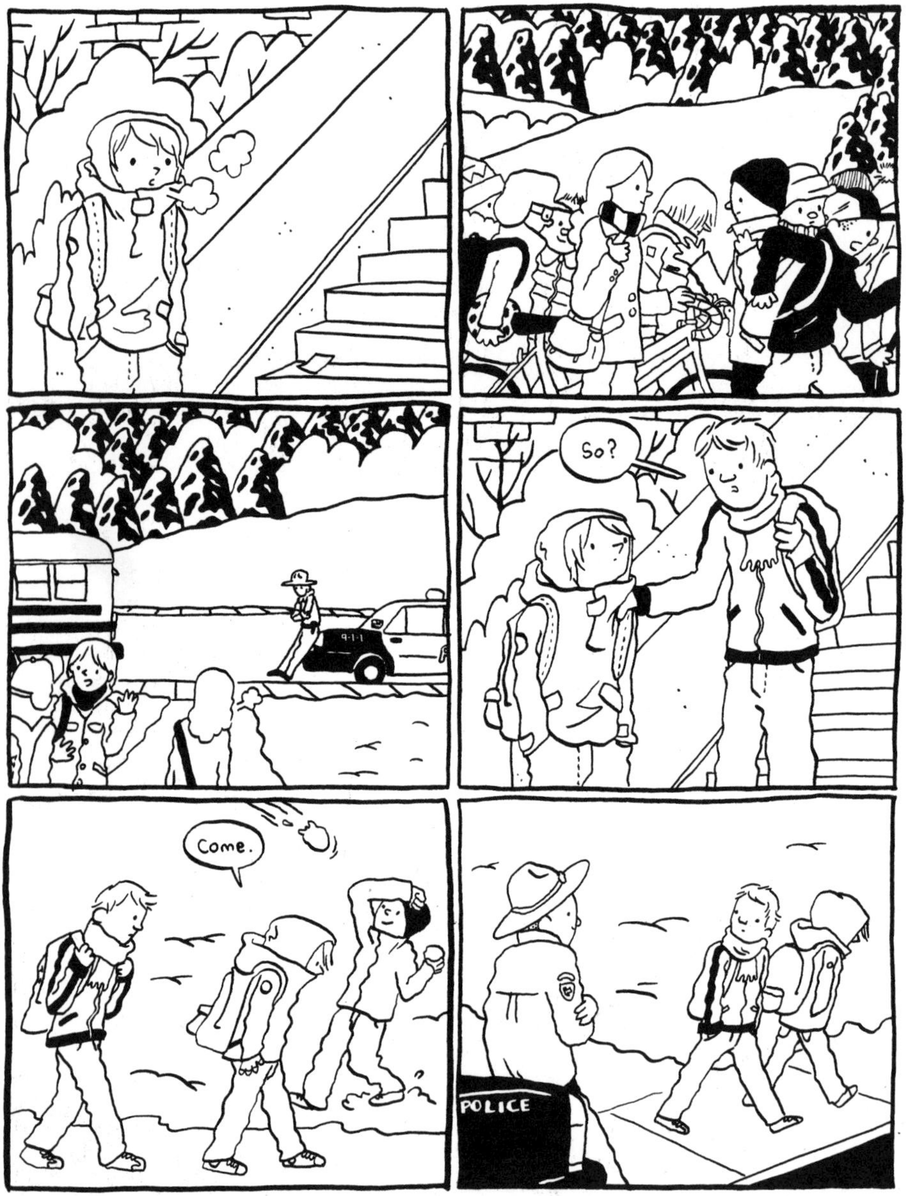
9-1-1
So?
Come.
POLICE

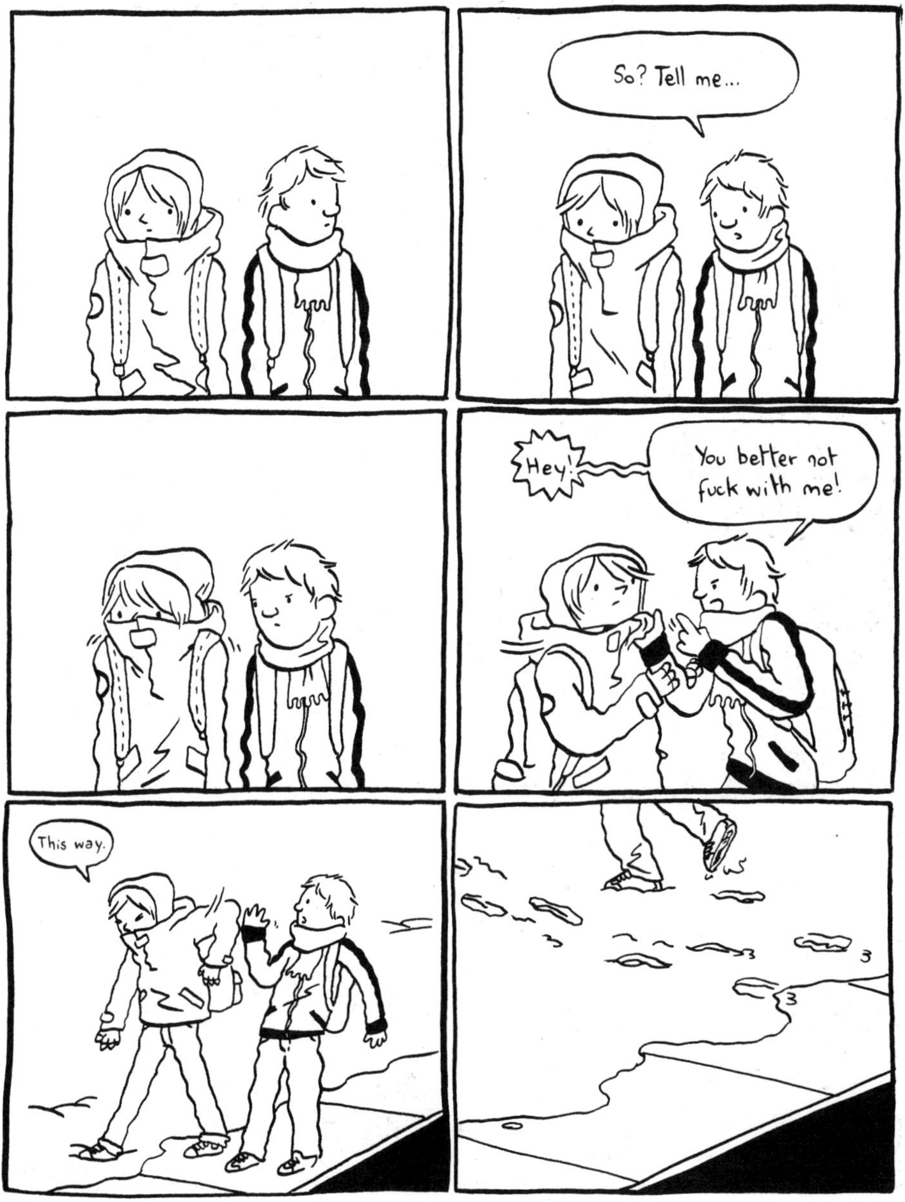
So? Tell me...
Hey!
You better not fuck with me!
This way.

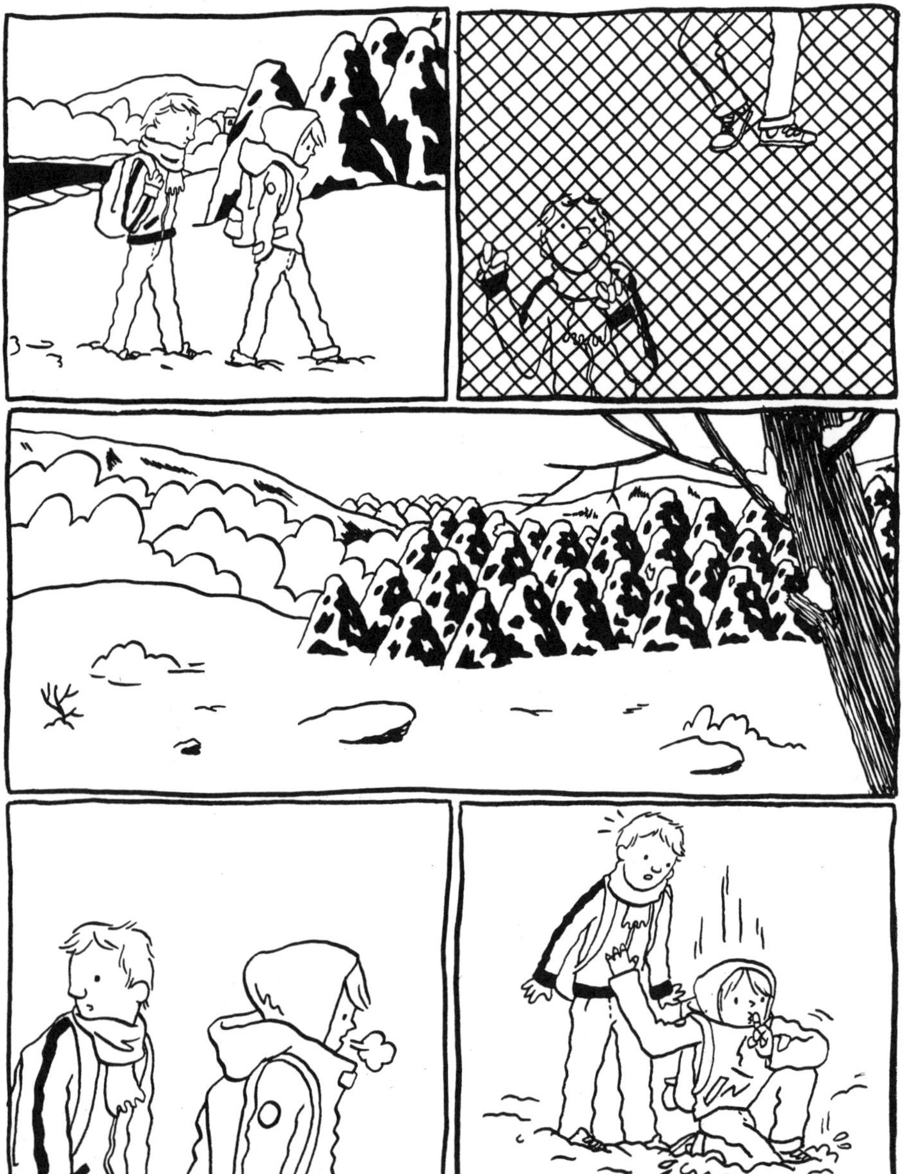

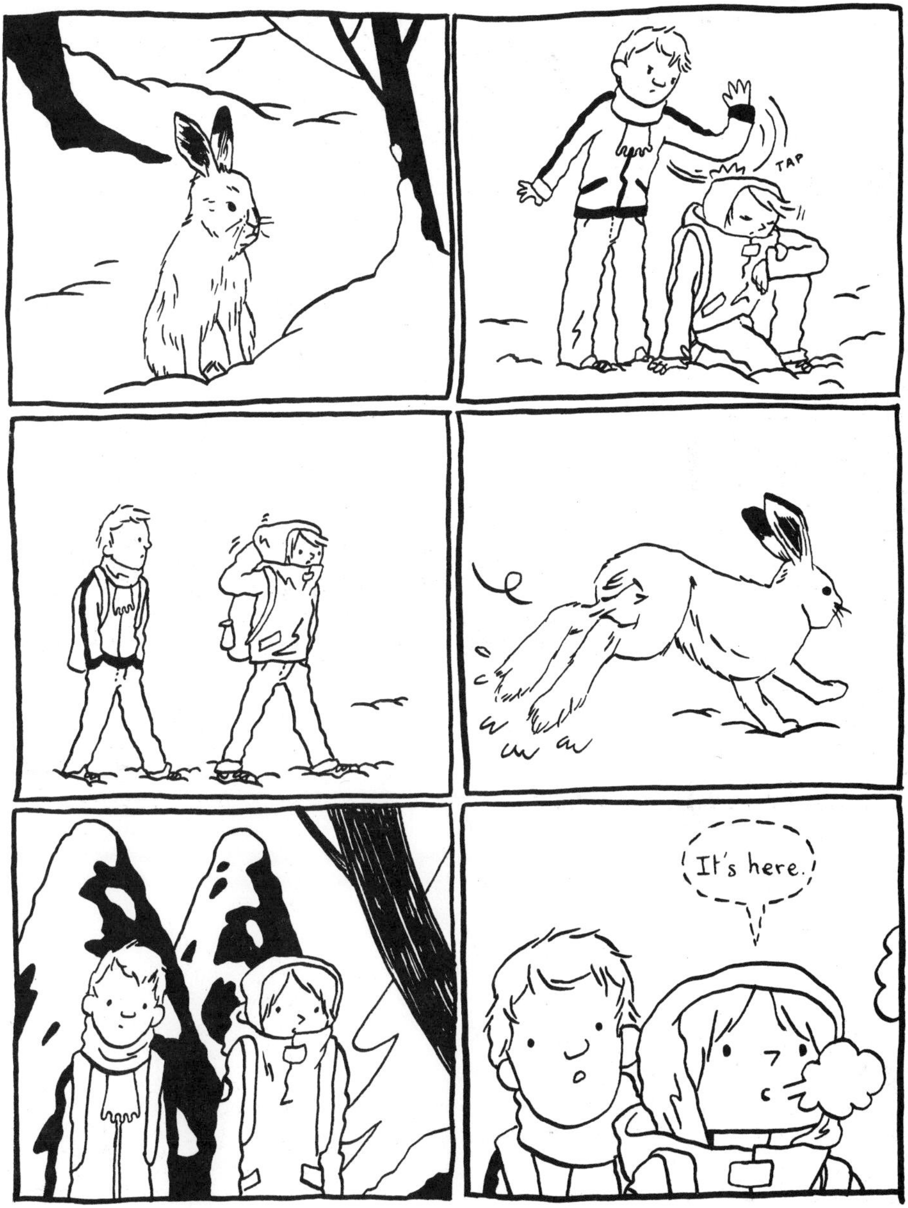
TAP
It's here.

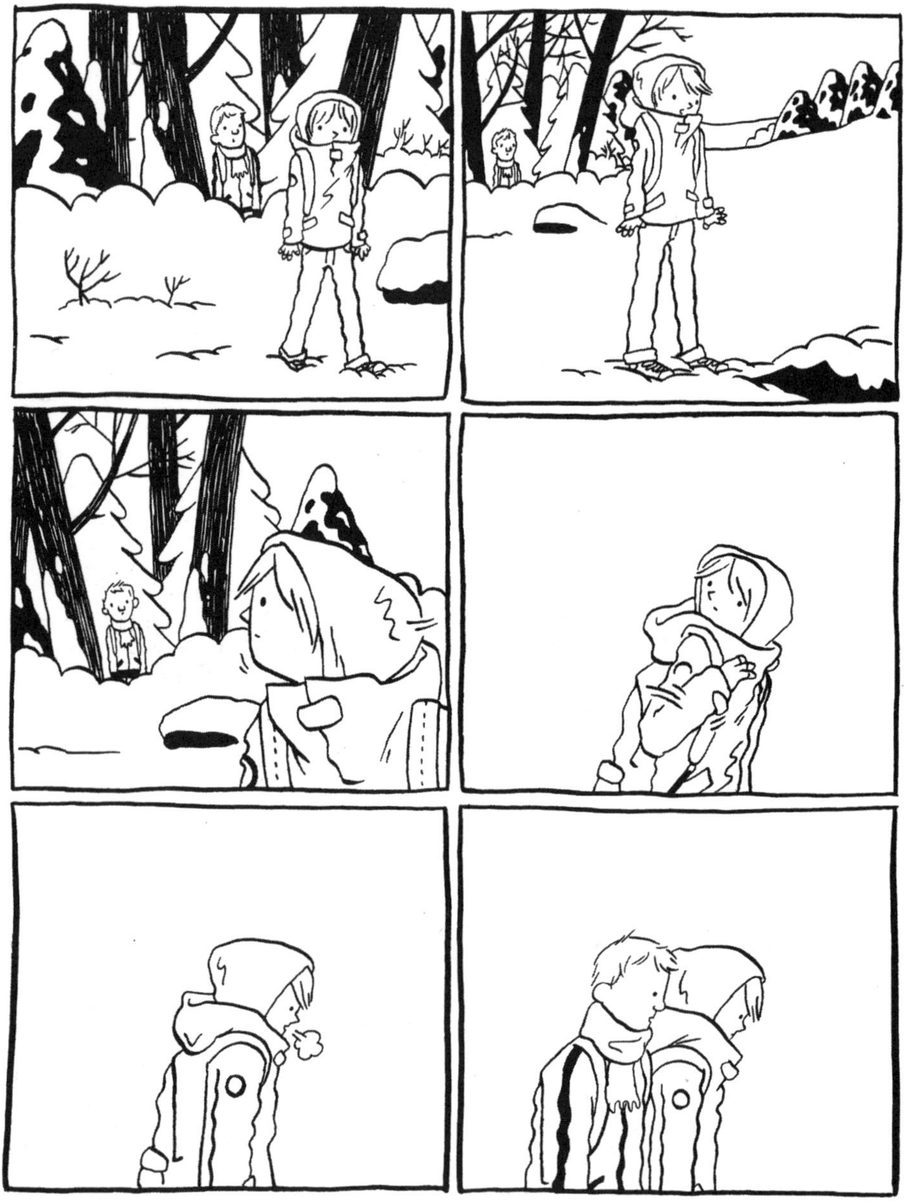

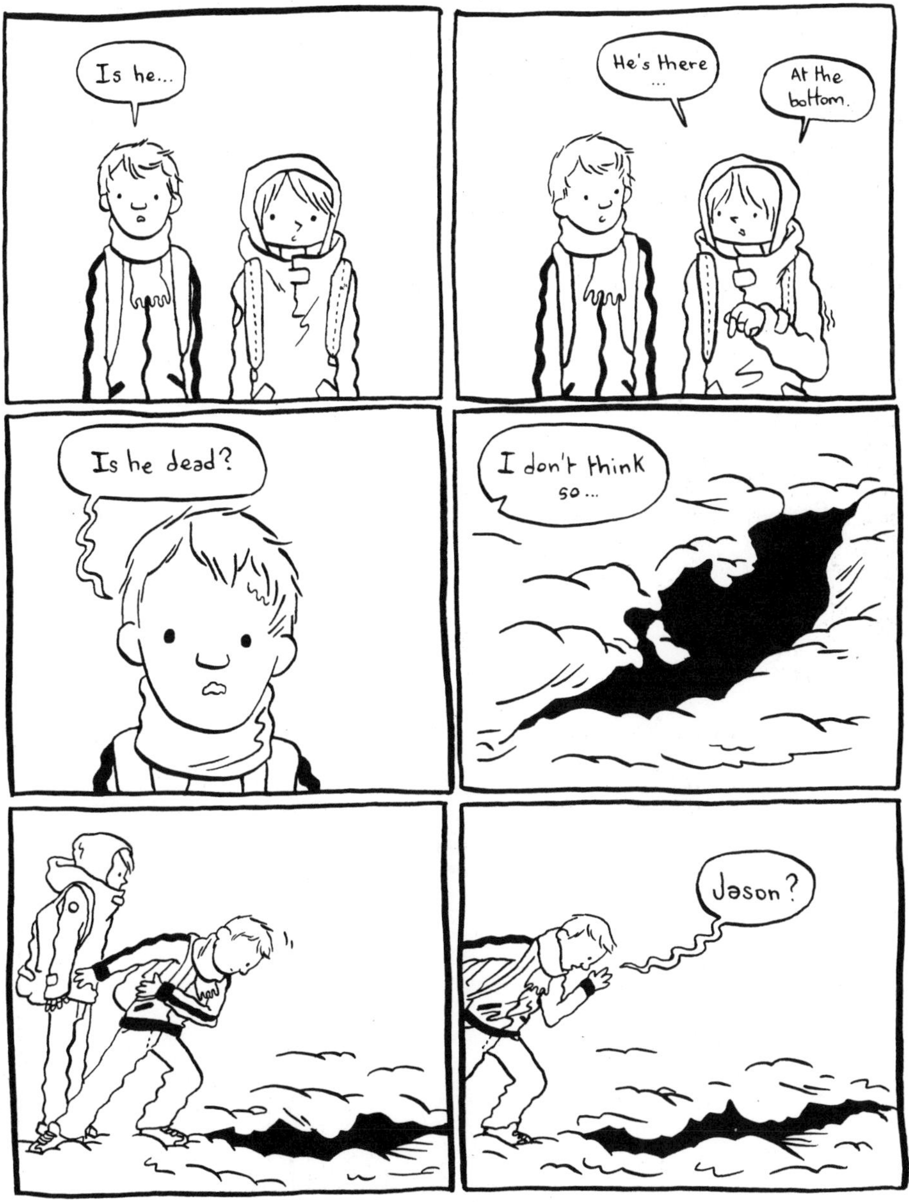
Is he...
He's there ...
At the bottom.
Is he dead?
I don't think so...
Jason?

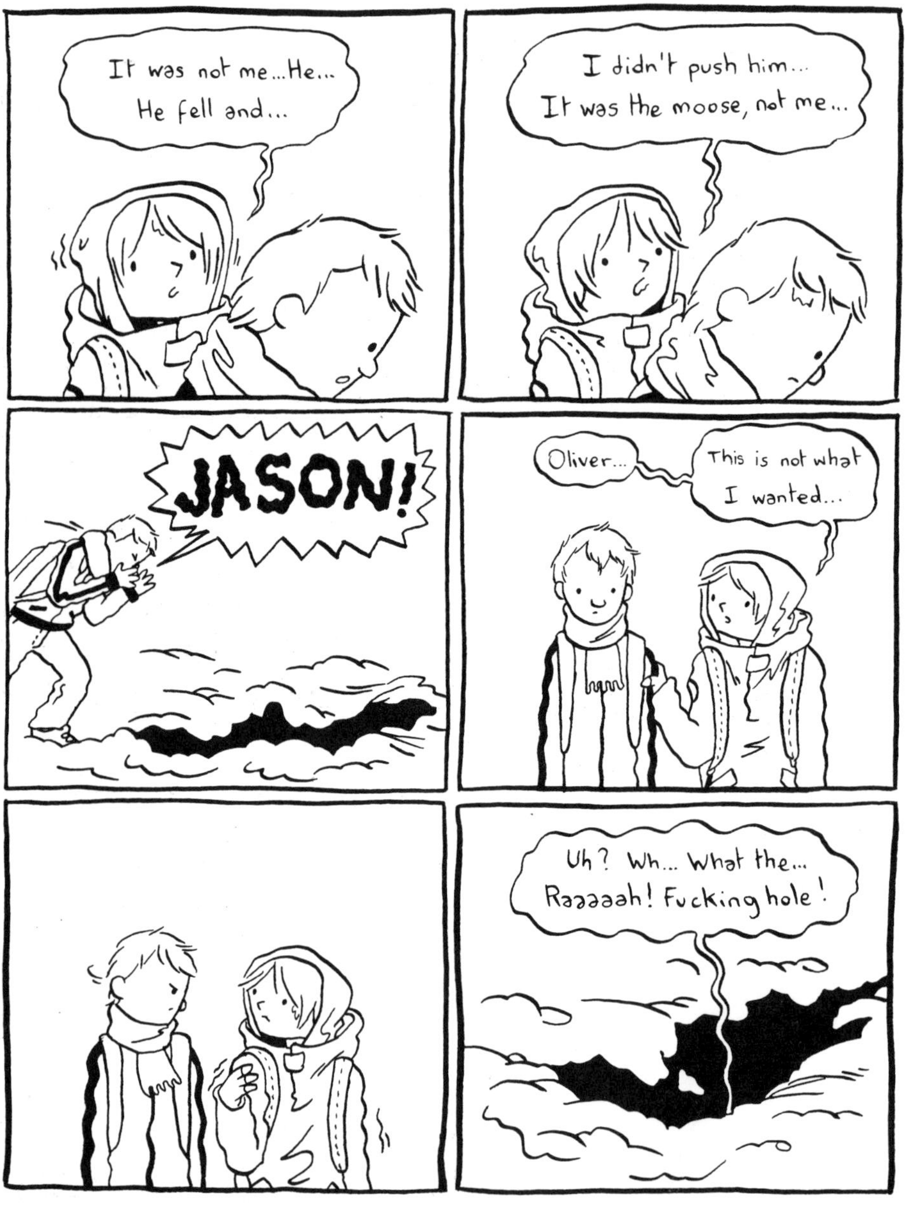
It was not me...He...
He fell and...
I didn't push him...
It was the moose, not me...
JASON!
Oliver...
This is not what
I wanted...
Uh? Wh... What the...
Raaaaah! Fucking hole!

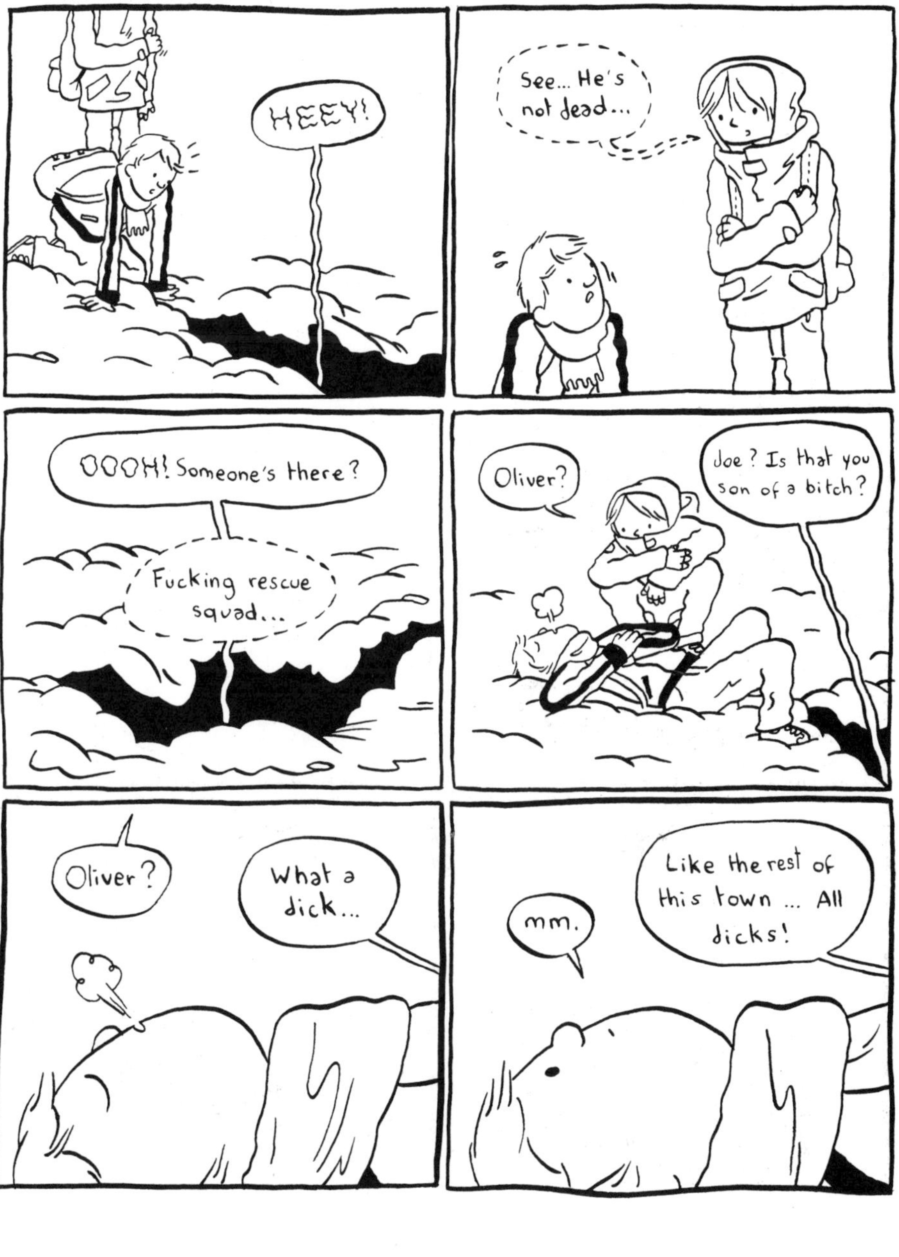
HEEY!
See... He's not dead...
OOOH! Someone's there?
Fucking rescue squad...
Oliver?
Joe? Is that you son of a bitch?
Oliver?
What a dick...
mm.
Like the rest of this town ... All dicks!

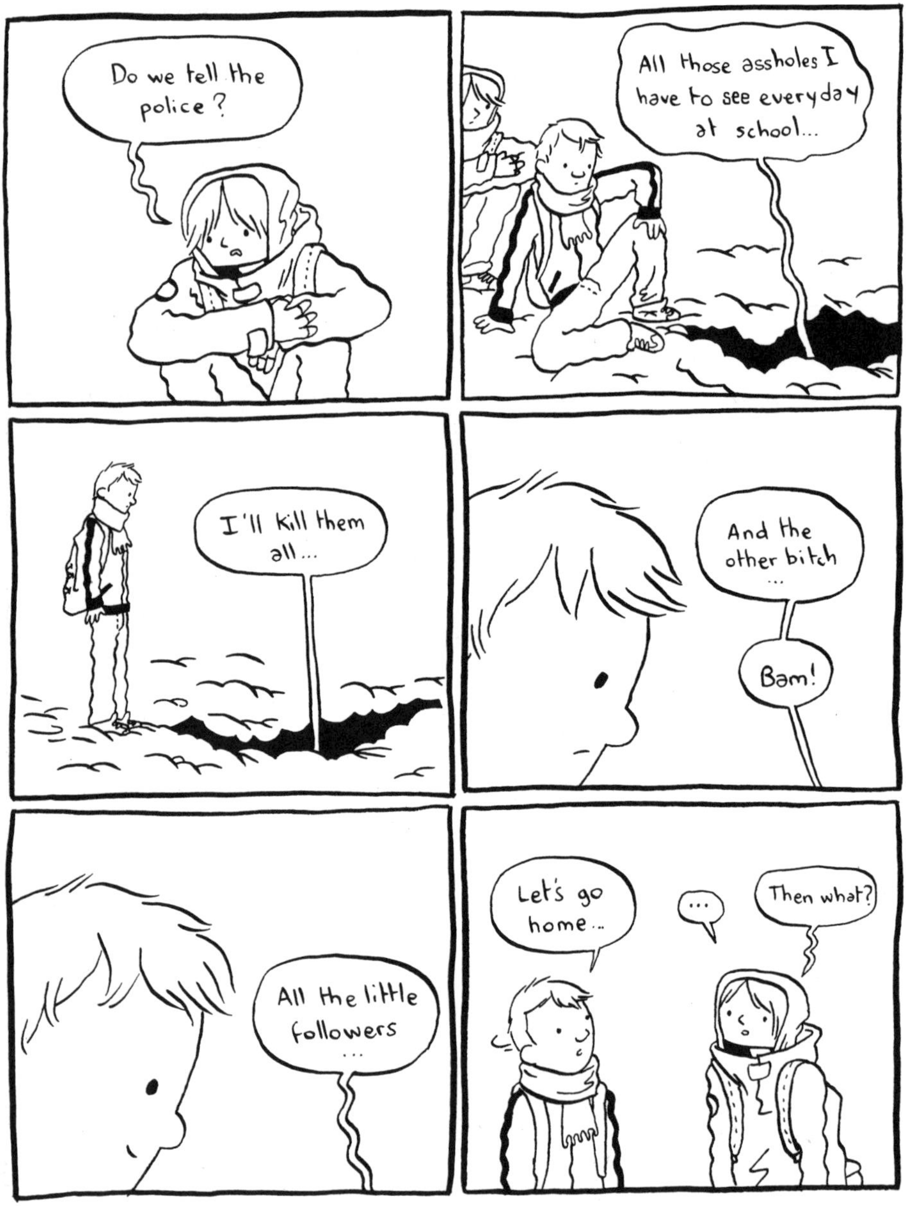
Do we tell the police?
All those assholes I have to see everyday at school...
I'll kill them all...
And the other bitch ...
Bam!
All the little followers ...
Let's go home...
...
Then what?

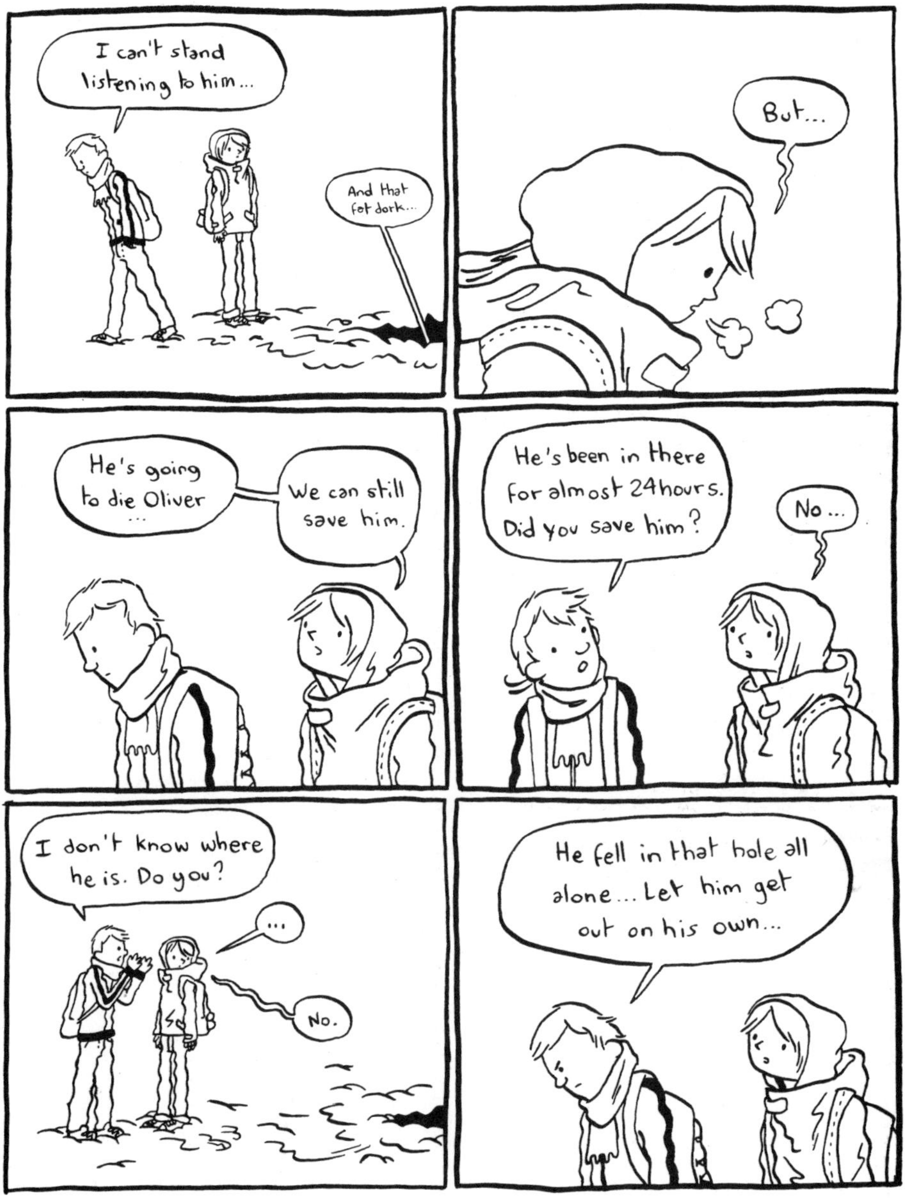
I can't stand listening to him...
And that fat dork...
But...
He's going to die Oliver ...
We can still save him.
He's been in there for almost 24hours. Did you save him?
No...
I don't know where he is. Do you?
...
No.
He fell in that hole all alone... Let him get out on his own...

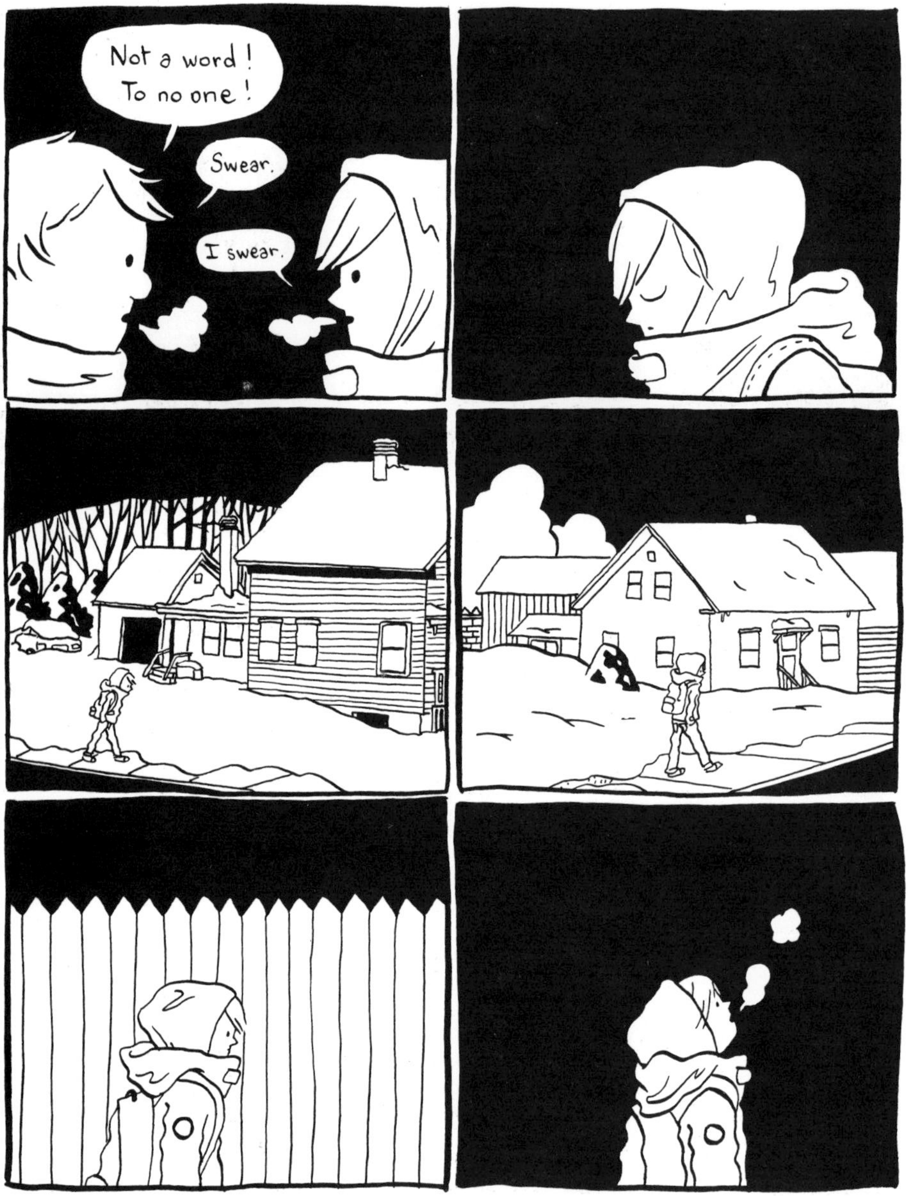
Not a word! To no one!
Swear.
I swear.

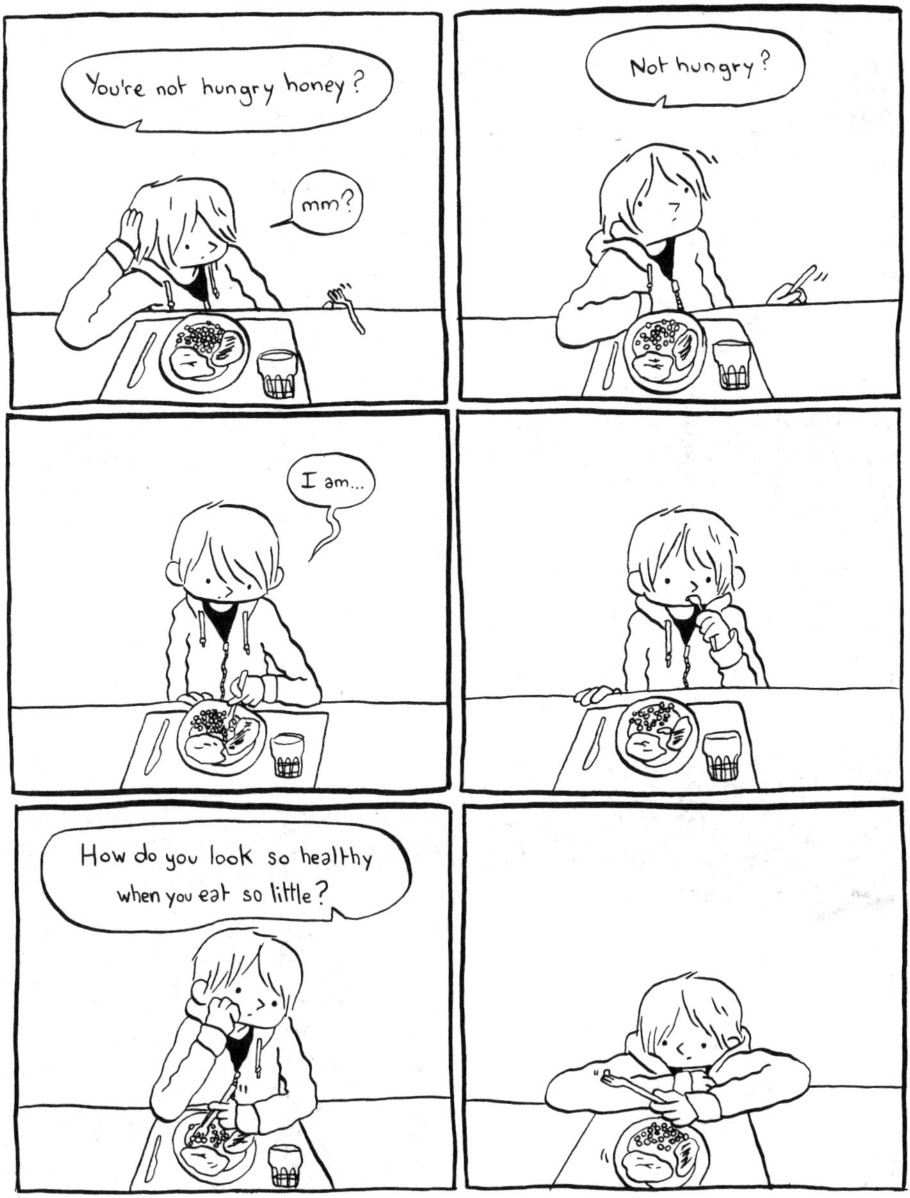

You're not hungry honey?
mm?
Not hungry?
I am...
How do you look so healthy when you eat so little?

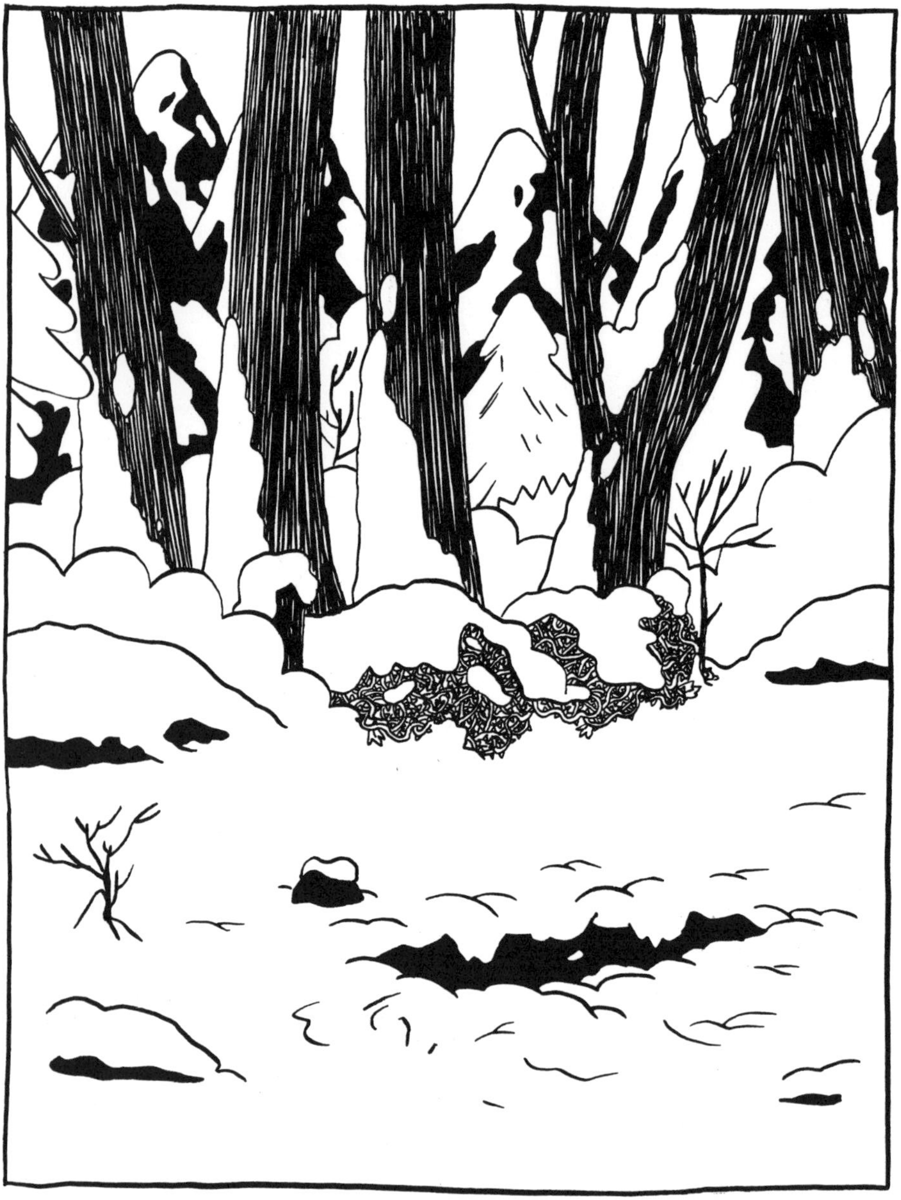

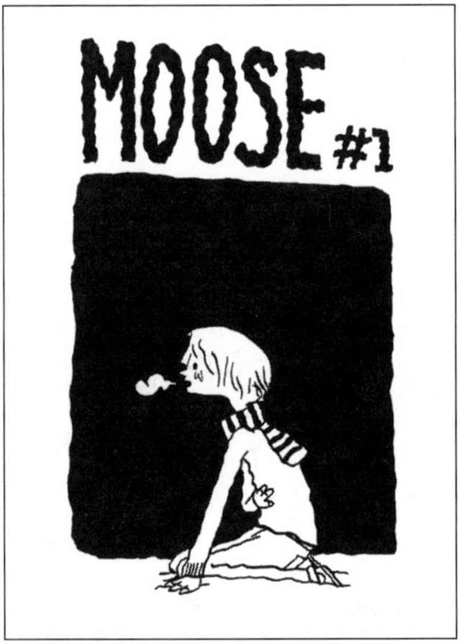
MOOSE #1

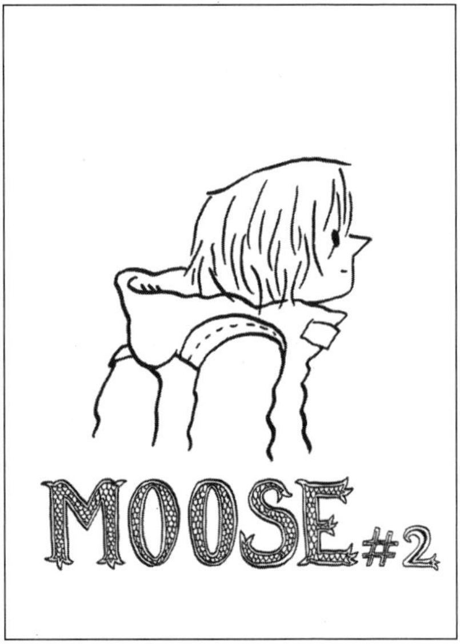
MOOSE #2

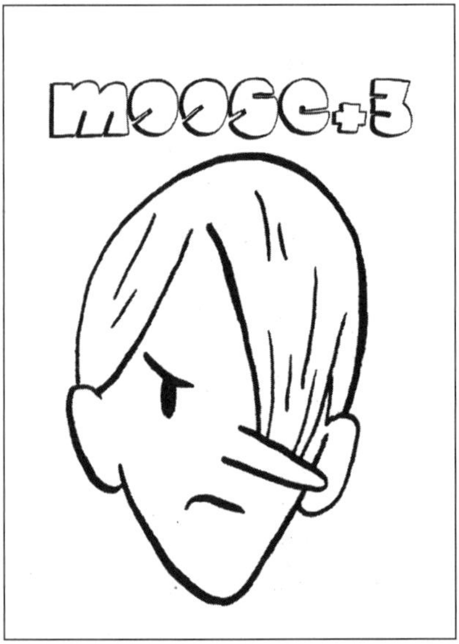
moose #3

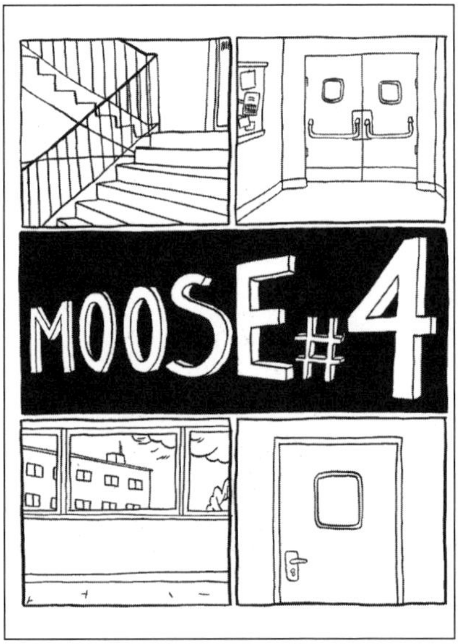
MOOSE #4

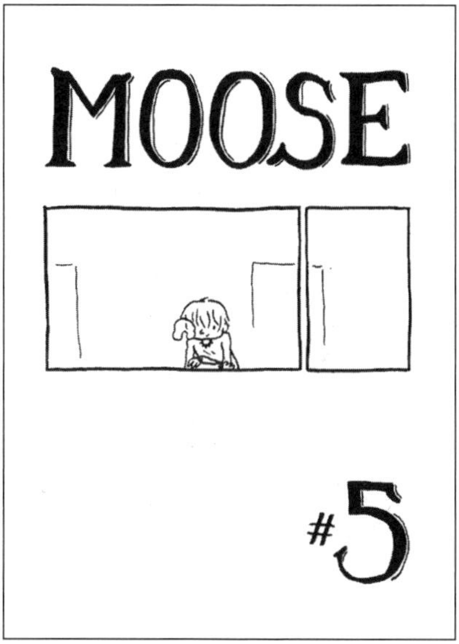
MOOSE
#5

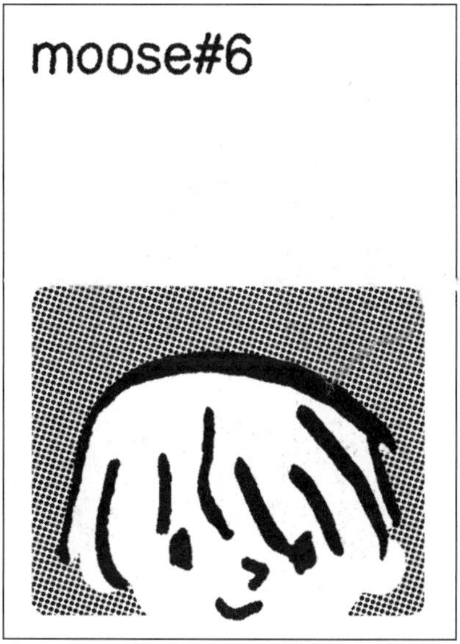
moose#6

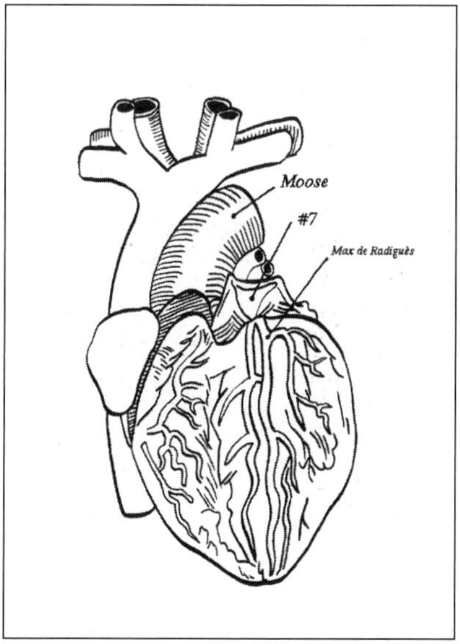
Moose
#7
Max de Radiguès

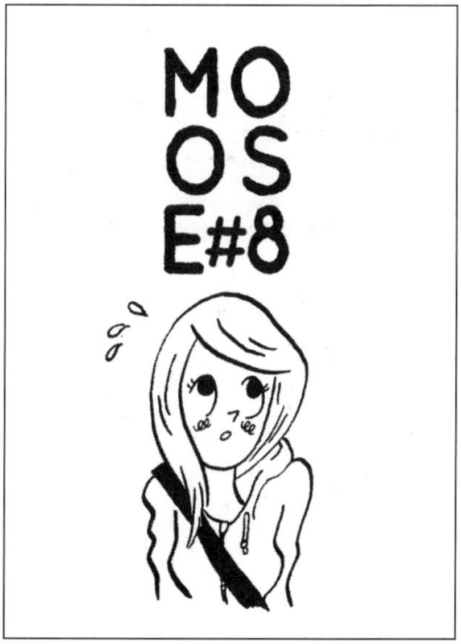
MO
OS
E#8

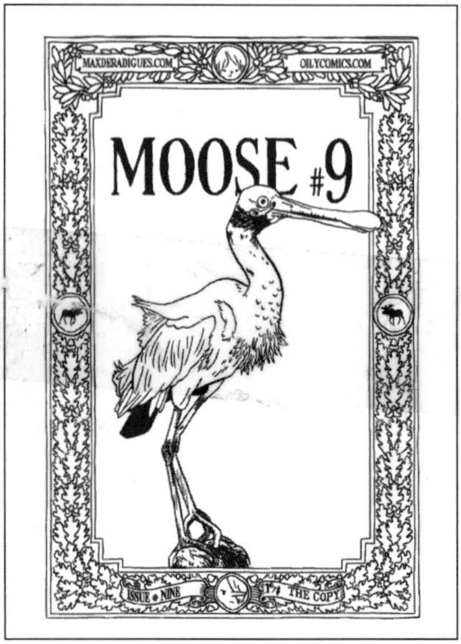
MAXDERADIGUES.COM
OILYCOMICS.COM
MOOSE #9
ISSUE # NINE
THE COPY

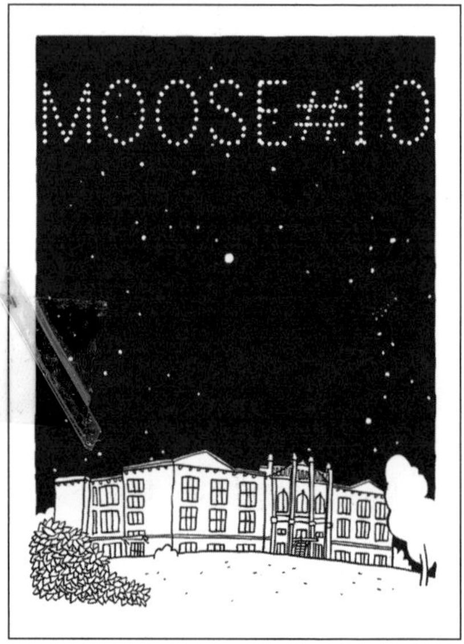
MOOSE#10

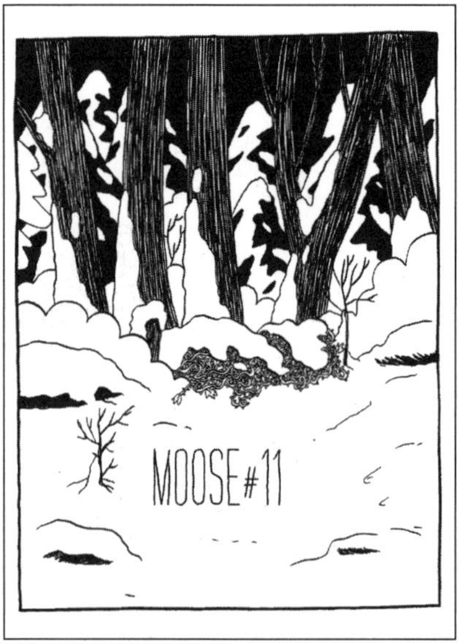
MOOSE#11

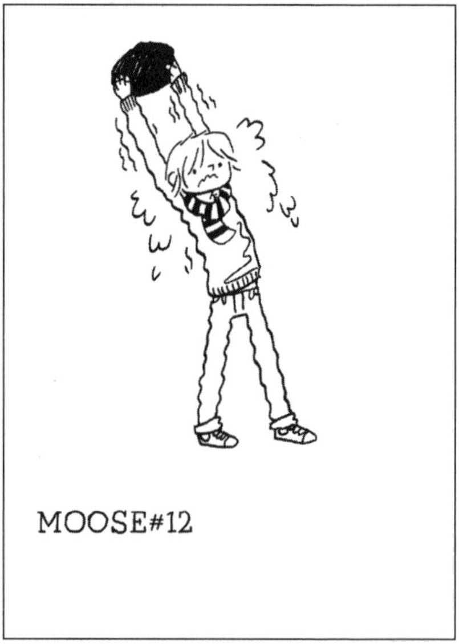
MOOSE#12

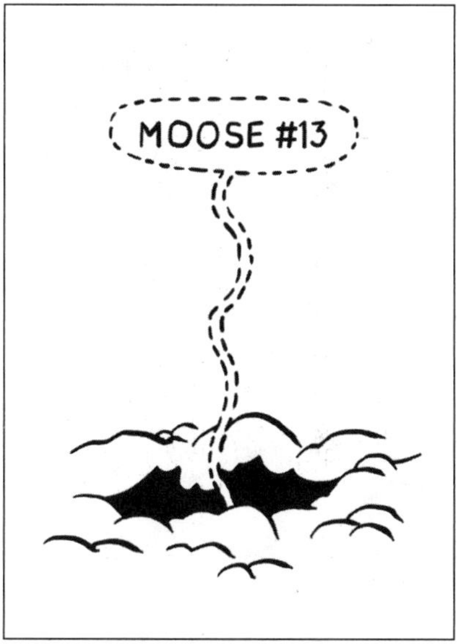
MOOSE #13

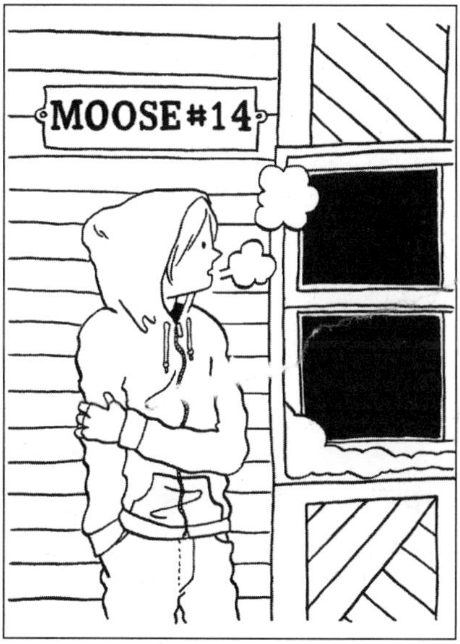
MOOSE #14

Max de Radiguès is a cartoonist and an editor at L'employé du moi. He is the creator of nine books and has contributed to countless anthologies in Europe and North America. He spent time as a fellow at the Center for Cartoon Studies in Vermont. He published *Rough Age* in English with One Percent Press in 2014. *Moose* was originally published as a series of mini-comics from Oily Comics. Special thanks to them. He currently lives in Belgium.

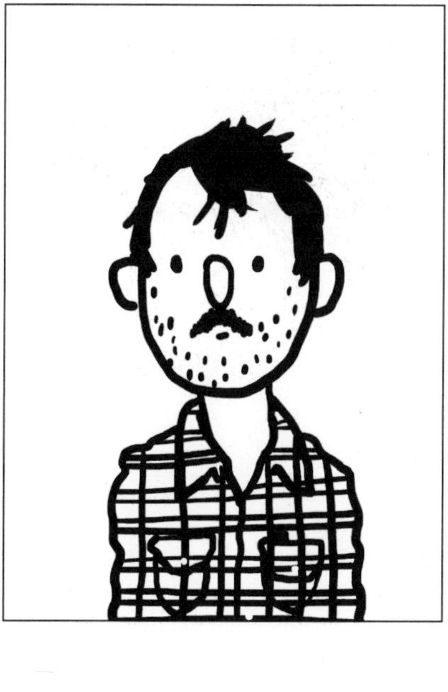